TINY
BUSINESS,
BIG
MONEY

TINY BUSINESS,

BIG
MONEY

Strategies for Creating a
High-Revenue Microbusiness

ELAINE POFELDT

The Countryman Press

An Imprint of W. W. Norton & Company
Independent Publishers Since 1923

*To my family, for inspiring me to take the leap
into running my business and to try a way of life that
I had no idea I would love this much.*

For information about permission to reproduce selections from this book, write to
Permissions, The Countryman Press, 500 Fifth Avenue, New York, NY 10110

For information about special discounts for bulk purchases, please contact
W. W. Norton Special Sales at specialsales@wwnorton.com or 800-233-4830

Manufacturing by Lakeside Book Company
Production manager: Devon Zahn

The Countryman Press
www.countrymanpress.com

A division of W. W. Norton & Company, Inc.
500 Fifth Avenue, New York, NY 10110
www.wwnorton.com

978-1-68268-643-0

10 9 8 7 6 5 4 3 2 1

CONTENTS

FOREWORD

Verne Harnish, Founder, Entrepreneurs' Organization

There's never been a better time to start and grow a business. As the world opens up after the COVID-19 pandemic, new opportunities are proliferating around the world. Many businesses can now be run from virtually any location. It's no wonder we've seen a record number of new business formations in recent months.

The challenge for many entrepreneurs is deciding where to focus their energy. There are riches in niches, but you've got to find the right one. *Tiny Business, Big Money* will help you do that, offering a detailed analysis of census data that highlights the industries that offer the biggest upside for microbusinesses with less than twenty employees, as well as the results of an original survey highlighting the best practices of nearly fifty entrepreneurs running the profitable seven-figure businesses that are profiled in this book.

These entrepreneurs have taken their businesses a step beyond the solo founders that Elaine Pofeldt profiled in *The Million-Dollar, One-Person Business*. They operate with very small teams, made up of either a consistent group of freelancers or a handful of employees. You'll learn how to set yourself up for success from their stories, with actionable strategies on how to develop the right mindset to create a business like this yourself; how to discover your ideal tiny business; how to find the money you need to start and grow it; how to connect with your first customers; and more. Running a tiny business that makes big money is ultimately about leveraging whatever resources you bring to the table for the best possible results.

Once you know how to create the foundations of a tiny business that makes big money, you'll have many options in front of you. Some owners will decide to keep their businesses at a boutique size. Others will find they want to take their business as far as they can go, and join the companies that have used the Scaling Up system for growing a company that I described in my book, *Scaling Up: Rockefeller Habits 2.0*. Both routes can help you achieve the one thing that drives all entrepreneurs—freedom—while allowing you to make a positive difference for your employees, your community, and the world beyond.

INTRODUCTION

Every day during the COVID-19 pandemic, my main escape from the Zoom calls in my home office was a daily walk. From the first days of the crisis to the lifting of the mask mandate for vaccinated people, I followed my route through the local downtown, whether it rained, the temperature hit 100 degrees, or I was sliding on ice or climbing over snowbanks. I'm a journalist, and I wanted to see what was happening for myself.

Many days, I took pictures so I wouldn't forget the details later—the signs of temporary store closures, announcements about new takeout and drive-up services, notices about reopening and the PPE customers would need to wear. During the winter, when I headed out a few hours after the morning darkness, I saw people huddled outside of restaurants, eating in the cold next to heat lamps, trying to support local businesses that were fighting to survive. Sometimes, when "going out of business" signs appeared in the windows of longtime family businesses, I cried. I run a business, and I've interviewed thousands of business owners over the years. I knew how hard they had worked to realize their dreams, and how some of them had fought to hang on.

Many of the businesses that made it to the other side were still trying hard to recover from the pandemic as I wrote the last pages of this book.

I had to ask myself if it still made sense to encourage people to start small businesses, after what we had been through. Did I really believe it was worth it?

And the answer, in my heart, was an emphatic yes.

Because, as hard as this latest crisis was for small business owners across America and around the world, there was still opportunity for people who want to earn a living in their own quirky way, with no boss and a blank slate for how to run things. Although many businesses had closed, just as in the Great Recession, others had thrived, and new ones were already sprouting up in some of the empty storefronts. With the pandemic lifting, restaurants near my home were getting crowded. Seeing people milling around outside, eager to see each other again, was a reminder of how important each small business is to the fabric of our communities and how much they are part of the glue that holds us together.

Meanwhile, lots of people had spent the pandemic building or growing thriving e-commerce businesses. US business formations skyrocketed by nearly 42 percent in 2020, as people put their time under lockdown to use in reinventing their careers.[1] That surge continued in 2021. In July 2021 alone, applications were up 98 percent, year over year.[2] Investors were racing to buy the tiniest, home-based operations to create a stable of e-commerce brands. Clearly, I wasn't the only one who was seeing opportunity.

I am a former senior editor at *Fortune Small Business* magazine and have contributed to CNBC, *Fortune, Forbes, Inc.,* and many other publications. I also wrote *The Million-Dollar, One-Person Business,* where I looked at the growing number of nonemployer businesses—those with no employees on payroll—that were hitting seven-figure revenue. Solo businesses often get ignored or even viewed as a nuisance, but it was clear there was an untold story about how much they could accomplish.

Tiny Business, Big Money looks at another greatly overlooked sector of small businesses: microbusinesses with just a few employees on payroll or that rely on a regular team of contractors who function as a cohesive team. Although all of the owners risk failure, they also have the potential for great success, as you'll see from the census data at the center of this book. You may be surprised to see which types of businesses topped the list of small

---

1 *Business Formation Statistics: June 2021* (Washington, DC: United States Census Bureau, July 15, 2021), https://www.census.gov/econ/bfs/index.html.

2 "Business Formation Statistics: Data Visualizations and Historic Releases," Business & Economy, United States Census Bureau, https://www.census.gov/econ/bfs/data.html.

businesses with the most cash left over after they make payroll, on average, in the charts in the appendices. Sometimes, the tiny businesses that bring in revenue in the high six and seven figures are very visible. Others, in true millionaire-next-door style, are churning out profits in a nondescript building or office on the side of the busy routes where we barely notice them (or, increasingly, in their home offices), doing work we seldom think about. Many, I found, are leading very creatively fulfilling and financially rewarding lives. To find out how the founders and owners in these pages uncovered the right businesses, grew them, and built the small teams that drive them, you'll be able to tap in to insights from interviews with nearly seventy entrepreneurs in more than sixty businesses.

In response to the numerous requests I've gotten from readers over the years, I also surveyed many of the entrepreneurs in this book to find out some of the things they had in common: How many years it took them to get to $1 million in revenue, whether they use contractors and automation, how much startup capital they had, where they get business advice and information, and what wellness practices they use to keep their lives balanced, whether it's powerlifting, yoga, meditation, or prayer. You'll see the results of that research in the appendices, as well.

I wish I could come up with one-size-fits-all instructions that would tell you how to build any business like a piece of Ikea furniture, as well, but it just doesn't work that way. Every business is different, and so is every entrepreneur. My hope is you'll get inspiration and practical advice from the entrepreneurs who generously shared their stories, so you can do things *your* way. Which is what running a tiny business that makes big money is all about.

CHAPTER 1

THE TINY BUSINESS REVOLUTION

Chris Meade, now 28, is living a life he never imagined was possible. After spending a month in San Diego, living in an Airbnb on Mission Beach near the cofounders of his company CROSSNET—his brother Gregory, 26, and their buddy Mike Delpapa, 27—he was getting ready to head to Tulum, Mexico, where the team was going to celebrate Thanksgiving together.

The four-way volleyball game the trio invented, CROSSNET, was selling like mad, and their company, headquartered in Meade's apartment in Miami, was on track to bring in $10–12 million for 2020, and was turning a profit. With California on lockdown during the coronavirus pandemic, Meade had been lucky to find a rental with a balcony. Every day, he'd head out there to work out with his girlfriend, Lyndsey—the company's head of brand communications and a Pilates instructor on the side—the high point of his day.

It wasn't always this way for Meade. Back in 2017, he rose most weekdays at 6:30 a.m. to head to the subway for a slow and grinding commute from Bushwick, Brooklyn, to Manhattan. He was working as an account executive at a rideshare company in New York City. When he got to the office at 8:30 a.m., he braced himself for a long day of cold calls to sell the company's food delivery services to local restaurants. He was grateful to be making a good living, but he didn't enjoy the work. He tried to ignore the dread he felt on Sunday nights and to enjoy what was left of the weekend until the jolt of his alarm on Monday morning. "I was stressed out, having to deal with constant rejection on the phone to build someone else's business, not my own," he recalls.

For a while, Meade felt he had no choice but to continue living that way. His father had passed away when he was a sophomore in college, and his mom was working as an Uber driver. He had more than $100,000 in student loans to repay after earning a BA in film, video, and interactive media at Quinnipiac University.

But something held him back from resigning himself to how he was making a living. "It was wanting happiness and knowing my current job was the bane of that," he recalls.

One night, Meade got together with Gregory and Delpapa in their hometown of Woodstock, Connecticut, to brainstorm a product they could invent together. His goal was to leave his job behind.

The three of them sat up all night, scribbling ideas on a notepad. One thing they'd always had in common was a passion for sports. As the sports highlights appeared on ESPN in the background, the ideas started flowing. What if they came up with a new spin on volleyball by combining the sport with the childhood game four square? If they divided the court into four quadrants, rather than into halves, they'd have a game that would be "insane," in a good way, they reckoned.

When they typed "four-way volleyball" into a search engine, it didn't look like anyone else had come up with an idea like this. They decided they would turn their concept into a product. To make sure their idea was marketable before they invested a lot of money, the partners bought a couple of volleyball nets from Walmart and set up a very rough prototype. "We made up a set of rules: Every man for himself in a free-for-all," recalls Meade. Each person would try to eliminate everyone else. They tested the idea by playing the game themselves.

That was in September 2017. Working during their commutes and on nights and weekends, the trio began taking the first steps to turn their idea into a real business. Delpapa, who is an engineer, drafted a prototype using the software AutoCAD. They found a manufacturer on the giant e-commerce marketplace Alibaba to create a sample for them for $250. Day by day, they tackled projects such as securing a trademark and a patent and recording videos to promote the product. Working with the same manufacturer, they ordered more than $20,000 worth of inventory to cover these startup costs, liquidating their collective savings.

That might seem risky, but to Meade, it was worth taking a chance. "I was $100,000 in debt," says Meade. "What did I have to lose? I had worked my ass off to get that college degree. I could always get another job."

Working without any employees, they grew the company to $85,000 in revenue in 2018. Meade quit his job on January 1, 2018, and moved to Miami, where he liked the weather and put his cold-calling skills to work. He dialed retail chains from his apartment to see if they would sell the brand-new product, propelled by enthusiasm for the game they'd invented. Meanwhile, Gregory worked on social media promotions as he traveled through Vietnam, while Delpapa refined the product, working from his home in Woodstock, Connecticut.

SCHEELS, a sporting goods chain in the Midwest, was the first to stock the game. When CROSSNET sold out in two SCHEELS stores, the retailer decided to carry it in twenty-two locations. That success opened the door to others, like winning distribution through the middleman Spreetail, which works with Amazon, Target, and Walmart and helped put Razor Scooters on the map. CROSSNET leaped to $2.25 million in revenue in 2019 before hiring a single employee or opening an office.

When the trio invented the game, they didn't realize they were creating the ultimate social-distancing sport, but with more people spending time at home during the coronavirus pandemic and schools looking for a safe activity for children in gym class, CROSSNET picked up momentum in 2020. It now sells its products through Amazon and 3,000 retail stores run by brands such as Academy Sports + Outdoors, DICK'S Sporting Goods, SCHEELS, Wegmans, and Walmart. "We're selling hundreds a day," Meade told me. "The stores can't keep it in stock." The education market has also been receptive: 10,000 schools have ordered a CROSSNET game, and the company had just donated 500 games to underfunded schools when I last spoke with Meade.

In 2020, CROSSNET broke eight figures in revenue. Meade and his partners have hired eighteen employees to handle work, such as marketing and managing a warehouse they opened in Canada, but when we last spoke, they planned to keep their operations lean so they could invest in building out their presence in Canada, and in Australia and the UK. They've self-funded the company and want to stretch every dollar. "We're paying ourselves humble salaries to get by," says Meade. "The money we make is constantly reinvested."

Meade and his partners are at the forefront of an exciting trend: tiny microbusinesses making big money—revenue in the high six figures, the seven figures, or beyond. It's never been easier for regular people to create a successful business with a tiny team of twenty people or fewer, whether it's made up of a regular group of contractors, traditional employees, or a hybrid team of both. Thanks to the explosion of free and low-cost digital tools, better digital payment options, the growth of freelance hubs, the ease of marketing on social media, the growth of online education via courses and masterclasses, and greater acceptance of remote work (which grew by leaps during the COVID-19 pandemic), small businesses can operate with new efficiencies and less startup capital than in years past.

"Tech has really leveled the playing field," says Steve King, partner in Emergent Research, a consultancy in Lafayette, California, that studies self-employment. "Larger businesses used to have a real, asymmetrical advantage in technology and data and information processing. Now, thanks to the platforms and marketplaces that the Amazons, Googles, and Shopifys of the world are putting out, small businesses can be as sophisticated as larger businesses."

Ben Leonard, who just sold his e-commerce company, Beast Gear, a provider of fitness equipment for weight lifters, and was launching a UK-based business brokerage, Ecom Brokers, when we spoke, calls it micro-agility. **"You can be a nimble little speedboat and turn around very quickly, as opposed to an enormous cruise ship,"** he says.

Meanwhile, some of the main barriers to starting a business have fallen away. "In terms of finding new clients and customers, the internet, social media, and online marketplaces make it much easier," King says. The "buy local" and "support small business" movements have picked up traction, too. "That ripples through the psyche of buyers," says King.

At the same time, it costs less to start a business of any size than in the past. "Whether you are a big business or a small business, there just aren't that many businesses that require huge amounts of capital to get going," says King. "Capital requirements have continued to fall over the last fifty years, and they will continue to fall. Thirty years ago, if you wanted to start a small business in manufacturing, you had to figure out a way to build your own manufacturing facility. Today even big companies outsource their manufacturing."

Other factors are driving the trend. In recent years, more leaders in government and academia are opening their minds to tiny businesses. Some are asking why is it better to create, say, one business that creates one hundred jobs than twenty-five businesses that create four jobs each—or even one hundred solo businesses? This has led to more programs to support small businesses—grant programs, incubators, accelerators, and even GoFundMe campaigns. "There's been a cultural shift to more broadly embracing small business and entrepreneurship," says King. And with many communities still reeling from the loss of small businesses in their downtowns and strip malls during the COVID crisis, those efforts are picking up traction. It's no fun to head downtown to meet a friend if there are no bars, coffee shops, restaurants, or bookstores.

Meanwhile, the government has created more of a safety net for freelancers, through measures such as the Affordable Care Act, which was being strengthened at the time of this writing. "Healthcare has gotten easier," notes King. That is not to mention that freelancers, contractors, and gig workers got access to unemployment insurance for the first time on a nationwide scale during the COVID-19 pandemic.

People's attitudes toward work are evolving, too. Almost everyone now realizes that traditional jobs, even those in the public sector, can be pretty shaky when the economy tanks. And even when people have jobs, the payoff isn't what it once was. People's salaries haven't kept pace with the cost of living, companies leave employees on the hook for more of their own healthcare costs, and housing, groceries, and education keep getting more expensive. And people feel like the hours they are working and the stress they're experiencing are slowly eroding their physical and emotional well-being. It's not surprising that 71 percent of self-employed workers said independent work is better for their health in a recent survey by MBO Partners, a provider of back-office services to the self-employed.[3]

Plus, more people are starting side hustles than ever before and building their entrepreneurship muscles. Many side hustlers discover they're good at entrepreneurship—a skill few of us learn in school—and that their part-time businesses have the potential to eventually replace their jobs, and then some. And they like the idea of building income streams no one can take away from them. "They are hoping, planning, and trying to turn it into a full-time business so they can better pursue their passion," says King.

Tiny businesses tend to get overlooked in the world of entrepreneurship, where the mindset is often "Go big or go home." Like one-person businesses, however, they represent a large portion of businesses in the United States and the world. Currently, there are 30.7 million small businesses in the United States, and of these, 5.3 million have between one and twenty employees. Another 26.4 million are nonemployer firms, meaning they have no paid employees on payroll—the group I covered in my first book, *The Million-Dollar, One-Person Business.*

In interviewing the owners of the fifty-plus businesses in this book, I've found that some nonemployer businesses operate more like employer firms than a traditional one-person business, and I have opted to include them, even though they don't run payroll. Unlike a one-person business that may use one or two contractors on an occasional basis—perhaps a bookkeeper and accountant—they depend on a regular team of freelancers and agencies, whom they coordinate almost like employees. Maybe these firms employ a virtual assistant, a bookkeeper, a social media agency, and a copywriter, all

---

3 *The State of Independence in America 2020* (Herndon, VA: MBO Partners, 2020), http:// info.mbopartners.com/rs/mbo/images/MBO_Partners_State_of_Independence_2020_ Report.pdf.

of whom operate their own businesses but come together once a week in a team Zoom call, similar to employees. Government and banking-industry researchers sometimes put these team-driven businesses into a special category, such as "high-propensity businesses," because they're likely to create traditional jobs at some point.

Tiny businesses are different from traditional solopreneur businesses, like freelance writing and design, in that they generally operate in fields where it's hard for one person to do all of the work, even with the use of automation, outsourcing, and contractors. For instance, Emily Tryon, RN, 46, who runs a medi-spa called Esthetic Solutions in Scottsdale, Arizona, grew her business to $1 million in revenue with the help of one assistant, who welcomed customers while Tryon was administering treatments such as Botox. Tryon now has five to ten employees on staff, depending on demand.

Like Meade, many entrepreneurs keep their tiny businesses lean by choice. Just as many people are seeking a simpler lifestyle and, in some cases, embracing trends like the "tiny house" movement, these entrepreneurs are deliberately opting for a minimalist approach to business. They pride themselves on traveling light—while still accomplishing what they set out to do: make a living, build economic security, have enough cash to do the things they want to do in life, and give back. "The big issue is control and lifestyle," says King. "For a lot of people who are starting businesses, their objectives are very idiosyncratic. Once they reach those objectives, they don't want to grow very much. The added benefit of growth is outweighed by the pain of managing the business."

But not for all. Some stay open to the possibility that the natural size of the business will reveal itself to them over time and that it may end up being larger than they can envision now. "They are business builders," says King.

Others start as one- or two-person operations that rely mainly on the occasional freelancer for help and move on to hiring employees. That's the case for Angie Lalla and Colin Raja, a married couple in their thirties that lives in Queens, New York. They were both working in corporate jobs on Wall Street when their passion for CrossFit and boxing inspired them to start a business. Angie noticed that most of the gear for women came in drab colors and thought they could make money manufacturing it in a prettier palette. To raise startup money, they bought a bunch of generic water bottles for $1 and sold them for $20 on eBay, then found a manufacturer that would make the gear for them. They grew their business, RIMSports, to $2 million as a two-person team. Today, they have fifteen employees located in Chennai, India, where Colin is from, to help with customer service. They brought in $3 million in revenue for 2020 and were projecting $5–6 million for 2021 when we last chatted.

While businesses like this offer many of the same freedoms and rewards of a one-person business, they also require more organization and systems in place to succeed. Being your own boss is one thing, but enlisting other people in achieving your vision is another—even if you run your business very informally compared to your past employers. We'll be looking at how the owners hold on to their lifestyle while building a team—the holy grail for many—in the chapters to come.

TINY BUSINESSES, BIG RESULTS

Although small businesses took a beating during the pandemic, there are still a lot of upsides to running one today, as the folks who are registering all of those new businesses understand. Many people don't realize what tiny businesses are accomplishing. Among those 5.3 million tiny businesses with employees, the average business had just four employees and an annual revenue of $816,180, with a payroll of $162,755, according to US Census Bureau statistics for 2017. (Payroll is the highest cost in many businesses, followed by real estate costs.) That leaves $654,425 to cover any remaining overhead and to take as profit.

Many small businesses bring in much more. If you look at the average revenue for firms with five to nine employees, it's $1.2 million, with 6.5 employees on average and a payroll of $252,033. That leaves about $950,000 to cover costs or to take as profit. And small businesses with ten to nineteen employees see average revenue of $2.5 million with an average of 13.5 employees and a payroll of $437,623. They come away with about $2 million to spend on overhead or to take as profit.

How much money is left over after they cover their costs? While overhead varies by industry—some owners must pay for a lease or mortgage—the rise of remote work has made it easier to keep real estate costs down. The Federal Reserve found that, even before the COVID-19 pandemic, 57 percent of small businesses were operating at a profit, and 18 percent were at break-even. Only 24 percent were operating at a loss.[4] Among the businesses the Fed surveyed, 55 percent had four employees or fewer, 18 percent had five to nine employees, and 13 percent had ten to nineteen employees. (If you don't run a business, bear in mind that business owners are taxed on their profits and tend to do all they can to minimize them on paper by, for instance, contributing to tax-advantaged retirement accounts and the like.)

Startups are staying lean, too. In 2017, the average startup employed 4.4 people, according to the US Small Business Administration.[5] This is compared to 7.5 in 1998, according to data from the Kauffman Foundation, which studies entrepreneurship.[6] While it's hard to measure startups' success by early revenue and profits—some successful startups don't make money the first few years, until they pick up traction—the startup community seems to be accomplishing just as much as ever with these smaller team sizes. The number of unicorn companies—those getting to a $1 billion valuation—is growing at a clip and has hit a record of more than 800, according to CB Insights.[7]

I believe that, as more people become aware of the income potential from very small businesses, we're going to see a lot more jumping on this trend. The average "rich" zip code in the United States has 19.1 microbusinesses per 1,000 people, compared to 13.1 in the highest-poverty zip codes, according

4 *Small Business Credit Survey: 2020 Report on Employer Firms* (Washington, DC: Federal Reserve Banks, April 7, 2020), https://www.fedsmallbusiness.org/medialibrary/FedSmallBusiness/files/2020/2020-sbcs-employer-firms-report.

5 *Frequently Asked Questions about Small Businesses* (Washington, DC: US Small Business Administration Office of Advocacy, October 2020), https://cdn.advocacy.sba.gov/wp-content/uploads/2019/09/24153946/Frequently-Asked-Questions-Small-Business-2019-1.pdf.

6 "Indicators of Entrepreneurship: Startup Early Job Creation," Early-Stage Entrepreneurship Series, Ewing Marion Kauffman Foundation, February 2021, https://indicators.kauffman.org/indicator/startup-early-job-creation.

7 "The Complete List Of Unicorn Companies," CB Insights, updated August 2021, https://www.cbinsights.com/research-unicorn-companies.

to census data.[8] How did the folks with the microbusinesses wind up living in the "rich" zip codes? No doubt the income from their businesses has helped.

Given that many of these firms first start out as one- or two-person businesses, this is a tremendously empowering trend. You don't have to have access to the clubby world of venture capital to participate, or even be able to qualify for bank loans in the beginning. The vast majority of tiny business owners are self-financing, using their personal funds, credit, and cash flow to do it on a shoestring,[9] with only 9 percent using outside funds. Many of the folks you'll read about in the pages to come simply used money they saved from their jobs or household income. Some launched with almost no startup cash, using methods like drop-shipping, where they brought in orders before they had to pay a manufacturer. Once they started growing their businesses and cash started flowing, they reinvested the money in the business.

Will starting a tiny, seven-figure business turn you into the next Elon Musk? In most cases, no—or at least not overnight. Tech moguls like that are running giant businesses they scaled up, often over many years, even though it often seems like they just got started. Still, once you subtract overhead, such as real estate costs and payroll, and pay taxes, you should be able to count on a comfortable six-figure income, without the hassles and frustrations of a traditional job—more than enough to live on, whether you live in the big city, a suburb in a good school district, a rural hideaway, or as a digital nomad.

WHERE THE ACTION IS

So which types of tiny businesses are the ones that make big money starting out? In *Tiny Business, Big Money*, you'll meet entrepreneurs running a wide

8 Peter W. Roberts and Deonta D. Wortham, "The Macro Benefits of Microbusinesses," *Stanford Social Innovation Review*, January 16, 2018, https://ssir.org/articles/entry/the_macro_benefits_of_microbusinesses.

9 *Small Business Credit Survey: 2020 Report on Employer Firms* (Washington, DC: Federal Reserve Banks, April 7, 2020), https://www.fedsmallbusiness.org/medialibrary/FedSmallBusiness/files/2020/2020-sbcs-employer-firms-report.

range of ventures that are breaking seven-figure revenue. They're doing all kinds of things that allow them to embrace their passions, talents, and expertise—designing and selling bikinis online, making high-end shampoo, prepping high school students for the SATs, doing app development, building homes, teaching other people how to podcast, and a lot more.

Based on my research, the industries that offer the best revenue and profit potential to the average person are:

- E-commerce
- High-end professional and personal services businesses
- Manufacturing
- Wholesaling
- Financial services/financial technology
- Transportation
- Construction and real estate

Are these the highest-profit microbusinesses in the country? No. As I'll explain in more detail later, I've weeded out businesses where there are steep barriers to entry, like a need for very specialized knowledge, enormous startup funding, or the right connections—or that are in industries that may not have wide appeal. To give you some examples, among businesses with fewer than five employees, casinos top the list of the tiny businesses with the most money left over, on average, after making payroll. Among those with five to nine employees, petroleum merchant wholesalers are number one, and in the ten to nineteen employee category, reinsurance carriers—the insurers of insurance companies—are top of the list. You can see the entire list in the appendices (I found it fascinating to see which businesses came out on top and where the money is flowing in America) and form your own judgments about which industry would be the best fit for you. Of course, there are many types of business in each industry, so you'll need to do some digging beyond that to find the niche that is right for you.

At the same time, while many people dream of running Main Street businesses where they can fulfill their creative passions—like hair-styling salons, bakeries, and photography studios—this book will not focus on these businesses, except those at the highest end of the market. While some do quite well, these had the least money left over after making payroll, on average, as you can see in the full data on tinybusinessbigmoney .com—at least on paper. And, as we saw during the coronavirus pandemic, brick-and-mortar stores that rely heavily on in-person sales are very vulnerable in the times we're living in. It's become essential in almost every industry today to do at least some sales online. This book will focus on businesses with the resilience to make it through booms, busts, and unpredictable events.

Who are the entrepreneurs running tiny businesses that make big money? They come from every age group and demographic. Here are just a few of the nearly sixty you will meet in this book.

Sean Kelly, 24, hoped to study business at Rutgers University, but when he couldn't pass the required math class in his freshman year, he took a leave of absence and started Jersey Champs, an online store that sells sports jerseys. He didn't have the cash to license the names of pro sports teams, so he approached rap and hip-hop artists and created jerseys with their names on them. He grew that business, which he runs from a laptop in his apartment, to more than $1 million in annual revenue. When the pandemic hit, he saw an opportunity to pivot to selling masks and, with a silent partner and two employees, grew a new business called PPE of America to $15 million in revenue.

Ana Gavia, 28, a medical student from Australia, loved sketching in her spare time. After coming up with a design for a bikini, she spent the $200 in her bank account to hire a factory to create a sample, posted it in a Facebook ad, and sold it to 100 customers who placed preorders and paid her ahead of time. She soon found a factory that was willing to do a small run and used the money left over from the sales to fund her next sample. Today she's built a brand called Pinkcolada, which grew to more than $1 million in annual revenue as a solo operation. It now brings in $2.5 million in annual revenue with eleven employees who handle customer service and warehouse work.

Julian O'hayon, 30, a digital nomad, created a streetwear brand called Blvck after images he created of black MacBook cases and black M&M's that went viral on Instagram. Today, he sells hoodies and other products, and his team of four employees brings in nearly $5 million in annual revenue.

Tal Masica, 32, and **Zeke Araki,** 33, built on what they learned through osmosis as the sons of local jewelry store owners and created PAVOI, a "fast-fashion" brand that sells inexpensive jewelry on Amazon. By learning how to optimize their Amazon listings, they built the two-man business to a whopping $5 million in annual revenue with no employees, relying heavily on automation and a virtual team of consultants to keep it growing. Now they have five employees and have continued to grow revenue.

Kish Vasnani, 36, and **Vanessa Jeswani,** 34, a married couple from New York City, started out working together at an Etsy store Vanessa launched to leave the corporate grind. When her travel-related pouches caught on, they decided to create a travel bag company called Nomad Lane, which sells lightweight nylon bags that fit perfectly under an airplane seat. They're currently running it from Florida and generating just under $1 million a year as they prepare to move from relying on contracted help to hiring an employee.

Steven Sudell, 37, a physical therapist from Venice Beach, California, got frustrated when he could not find a good neck traction device for his patients. Tinkering in his office, he created a makeshift contraption that would hang from a door handle. After hiring an industrial designer to turn it into a product sample, he raised more than $1 million to test and manufacture it on Kickstarter and Indiegogo. For several years he ran his physical therapy practice—his passion is working one-on-one with patients—while selling the Neck Hammock online on Amazon and through his e-commerce store. In early 2021, he sold the business for a seven-figure amount.

Jason Martin, 40, and **Patrick Falvey,** 38, best friends and ultramarathoners from Boise, Idaho, founded AppEvolve, a software firm, on the freelance platform Upwork—far from the traditional startup scene—and used energetic customer service to get to $1 million, despite intense price competition on the platform. They rely on a team of twenty to twenty-five contractors and just hired their first employee, an office manager.

Tiffany Williams, 40, who, upon hearing that her sales job at a daily deals site was about to dry up during a layoff, started selling print-on-demand T-shirts inspired by her Yorkie, Prada. She soon graduated to selling basic household items on Amazon that she purchased at a discount at big box stores and marked up, and eventually began training other women on how to start businesses through courses at her brand, Rich Girl Collective. She brought in more than $1 million last year with a regular team of six contractors and one employee, her mother.

Abby Walker, 44, wished she could find a way to make a living that allowed her to be home when her children's school bus arrived, but couldn't afford to quit her corporate job. She found her escape hatch by creating Vivian Lou, a home-based business in Denver, Colorado, that creates insoles that make high heels more comfortable, licensing the insole design from a group of MIT scientists she partners with. The company now brings in $1.5 million in annual revenue.

Wes Johnson, 47, got worried about his future when his work in a home-construction business slowed down during the Great Recession. To create a new income stream, the avid outdoorsman started a side business selling hammocks from his home in Raleigh, North Carolina. At first, he hired local seamstresses to sew custom-made hammocks and then, as the business grew big enough for him to quit his job, he moved on to manufacturing them. Today the business brings in $1 million in annual revenue.

Kenric Hwang, 49, is the proud pet parent to a Belgian Malinois named Shara, and foster parent to a menagerie of rescue dogs. The former insurance company program manager runs Max & Neo, an online store that sells items such as dog leashes and collars and donates one of each item that customers buy to a rescue organization. He brings in $4.5 million in annual revenue with three employees.

Alicia Schiro runs the three-person event-planning business Aced It Events. Schiro had to reinvent her business overnight when the COVID-19 pandemic hit and pivoted from planning live events to virtual ones—and grew her New York City-based business to $1.5 million in annual revenue.

Sonsoles Gonzalez, 52, realized that there were few hair care products targeting midlife women during a long career at companies such as P&G and L'Oréal, though they sometimes have to deal with challenges such as hair thinning and dryness related to coloring their hair. So, after she retired, she used some of her savings to launch Better Not Younger, which sells shampoos and other products targeting this demographic. The business brought in $2 million in revenue in 2020, with six employees, and was on track for $10–12 million for 2021.

Kathy Goughenour, 64, a former marketing manager, went back to school to earn an MBA when her boss at a telecom company said she needed the credential to get promoted. But after she came back to him with her degree, he told her he had no intention of promoting her. Tired of being denied opportunities to advance, she quit her corporate career, became a type of remote administrative pro called a virtual assistant (VA), and developed online classes and mastermind groups to teach other VAs how to run their own businesses. She's bringing in $1 million in revenue in 2021.

Geoffrey Stern, 64, runs the manufacturing business Voice Express Corp. in Fairfield, Connecticut, which makes the devices that let the teddy bears at Build-A-Bear Workshop talk and that power talking greeting cards. The twenty-year-old company brings in about $4 million in annual revenue. It is currently operating with an extended team of contractors, but has also had employees at some points.

Johan Hattingh, 71, once an executive in the financial planning world, ran through his savings and exhausted his disability insurance when a heart problem prevented him from working in his early sixties. Looking for a way to earn money that didn't require driving—he suffered fainting spells—he now runs Ain't It Nice, a garden ornament store, on Amazon. It's grown so fast he now partners with his son, a military veteran, and brings in close to $2 million in annual revenue.

Of course, building a business like any of these examples doesn't happen by accident. As you read on, you'll learn how entrepreneurs like Chris Meade and his partners—and the founders of nearly sixty other businesses—built six- and seven-figure businesses with tiny teams. All of them have valuable lessons to share about how to get off to a strong start in your business and, if you already own a business, how to fine-tune the way you work to take it to the next level.

In the pages to come, you'll learn some things that will help you start or grow your own tiny business:

- How to break out of the "employee" mindset you may have learned in school, at work, and maybe from the people who love you most—and think like the owners of today's mighty microbusinesses.
- Quick ways to generate great business ideas and to test them for viability and potential impact before you risk your time and money.
- Where to find the cash you need to bring your idea to fruition—no matter how little you have in the bank or how much debt you're in.
- What systems to put in place so you can maximize the resources you've brought to the business and protect your time.
- The best ways to spread the word about what you're selling and to build an authentic, high-personality brand without posing on Instagram in a bathing suit (unless you happen to like doing that).
- Where to find the talent you need to grow your business, whether you need a freelance web designer or your first full-time administrative assistant, and learning the ropes of managing your team (without turning into your worst corporate boss) and building a culture.
- How to master the skills you need to keep growing as an entrepreneur and to bust through revenue barriers.

You'll also learn which practices and habits contribute to the success of these entrepreneurs. When I interviewed them, I also asked them to complete a survey looking at their use of contractors, employees, and automation; where they turn when they need information and support; how they ensure growth and their mind-body routines for peak performance, among other things. You'll see the results in the appendices.

What if freeing more time to live the life you want is more important to you than money? You should come away with many tips you can use to optimize what you and your team can do, so you can earn more in less time and spend most of your day doing what you love with the people you enjoy most. You'll also be in a position to make an impact, whether it's by treating your team well, acing customer service, donating to worthy causes in your community, or becoming an influencer in your field and sharing your knowledge with thousands of other people.

To help you navigate the unexpected situations that can blindside you as an entrepreneur, each chapter includes Streetfighter Strategies that'll help you land on your feet even stronger. Much as I love discovering and writing about tiny businesses that make big money, I also run my own business and know that it's full of surprises and not always easy. Making it through the ups and downs of the economic cycle requires what my children's karate school, Tiger Schulmann's Martial Arts, calls "the non-quitting spirit." Most of us can use a refill of it from time to time, and these Streetfighter tips will give you quick ideas to help you navigate situations when you're in an environment that seems to have no rules, conditions that are unpredictable, and where you may need both conventional and unconventional approaches to navigate situations that arise spontaneously.

The foundation of it all is developing the mindset that will help you succeed in a microbusiness. In the next chapter, we'll look at how to develop the outlook you need for tiny business success.

CHAPTER 2

MINDSET MAKEOVER

Chris Meade, the entrepreneur who started CROSSNET, took a step that many people consider out of their reach. He left behind the weekly paycheck from his job in sales and dove into the business of selling a brand-new product he and his cofounder invented—while he was paying down $100,000 in student loan debt.

It was a giant leap of faith, but his desire to be his own boss and to spend his time on work that truly mattered to him was strong enough to override any doubts. Now he spends his days working on creative challenges, like perfecting the beach version of CROSSNET, while traveling with his team to work from various sunny places around the globe, whether it's an Airbnb in San Diego or Tulum, Mexico, or his home in Miami.

Meade didn't start out knowing how to run a business. He was simply tired of working in a traditional job and looking for a way out. The idea of moving to a rival company in a year to get a pay raise—the most promising option if he stayed on the conventional career track—just didn't excite him. Losing his father during his sophomore year of college had brought some urgency to his decision about whether he was on the right path. Grieving led him to ask questions about his purpose in life that many people wait decades to ask themselves. "Life is short," he would find himself thinking. "Why wake up and be unhappy?"

So, Meade took the courageous step of daring to imagine another life, one where he did what he loved. Taking the very first step—getting together with his brother Greg and their friend Mike Delpapa to brainstorm a product they could build a business around—didn't seem like a big move at the time. However, **that simple act put his life on a completely different trajectory.** Allowing himself to picture a different way of living, even when he was not completely sure of what it would look like, unlocked new energy and momentum in his life, along with reserves of creativity and resourcefulness he didn't know he had. Many of us don't realize how draining it is to suppress dreams of what we want to do until we allow ourselves to consider going after them.

After the brainstorming session, Meade wished he could start working on his business full time, but he still had to pay the bills, including those massive student loans. He couldn't just assume he'd make enough money from the business to stay solvent. So, he did the next best thing: He worked on the business in whatever time he had available. That meant breaking out his laptop on the subway and hunkering down over cartons of takeout food to do a second shift at night and on weekends for close to a year. It was during that time that he tackled big projects, such as patenting and trademarking the CROSSNET game and building the company's website, one hour at a time. Meanwhile, Delpapa, working from Connecticut, located the manufacturer on Alibaba and developed the prototype for CROSSNET. Greg Meade, who was running his own digital marketing company at the time, started setting up CROSSNET's social media presence, as he traveled around the world.

By the time they had a product to sell, the three partners were well prepared to drive customers to the website Meade had built, paying for ads on Facebook, Instagram, and Twitter. That enabled the trio to find out if customers would buy the game and to conduct experiments on how to price it. Seeing that CROSSNET was moving quickly at $100, they raised the prices to $150. "Customers were just as receptive," Meade recalls. That gave them the confidence they needed to move ahead.

THE TINY BUSINESS, BIG MONEY MINDSET

Meade and his cofounders had a fresh, innovative idea but that was only one contributor to their success. What allowed them to build a successful business was a particular mindset—the mindset that unites owners of tiny businesses that make big money.

What is that mindset? MBO Partners' founder Gene Zaino says successful owners of the high-revenue tiny businesses he works with fall into two categories (or both): (1) confident and determined or (2) very skilled or talented in a specific niche to the point that other people are already coming to them for help—and they are willing to respond to those requests. Regardless, they don't take their success for granted. "Every day, they rewind the clock and say, 'I've got to go get it again—go get that sale or extra project,'" Zaino explains. "They don't just assume that what was good yesterday will be good again today. They don't feel entitled."

After interviewing the founders and owners of the businesses you'll read about in this book, I've found they also share certain attitudes about starting and growing a business. Based on my interviews, you'll have a better chance of building a tiny business that makes big money if you share these five key attitudes.

1. You Are Ready and Willing to Define Your Future

What your teachers, parents, romantic partners, family members, professors, bosses, mentors, professional contacts, and friends think of your natural gifts and capabilities can offer tremendous insight in choosing your path in life . . . but ultimately, you must be willing to make the judgment call on whether you have the talent, experience, skill, and capacity to build a business that makes six or seven figures and beyond. And only you can decide if the freedom to be your own boss, choose the work you do, and set your daily schedule are worth enough to you to justify the challenge of starting or growing a business, *no matter what outcome that decision brings.*

Kathy Goughenour, a former marketing manager, decided she had what it takes—and was willing to leave the trappings of corporate life behind—when she started her journey to launching Expert VA Training.

Today, at age sixty-four, she brings in $1 million a year in annual revenue teaching women how to start and manage their own businesses as virtual assistants, or VAs—a type of remote administrative assistant. Her story embodies the mindset of being willing to define your own future, even if that means making a big change of career plans.

At the time Goughenour decided to become an entrepreneur, she was working at a telecom company with her feet planted firmly on the corporate track. She had just attended business school at night and on weekends to earn an MBA—a degree her manager said she needed to get a promotion. Finally, the day came when she felt confident enough to step into her boss's office and ask him for a better job. He rebuffed her. The "real" reason he'd never promote her, he said, wasn't that she lacked an MBA. "You laugh and smile too much," he lectured her.

Once the sting of his remark wore off, Goughenour realized the incident was a blessing. She was tired of the constant rounds of layoffs at her firm, cruelly punctuated by the appearance of the packing boxes in the hallway just before everyone on the team learned who would be let go next. She didn't want to spend the rest of her career worried that the stress of her job would give her a heart attack. **"I asked myself, 'If I don't get out of this job, what is going to be harder—death or taking this risk?'"** she recalls. "I felt that was the choice I was facing. It was very easy for me, after I made it, to always know what my next step would be. All I had to do was ask: Will this bring me joy or be more like that corporate world? Anything that would bring me joy was what I was going to do."

Not long after that conversation with her boss, Goughenour marched back into his office. This time, she handed him her resignation letter. She told him she planned to start a business. "You're making the biggest mistake you'll ever make," he said. "You'll never make this kind of money again."

"Not only will I make more," she told him, "but I'll be happier than I've ever been before."

That was in 1995. Unfortunately, when Goughenour plunged into her business, where she did direct sales of candles, she didn't like it as much as she expected. It was heavy on travel, and she discovered she preferred to work from home. Still, after what she'd been through at the telecom company, she wasn't ready to give up on the idea of self-employment. She kept working in the candle business while keeping her eye out for other possibilities.

Goughenour finally found the right business opportunity in 2001, when she hired a real estate broker to help her find a home. When she gave the broker some free advice on how to improve his website, he told her that many real estate agents were looking for exactly the type of help she'd offered. They were turning to VAs to do it.

To start making connections that might lead to work, Goughenour began phoning local real estate agencies to offer them free marketing training, then branched out into offering webinars to expand her reach. That helped her attract clients who needed her to write web content, such as blogs. Goughenour eventually built a membership site called the Lead Boost Club, where agents could access twenty blog posts a month that they could easily customize and post on their websites.

Getting started in the new business was not easy. Internet speeds back then weren't what they are today. "It was like the pioneer days," she recalls. But Goughenour was determined to stay in control of her own career, so she applied herself to figuring out technology. Within a few years, she had built a roster of seventy clients. Soon, however, she found there was a downside to all of the business growth: Writing all those blogs got exhausting. "You can't imagine how burned out I was," Goughenour says. She ended up selling the business in 2012.

Goughenour remained committed to staying self-employed and defining her own path, though, and was already on her way to running a new type of business by that point. Since 2010, she'd been offering both administrative and marketing services to authors, speakers, trainers, and coaches. She was seeing high demand, particularly from the professional speakers. As her workload grew, she began subcontracting work to five other VAs, referred to her by friends and contacts from her corporate career. To maintain quality control, she trained the VAs in the processes she used, designating one VA with excellent organizational skills as their project manager.

It was then that Goughenour discovered how much she enjoyed guiding other VAs—and found an ideal way to make her self-employment even more sustainable. Many of the VAs she hired were women who couldn't find the rewards they were seeking in traditional jobs—or who needed more flexibility. However, they hadn't quite mastered how to run their VA businesses profitably, and some were selling themselves short by undercharging or not setting boundaries with other clients. "Women are so giving," says Goughenour. "They really want to help." Goughenour had learned a lot over the years and knew that she could enable them to build stronger businesses.

In 2008, Goughenour decided to turn her training system for subcontractors into an online course, which she now offers at her company website, ExpertVATraining.com. She uses the course to teach students how to launch their own home-based VA businesses, offering weekly Zoom meetings with her (she keeps things lively by wearing tiaras) and one-on-one coaching, with unlimited email access. The message of her marketing for this and other services is, "What one woman can do, another can do." By showing them how to bring in more revenue by, for instance, delivering premium services that command higher pay, she was certain she could make an impact. "I fell in love with helping other women who were in the same position I was—not having people see their value," she says.

The course took off. Goughenour has found that her offerings resonate particularly well with women in the forty- to fifty-five-year-old age group, who are ready for a career change and have plenty of energy to build a business. Many of Goughenour's clients are married to men with disabilities and are the main breadwinners in their families. They need to earn enough income to pay the household bills but also to juggle their many family responsibilities. "I'm teaching them to become the 1 percent—the best there is," she says.

To stay in control of her destiny and to continue to grow her business, Goughenour has invested in her own education. About five years ago, she signed up for a mastermind with Ryan Levesque, author of the books *Ask*, a marketing guide, and *Choose*, a book on which type of business you should start. It was a big investment—$35,000—and she didn't have the money saved at the time. She made a bet on herself and her ability to learn from Levesque and took out a loan from Discover. Her business was bringing in about $100,000 annually, and she wanted to grow it to $1 million. "I needed someone who would take me higher," she says. "I never looked back."

It was at that event she met her current business coach, Jennifer Kem, who is helping her to embrace the mindset of "progress, not perfection." Under Kem's guidance, Goughenour has continued to improve on offerings such as her Virtual Expert Certification, a program designed to help VAs earn at least $80,000 a year, or half of that if they want to work part time. The program costs either $3,500 or $8,000, depending on whether they want to go part time or full time. Goughenour also now offers a mastermind called 6-Figure Virtual Expert, which costs participants anywhere from $10,000 to $25,000, depending on the level. "I'm constantly pivoting, constantly redoing," she says. Fortunately, she's built a team of about twenty reliable contractors—many of them VAs who help her with various aspects of the business.

Hearing the women's success stories keeps Goughenour motivated to see how far she can take the business. One woman, who posted her story on Goughenour's Facebook page, shared how she lost her job as she juggled medical appointments for both her husband and child, who each have health challenges. She started a VA business to pay the bills. "In just a few months she has made more working from home per month than she did in that job," says Goughenour. Another woman is on track to bring in $500,000. "We're having a lot of successes," she says. "That's what keeps me going."

For Goughenour, what she's doing is more than a business. She has created a community, where she brings clients together through online activities, such as a "show-and-tell," where they share things from their lives, whether it's the latest scarf they've knit, a cake they've baked, or a great story about their grandchildren. "I'm developing a community of women who truly support each other," says Goughenour. In 2020, she released a new book, *Leaving the Grind Behind*, to help VAs start their businesses.

Goughenour loves her lifestyle, where she and her husband live in Black, Missouri, in the middle of a national forest two hours from St. Louis. Looking back with 20/20 hindsight, she has no regrets about leaving the traditional career track to define her own future. She's free to laugh and smile all she wants—with no career penalties—and she has plenty of reason to

ARE YOU READY TO CHANGE YOUR WORK LIFE?

Below are common threads among many of the entrepreneurs you'll meet on these pages. To create a business that allows for a better income and a happier, healthier way to work, how ready and willing are you to:

1. Evaluate your capability to run a business—regardless of what others think?
   - ☐ Very ready
   - ☐ Somewhat ready
   - ☐ In between
   - ☐ Almost ready and willing
   - ☐ Not ready and willing

2. Change how you handle your personal finances to free cash to put your dreams in motion without undue financial stress?
   - ☐ Very ready
   - ☐ Somewhat ready
   - ☐ In between
   - ☐ Almost ready and willing
   - ☐ Not ready and willing

3. Adjust to a new way of working?
   - ☐ Very ready
   - ☐ Somewhat ready
   - ☐ In between
   - ☐ Almost ready and willing
   - ☐ Not ready and willing

4. Educate yourself about how to start and improve your business, whether through formal methods, like classes, or by reading, listening to podcasts, attending online events, or working with a coach?
   - ☐ Very ready
   - ☐ Somewhat ready

(continued)

☐ In between

☐ Almost ready and willing

☐ Not ready and willing

5. Take the time to set up an organized business—or hire someone to do it for you?

☐ Very ready

☐ Somewhat ready

☐ In between

☐ Almost ready and willing

☐ Not ready and willing

6. Prioritize eating healthy, getting exercise, and getting good-quality sleep so you have the stamina to run a business?

☐ Very ready

☐ Somewhat ready

☐ In between

☐ Almost ready and willing

☐ Not ready and willing

7. Find a mind-body or spiritual practice (meditation, prayer, etc.) to help you stay resilient?

☐ Very ready

☐ Somewhat ready

☐ In between

☐ Almost ready and willing

☐ Not ready and willing

8. Build a support system to help you stay committed to your business—even if it means looking beyond your existing network?

☐ Very ready

☐ Somewhat ready

☐ In between

☐ Almost ready and willing

☐ Not ready and willing

Give yourself a 5 for every "very ready," a 4 for every "somewhat ready," a 3 for every "in between," a 2 for every "almost ready and willing," and a 1 for every "not ready and willing."

If most of your scores are a 4 or 5, you are showing indicators that you are ready to start a business and to stick with it. If you're mostly scoring 3s, you're in the "thinking about it" stage. Scoring a lot of 1s and 2s suggests you probably are not ready at the moment. That doesn't mean you'll never be ready. The timing may not be right for you now, but no one knows what the future may bring.

do both. "I love what I do," she says. "It doesn't feel like work." She's got all the free time she wants to spend time with her husband or go to yoga classes with her friends. She does have one regret, though: The times she hesitated to take a chance on herself and her business. "My business could be ten times bigger than it is now if I had taken bigger risks earlier," she says. With no plans to retire, she's fortunately got many opportunities ahead to test her mettle and to continue to control her destiny.

2. You Look at Risk through a Different Lens than the Average Person

Many people in traditional careers view starting a business as something only other people can do—people with no bills to pay or dependents to support. Perhaps over the years, well-meaning parents and teachers have told you that starting a business is "risky" because it might not work out, and that "responsible" people get steady jobs that deliver a regular paycheck.

But what's risky has changed dramatically in an economy where nearly 15 percent of the population was thrown out of work almost overnight in the COVID-19 pandemic, and joblessness went as high as 39 percent in hard-hit industries like hospitality.[10] People who run thriving tiny busi-

---

10 *Unemployment Rates During the COVID-19 Pandemic* (Washington, DC: Congressional Research Service, July 20, 2021), https://crsreports.congress.gov/product/pdf/R/R46554.

nesses often feel it is safer to run a business where they call the shots than to rely on a job as their sole source of income, even if that means they could have to rustle up new revenue streams during a global health crisis. They trust themselves to hustle more than they are willing to put their economic well-being in the hands of any company they might work for. If you have that mindset or feel the seeds of it taking root, you've got a lot in common with many of the entrepreneurs in this book.

Anthony Coombs, 40, founder of Splendies, a Los Angeles–based company that brings in $13 million in annual revenue selling women's underwear via monthly subscription, embodies this way of thinking. "If you were to ask me, 'What is a greater risk—to put my future in the hands of a company owned by someone else or myself?'—I'd say working for someone else is a much greater risk," Coombs says.

Coombs, whose story you'll read in more depth in Chapter 8, started to learn about business at age eleven, when he began helping his grandparents, who lived in the same household, at a flea market stand where they sold odds and ends they found around town to make money. It was there he learned about pricing, negotiation, and the thrill of making a sale. "I'd always get a high when people would come up to the stand, and I'd think, *How do you get them to buy something?*" he recalls. Without knowing it at the time, he was starting his journey to becoming an entrepreneur.

Armed with that early understanding of how businesses worked, he developed the desire to run his own business at age sixteen, when his mother, a single parent, got laid off from her job with the state of Florida after the governor changed. The family had to go on public assistance until his mom found another job, in retail. "It was very, very difficult," says Coombs. "I remember thinking right then I never want to put my future in someone else's hands."

After going to the University of Pennsylvania, Coombs started a series of businesses, including an app that helped people connect to others nearby (it failed) and an online marketplace for used cars (it succeeded, but he was ready for bigger things). He launched Splendies in 2013, with $500, after his cousin told him about a gap in the marketplace: Almost no one was making cute underwear for full-figured women.

Fortunately, Coombs's bet on Splendies paid off. He was on track for

$17–18 million in annual revenue when we last spoke in mid-2021. To keep up with orders, he now relies on help from a robust team of contractors.

But, having experienced both business failure and success in the past, Coombs recognizes—and accepts—that the story could have turned out differently. He suggests that other entrepreneurs consider whether they could live with the possibility their business might fail before they even start one. "I have a lot of friends who say they want to run their own company," he says. "Let's say you're making $70,000 a year and working thirty to forty hours per week. The test is this: Are you willing to work sixty to eighty hours, or more, for no income with the great possibility of a loss of income for an undetermined period, with zero guarantees you'll ever get to $70,000, all for the possibility you can run a company that makes more than what you are making—and can work less? If any part of that gives you pause, I would say not to do it."

And if you do think you want to run a business, how do you feel about the fact that managing the risks that come with it will be your job, 24/7, not someone else's? "When someone has been in school and has been taught the ideas of how to be a good employee, then it's really hard to understand that running a company means you are 100 percent responsible for everything at the end of the day," Coombs says. "I don't think a lot of people embrace or want that responsibility. They'll say it, but when it comes down to it, they want to have someone else handle the big issues and problems."

Coombs got a reminder of this after he raced out to Staples in his pajamas at 11:00 a.m. one morning. The cashier, perhaps curious about the PJs, asked what type of work he did. When he said he was an entrepreneur, she confided, "I've always wanted to do that."

"You should," Coombs told her. "Why don't you?"

"I'm really scared of making mistakes," she said.

"I've already made ten mistakes and it's only 11:00 a.m.," Coombs told her.

Coombs thrives on learning from those mistakes and figuring his way out of challenges as he goes along; other people might find working that way very stressful and prefer to be part of a team where someone else is ultimately responsible for keeping the ship at sea. The question is, which scenario gives *you* the chance to do your best work and be happiest?

Streetfighter Strategy
KNOW YOUR RISK PROFILE

Examining how you view risk in your career can open up new possibilities for your work life—and help you avoid getting upset by friends and relatives who drop love bombs like, "Do you know that X percent of businesses fail?"

While many people grew up believing that getting a job was the ticket to economic security, that's changing. According to the 2020 State of Independence Report by MBO Partners, 56 percent of Americans said they'd be more secure working for themselves than in a traditional job, up from 32 percent in 2011.*

Why do so many people now see self-employment as more secure than traditional jobs? MBO Partners point to trends such as businesses' greater use of "non-employee" labor (meaning labor provided by independent workers and small businesses), easier access to healthcare through the Affordable Care Act, and the growth of online marketplaces and cloud-based software that made it "cheaper, easier, and less risky" to start and run an independent business and to find customers.

Another factor is the declining quality of traditional jobs. "Even amid the long-running expansion, companies were often ruthless about cutting jobs, restructuring, and outsourcing—all of which led to a decline in people's perception about the relative security of traditional work, and their comparative comfort with spreading the risk across multiple independent projects," the MBO Partners report adds.

Or, as Steve King at Emergent Research, which conducted the study, puts it, "[People] want control over their future and their life, instead of being at the whim of mercurial bosses and decisions made far away in corporate headquarters. If you ask them in interviews why they feel more secure, they'll tell you, 'I have control over my destiny and multiple sources of income.'"

* *The State of Independence in America 2020* (Herndon, VA: MBO Partners, 2020), http://info.mbopartners.com/rs/mbo/images/MBO_Partners_State_of_Independence_2020_Report.pdf.

That said, no one can deny running a business does come with risks, from not being able to make sales to being forced to shut your doors during a global pandemic, as many small businesses were. "A lot of this gets back to the risk-profile differences between people who start businesses and people who don't," says King. "About 40 percent of America has a risk profile that fits going out on your own to some degree. About 60 percent of the people in our studies say, 'Nah, I'd rather have a regular job.'"

Knowing which category you fit into can help you make the right decision about starting a business. Would you rather live with the risk that you might start a business that fails—or that the world of traditional work might fail you as you attempt to get a job, keep your job, or find another job after a layoff? Only you can answer that question.

What if you fall somewhere in the middle of the risk-tolerance spectrum? One way to have the best of both the world of traditional jobs and entrepreneurship is starting a business on the side and hiring someone else to run it for you. Andy Humphrey, 41, a landscape architect from Traverse City, Michigan, took this route at his e-commerce business, Sprinkler Supply Store, which he founded in 2010. The father of three started it as a side business, along with a second store that sells Christmas lights, while working at an irrigation-supply distributor. But he doesn't work in these businesses during the day: he spends his time doing full-time freelance consulting on irrigation. He's worked on high-profile construction projects, such as Hudson Yards and Battery Park in New York City. He also runs a podcast called Sprinkler Nerd, where he talks about topics like winter watering and soil-moisture technology with other enthusiasts.

In 2008, Humphrey hired the first of four employees, who now handle customer service, marketing, logistics, and website merchandising for both e-commerce businesses. He has no intention of leaving his consultancy behind. "I only believe you should quit your job if it's something you don't like doing," he says. "There's no reason to quit if it's putting money on the table. I enjoy the irrigation industry. I choose to stay connected outside of e-commerce. I think that's a shift we're seeing: trying to find employment happiness."

3. You're Willing to Learn What You Need to Know as You Go Along

Starting a business, even a tiny one, can be a little intimidating if you've never done it before. That may be especially true if you've done well in school and in the world of traditional work, where the path to success is much clearer and more linear and, if you have any doubt you'll be able to handle your next move, there are plenty of credentials to earn—titles, degrees and certificates, and continuing education hours—to boost your own confidence that you're "ready."

Things don't work that way when you run your own business. Even if you've earned an MBA or a degree in entrepreneurship, it does not guarantee you're "qualified." There is so much to do in a business that, from day one, you'll need to dive into doing things way outside of your professional skill set. If your business is very innovative, you may have to take on new tasks for which *no one* is officially qualified.

To start and run a tiny business that makes big money, you'll need to embrace that, and be ready to move ahead long before you've figured everything out. "Everyone is chasing confidence," says Micala Quinn, who trains women on how to start home-based businesses and hosts the *Live Free Podcast* for entrepreneurs. Learning by doing is so valuable that she suggests you don't wait until the day you feel like you're perfectly prepared—because it will never come. "We need to put our focus on having the courage to try," she says.

It's a little like taking up a practice like yoga or martial arts. In my hot yoga class, the teachers often remind us that it's okay to "get messy" in a posture that we're still learning. You can't learn to do a handstand if you don't risk trying it by at least putting your hands on the floor and lifting a single leg, or propping yourself against the wall. Inevitably, if you keep trying, you'll find that all of those imperfect handstands are getting you somewhere you couldn't go before. One day, you'll walk into the studio and be able to do a handstand without thinking about it. But you never know exactly when that day will arrive. You'll only learn it if you keep showing up.

Elizabeth Davis, 35, an engineer, was willing to learn in this way—and it has paid big dividends. She was working as an assistant project manager at an engineering firm when she started her Atlanta, Georgia–based business, Shedavi, which sells shampoos and other products aimed at women who want to grow longer hair. During the day, she worked on plans for the construction of Porsche's North American headquarters in Hapeville, Georgia, and was on the team that built the MGM Casino at the National Harbor in Washington, DC. Davis liked her job but knew that working as a project manager wasn't her life's passion. She'd always known she wanted to start her own business, but hadn't yet pursued the idea. "I didn't know what it was going to be," she explains.

Davis let the idea of starting a business percolate, staying open to clues from her daily life on what direction to take. The first major hint came when she thought about what she liked to do when she got home at night. In a perpetual quest for longer hair, Davis would mix up natural elixirs and other products she made with herbs, essential oils, and Ayurvedic products.

As she tested her hair products on herself and her friends—and found, over the months, that they worked—it dawned on her that she had already started the business. Nonetheless, part of her resisted the idea that running one could be this much fun. "A hair care business sounds too easy or too good to be true," she says, "but that's what I did."

In 2014, Davis finally decided to take her passion seriously and formed Shedavi as a side business. "What inspired me to be an entrepreneur was really to be able to build something from the ground up and build a legacy for myself, my community, and the African American community," she says. She registered the company with the state of Georgia in 2014, then worked on it during every spare moment. "It took me time to develop the product, get the branding done, and do all of the basic things I needed to launch," she recalls.

Although Davis had saved up about six months of living and business expenses before the launch, she didn't want to burn through it quickly. To make her money last, she turned to two credit cards with zero-percent interest deals for eighteen months. That gave her about $25,000 to spend on research and development, raw goods, tools, and packaging, and for work on branding. "All I had to do was make a minimum payment on my credit card," she says. She paid off the balance once she started making sales.

Still, Davis's budget was limited. Instead of renting a commercial facility to create her first batch of hair products, she mixed them up in her kitchen, experimenting as she went along and learning from each experiment. That was where she made the first 1,000 units of her first product, a hair and scalp elixir, pouring it into bottles she ordered online from a packaging store and adding labels from a label company. She found resources like this by doing online research.

Davis also introduced a vitamin to support healthy hair. Vitamins can't be made in a home kitchen, under health and safety laws. To make sure her products were made properly, Davis used part of her budget to hire an FDA-approved factory.

Then it came time to develop the look and feel of the brand. Davis, who'd studied architecture her first year in college, always had an eye for design and loved to draw, so she tapped that hidden talent and sketched the company's bottle designs and label before having a graphic designer polish her work. "I wanted the packaging to be gorgeous," she recalls. "I wanted it to look clean, simple, and clear, but I also wanted it to have a luxurious side to it."

Davis was just as willing to experiment with marketing. Long before she had a product to sell, Davis put up an Instagram page where she shared tips and information about healthy hair. By the time she introduced her hair and scalp elixir and the vitamin, she had attracted 10,000 followers who shared her passion. "I put videos together myself on how to use the product," she recalls. "We distributed them through social marketing channels. That's how I was able to get so many people."

All this experimenting took time, but Davis was willing to spend it doing something she loved. By February 2016, she was finally ready to begin selling the elixir and vitamins. Her family, friends, and Instagram followers became her first customers after she did a countdown to the launch. Davis got her first taste of the rewards of all her experiments when she made about $2,000 the first weekend after her product launch. Having an audience helped her as she did the countdown to the release of her first product.

Fortunately, Shedavi grew quickly. Rather than focus on selling her products one $25 bottle at a time, Davis experimented with grouping them according to her customers' needs, which helped in selling more products. Her first kit was the Hair Starter Bundle ($49). "Customers like the recommendation and prescription of the 'bundle,'" she explains. "They know the bundle caters toward their specific problem or issues."

Davis also experimented with production and shipping. Like many solo entrepreneurs, Davis wasn't in a position to open a factory—so she did the next best thing and tried working with an outsourced manufacturer called a co-packer to make the formulas and to put them into the bottles she designed. This gave her access to the manufacturer's knowledge and experience, reducing the learning curve and newbie mistakes. "That's something I recommend initially," says Davis. "When you first start your business, you should probably outsource." When it came time to ship her products, Davis didn't pack them up in boxes herself to mail them to consumers, either. She also took a chance on working with an outsourced partner that does third-party logistics, sometimes called 3PL, so she could concentrate on building the brand.

To expand her marketing efforts as the company grew, Davis tried working with other professionals. When she needed a graphic designer, social media manager, videographer, and digital marketing manager, she turned to freelancers, finding them through word-of-mouth recommendations from her network, and even on Instagram. She focused on building long-term relationships with them, so she had a team she could count on. "It's not a one-off thing," she says. "I work with them consistently."

All of this cost money, of course. Davis had to pay everyone—the factory, the shipping partner, and the freelancers. With the company bringing in $1 million in revenue from February 2016 to February 2017, Davis finally felt comfortable leaving her job in March 2017, when she knew she could cover both her personal expenses and business overhead. But her openness to learning while she went along paid off. Davis, whose business has more than 65,000 followers on Instagram, was expecting to double its size in 2021. "The most important thing is to distinguish yourself," she says. "No one else is selling my product."

4. You Are Prepared to Create the Financial Base You Need to Embrace Business Ownership—Even if You Can't Quit Your Day Job

If you're beyond the stage where you can crash on your parents' couch if you go broke, there's no way around planning your finances carefully before you start your business. For many of the entrepreneurs in this book, starting a business on the side while they worked at a day job was the best way to do this. Sometimes, that can mean working very long days for a year or two. But it isn't permanent. Owners of tiny businesses that make big money frame this phase in their mind as a bridge to carving out a new way of working, and living, that will be much more rewarding on every front. And you may be surprised by how much energy you have when it comes to building something you love—for yourself and your loved ones. As the poet David Whyte says, "The antidote to exhaustion is wholeheartedness."

Brian Abrams, 46, a father of two, could not quit working when he decided to start his own business, so he spent some time planning how he'd exit from a stressful job at a Boston-based staffing firm. He'd just joined that company, but it was sold four months after he got there—"Not what I signed up for," he recalls—and he had no desire to hunt for another job in staffing, a demanding field where disengagement was rampant. "I'm probably going to have an uninspired boss and work with people who didn't have the kind of motor I have," he reasoned.

So, in August 2014, Abrams went out on his own and created PMO Partners, his information technology (IT) project-management consulting firm in Groton, Massachusetts. But before he quit his job and went all-in with the business, Abrams did short-term consulting work. "It was a good way for me to keep making money while I was planning," he says. It also freed him from his one-and-a-half-hour commute each way, giving him more time to work on the business. During that time, his wife paid most of the household bills with her salary, after they discussed what it might be like if she became the main earner for a while and she agreed to take that on. Although Abrams was excited about the potential rewards of running his own business, he knew he might not make money for the first six months. That possibility didn't dampen his wife's enthusiasm for his new venture.

"She thought it was a good idea," he recalls. And they had saved $5,000 so he could pay for basic startup costs such as putting up a website, getting incorporated, and putting the right legal documents in place.

With his wife's vote of confidence, Abrams began planning what he would do at his company on his evenings and weekends for a year, so when he was ready to start up, he could build momentum quickly. Finally, when his last consulting gig ended, he dove into building PMO Partners full time. "I knew, going into it, that there were going to be bumps in the road and mistakes along the way," he says. "I wasn't afraid of that. My feeling was just 'Be really good at what you do and acknowledge you're going to run into challenges. Hustle.'"

So how did Abrams build a sustainable enough income to leave his corporate career permanently? One way was by specializing in a narrow, in-demand niche that he knew well. Abrams had enough knowledge of his field to start a more general staffing agency, but he decided to focus on placing IT project managers because he knew other firms were not paying much attention to this space—meaning he'd have a better flow of work. "There's a lot of competition in the staffing world," says Abrams.

Abrams also knew he could earn more by working with project managers, particularly those at the senior level, than other types of professionals. In the staffing industry, recruiters' commissions are tied to the salaries of the people they place in jobs. Senior-level project managers generally earn $80,000 to $150,000 a year, or more in some cases, he says. That meant Abrams's commissions, in the range of 20 percent, would add up quickly. "If I place someone in a permanent position, and they are making $100,000, the client might pay $20,000," he says. Similar rewards would come into play even when he placed project managers in shorter-term, temporary gigs, with their high hourly rates translating into substantial commissions. "I'm billing them out at $100 an hour, $130 an hour, $150 an hour—that's what drives the revenue so high," he says.

Abrams's decision to focus on project-management professionals helped him get to $760,000 in revenue by the end of 2015. Determined to grow the business, Abrams resisted the temptation to do everything himself and brought in professionals to tackle assignments outside of his area of expertise. Instead of trying to learn marketing, for instance, Abrams retained an outside marketing firm that does most of his marketing and social media. "I'm laser-focused on the recruiting and staffing world," he says. "That stuff, I know."

Within his own realm, Abrams made time to network, both online and off, to keep the business growing. He attends a lot of industry events, such as user groups for project managers, holds a monthly webinar on a topic relevant to project-management pros, and frequently posts on LinkedIn about topics that will interest those in the field. "There's that balance between getting my name out there and actually running the business," says Abrams.

By focusing on delivering excellent service to his existing customers and on meeting new ones, Abrams got to $1.5 million in annual revenue by 2016—while enjoying a lot of professional satisfaction along the way. "I really like connecting with candidates and working with them through-out the job search process," he says. "I like working with clients, under-standing their needs, helping them find the ideal employee, and creating a great match."

Just as he approached $1 million for the first time, Abrams realized he needed a director of operations to handle back-office work, such as finan-cial documents and candidate paperwork, and made his first hire. With his operations chief handling tasks that were bogging him down, he found, growth started to take off. "She brought a lot of structure to the com-pany," he says.

As the business has continued to expand, Abrams hasn't hesitated to seek advice from outside experts with the knowledge to help him grow his firm. Through his marketing firm, Abrams learned about Tom Erb, a con-sultant in the staffing and consulting industry, whom he hired to assess his firm, to help him identify and shore up any gaps in what he was doing. He also attended a two-day conference with Mike Gionta, a successful recruiter who now teaches other recruiters how to build their sales pipelines. Though he knows his specialty well, he also realizes he's still relatively new to run-ning a business. "To this day I'm still learning," says Abrams. "I've never built a business before."

In the meantime, Abrams has started to build a board of advisors. "These were people I knew and trusted who could advise me on things I was stuck on," he says. Focused on building his business, Abrams never looks at placements of project managers as one-time relationships: "I always say, 'I am looking forward to working with you for years to come.'"

Many take him up on that—and this has added to the flow of work that makes his now three-employee business sustainable. "One of the things that makes me proud is that some of these candidates I've known for years and years always think of me when they're becoming available again," he says. "Earlier this year I placed a consultant I've known for ten years. I never had a chance to place him before, due to timing. I finally placed him."

During the COVID-19 pandemic, Abrams found that all of the efforts he put in to build a strong foundation for the business paid off. "We stayed busy," he says. "We got lucky in connecting with organizations that had an uptick in business." For instance, he took on a couple of food-manufacturing clients and one that specialized in developing online college courses for colleges and universities. He also participated in a network of a couple of thousand recruiters. They help each other find good candidates and make placements in their areas of expertise. "If I'm successful in placing these candidates, I get half the fee," he says.

All of this takes continuous effort and an ongoing commitment to reinvest in the business, but Abrams is okay with that. He's built a career where he can work on his terms and a business that has become a valuable asset. "I'm never going back to corporate America—I promise you that," says Abrams. "I'm never going to have a boss again. That's not the plan."

5. You Are Willing to Keep Showing Up

No one can start or grow a business by just thinking about it. You have to make time to work on it, a little bit at a time, even if you have to squeeze it into your morning commute, as Chris Meade did, or evenings when you'd rather crash and watch Netflix. Without exception, every very successful tiny business owner I've interviewed commits to showing up for business regularly. Fortunately, making small, consistent efforts can get you somewhere over weeks or months.

HOW CLOSE ARE YOU TO MAKING
A BIG CHANGE IN YOUR WORK LIFE?

The fact that you've picked up this book suggests that when it comes to
your career, you're very likely entering one of the stages of change that the
psychotherapists James O. Prochaska, John Norcross, and Carlo DiCle-
mente describe in the book *Changing for Good*. By figuring out where you
are now, you'll be able to set the stage to move forward with your dream
of starting or growing your business, stay motivated, overcome obstacles
and, when ready, actually start running your business. Sometimes, change
may not come at the pace you expect, but eventually, you'll be surprised
to find you've moved into the next stage—or realize you've gone as far with
this as you ever will. These are the changes they describe, and how they
apply to where you might be in your journey to building a business.

Precontemplation: You may be in a stage of questioning your current work
situation and opening up to the possibility of change. You're not yet doing
anything to actively move toward changing it. You may not even be sure yet
that you dislike your current work situation enough to change it.

Contemplation: Evidence is mounting that your current situation—
whether it is a job, a period of not working, or the way you are running your
current business—may be causing dissatisfaction or even harming you.
You may be open to the idea of starting a business, or optimizing a current
one that you've been growing on the side but are still a little unsure that
by changing your work situation, you could improve your life. At the same
time, you're willing to learn more about your options to start a business,
perhaps going into this with the idea: "Maybe I'll pick up one or two good
ideas I can apply to my life, even if I never start a business."

Determination: You're on the verge of taking concrete steps to change
your work life. You start using the methods you learn in *Tiny Business,
Big Money* and other sources to test your business idea and to get it rolling, and begin to see momentum and results, like getting leads to new
business and actual sales. You start to experience positive changes in

your well-being as you leave behind ways of working (or a situation where perhaps you were not able to work) that were detrimental to your life and embrace new ones. Once you're ready, this leads to the next critical step: action.

Maintenance: You've started the business and are getting into a rhythm of earning money from it. You may encounter setbacks as you experiment, finding that not all of your offerings succeed, some clients turn out to be more trouble than they're worth, or you have inner obstacles to overcome, like asking customers to pay you when they're late. The key to this stage is to realize that even the most successful entrepreneurs in the world encounter setbacks. Sir Richard Branson, the founder of Virgin, had to cope with his airline and travel empire being all but grounded during COVID-19, to name one example. Once you're in the maintenance stage, the key to sustaining your new work situation is to find ways to stay resilient so you can keep on keeping on. You'll learn more about how to do that through all the case studies in this book. This brings us to our next point . . .

That was what Abby Walker, 44, did when she started Vivian Lou, a Denver-based company that sells insoles for high heels and brings in $3 million in annual revenue.

Walker was the chief marketing officer for a natural-products company when she happened upon the idea for her business. During her fifteen-year corporate career, she'd always loved dressing up in stylish stilettos. "I wore high heels every single day," she recalls. Though she was juggling a career in communications and marketing with raising two children, now ages eight and ten, Walker somehow managed to fit in time to write a blog on high heels called *Mama's Shoes*.

However, Walker's passion came with a price. Some of those pretty high heels turned out to be cruel shoes. Tired of sore feet, Walker began looking into the idea of creating a natural foot spray that would lessen the pain of high heels. In doing her market research, however, she came across a type of insole that made it possible to wear her favorite shoes comfortably, and realized there was a better way to solve what was a literal pain point for many high-heel lovers.

Walker had soon called the head of the insole company, Insolia, to ask why she had never heard of its brand. "We're a bunch of MIT engineers who don't know how to market the product to women," he told her. Walker offered to help him in exchange for a cut in the sales. She licensed the right to sell the insoles in North America under a brand she created, Vivian Lou, with Insolia handling the manufacturing on contract, tapping into $7,500 in startup cash she and her husband had set aside. That was in 2014.

Although Walker believed in her product, she had a lot of work ahead of her. The makers of Insolia had built an email distribution list with 18,000 names of past customers, but it was inactive. She set to work resuscitating the list by sending out mailings again, so visitors would come to the website she put up using Shopify, an inexpensive e-commerce platform, chipping away at it in her time off from work. "I was able to revive a lot of those customers," she says. Nonetheless, the business grew slowly, given her already packed schedule. "In a good month, I'd make $1,500 worth of sales," she recalls.

To free more time for the business, Walker quit her job—a big financial decision for her family. She and her husband agreed she would devote herself to Vivian Lou for the summer of 2015 and see where things led. Aiming to make the most of her summer off, Walker hired a fulfillment house to send the insoles to customers, realizing she was too busy to do it. "I knew if it were on me to get the orders out the door, the business was doomed," she says.

She also attended a sales seminar in Minneapolis to learn more about pricing—a critical decision for someone who only sold one product. When Walker told the seminar leader she was selling her insoles at two pairs for $19.95, the sales trainer told her they were way underpriced and encouraged her to sell a single pair for that price. "When should I raise my prices?" Walker asked.

"Tomorrow," the seminar leader told her.

Walker swallowed hard and raised her prices the next day. "I only got two pieces of hate mail from my customers—and started having more sales," she says.

Although Walker has since raised her price to $29 for a pair of insoles to make sure she is covering her overhead, customers continue to flock. "It doesn't do anyone any good to underprice your product," she says.

Walker was bringing in more money, but she still wasn't making enough from the business to say goodbye permanently to corporate life by the end of the summer, so she decided to take another corporate marketing job, this time at Ameriprise Financial Services. Still, she didn't give up on taking the business full time, given the feedback she was getting from customers on the insoles. "I knew this company was going to be something," she recalls.

Her big break came when she applied for and was accepted to a pitch night for Story, a gallery-like shop in New York City. Besides pitching founder Rachel Shechtman, Walker found herself telling her story to *Good Morning America* and HSN that night. On Shechtman's recommendation, she says, HSN fast-tracked the approval process for her insoles, and her products sold out the first time she went on the air, in January 2016. Walker took Shechtman's advice to redesign her packaging and, inspired by Spanx, opted for one in a cheerful red.

Walker persuaded her husband it was time to quit corporate America again after that success and doubled down on her efforts to grow the business. She began learning all she could about Facebook advertising and plunged into it in earnest. By September 2016, she had a "phenomenal" sales month and was featured on *The View*. The ensuing sales enabled her to pay off $80,000 in debt used for advertising, inventory, packaging, and warehousing of the insoles. In 2016, she hit $600,000 in annual revenue. With the business humming, Walker expanded internationally and introduced an insole design for flats. She grew the business to $3 million in annual revenue, a level at which it was profitable by 2018.

Although Walker still hasn't hired any employees, she has managed to operate like a much bigger company by finding inexpensive ways to extend what she can do in her one-woman, work-from-home business. For instance, Walker outsources the packaging and shipping of her products to a warehouse in Denver. She has relied over time on contractors to help her with website design, social media advertising, and A/B testing, a process to determine how customers are responding to a website. Similarly, she outsources customer service.

She also relies on automation to handle tasks like eliciting reviews from customers, for which she relies on a tool called Yotpo. This has helped Vivian Lou get nearly 2,500 reviews. "Reviews are critically important," she says. However, the tool, while efficient, doesn't do all of the work for her. She offers a 20-percent discount on a customer's next purchase if they post a review. She also guarantees that if the insoles don't work for someone, she will happily refund 100 percent of the purchase price.

When COVID-19 hit, many of Walker's stylish customers were working from home and had traded their dress shoes for fuzzy slippers. And with events like weddings shut down for an extended period, no one was going out in stilettos on the weekend. Sales took a frightening nose-dive but Walker found that the pause allowed her to get back into the weeds of her company and to reconnect with what made her launch it in the first place. "It was an opportunity to step back and look at what I loved about my company, and wanted to change," she says. Working from home in her favorite high heels to keep her spirits up—"I felt I could breathe a little better," she says—she battened down the hatches, canceling subscriptions she no longer needed, and let go of her customer service team and Facebook ad agency, taking on that work herself. Then she set to work introducing an insole for athletic and athleisure shoes. "It just made sense, given the current climate," she told me.

It wasn't easy, given that her two children were also home, doing online school. She stayed focused by keeping her eye on one metric each day: the cost of acquiring each sale. "If I spend X amount on advertising to get that order, I'll be within my profitability goal," she says. Because she continued to show up for herself and her business, even when she was stretched to the max and facing circumstances beyond her control, her business ended up more profitable than ever when she closed 2020, even though revenue had declined to $1.5 million.

There is a lifestyle reason for this. Now relocated to Denver with her family after living in Minneapolis and then Milwaukee, Walker wants to be present for her kids. "My mission as a CEO and business owner is peace and freedom," she says. "I don't do things that take away from my freedom as a business owner or jeopardize my peace. I manage my business very simply."

As Walker found, it's easier to tough it out in a small business during tough times if you start in an industry you love. In the next chapter, we'll look at how to uncover the field where you can run a tiny business that makes big money, and how to conduct the small experiments that will enable you to determine if your idea will work.

CHAPTER 3

FIND YOUR IDEAL TINY BUSINESS
(OR LET IT FIND YOU)

Greg Berry was serving on his town council in Pottstown, Pennsylvania, when he discovered his community was facing a big challenge. Whenever the town needed to sell a used item, such as a police car, it was difficult to find buyers. "No one knew it was for sale," he says. The town couldn't just post a listing on eBay. It had to sell everything in closed bidding. With little competition, the bidders would often be able to buy valuable items for a song—say $300 for a police car worth $3,000. Meanwhile, the town council struggled to find the money to pay for community events, like parades.

Berry, then 26, had worked in IT and saw an opportunity to help. Assuming other towns had the same problem, he believed they would be open to using a central marketplace designed to follow government regulations. He made a few calls to friends in other municipalities to see if his hunch was correct. When they sounded excited about his idea, he put up a simple auction website called Municibid. There, towns could post what they wanted to sell. He made sure the site was compliant with the rules governments need to follow.

It wasn't long before he found his first customer: a town that wanted to sell a lawnmower. "They were hoping to get $100," he recalls. "They got $500. They couldn't believe it." Not long after that, Municibid sold a police car. "It had a blown engine," he recalls. "They were hoping they would get a few hundred bucks for it. They got $3,000. We were able to get true market value for things that were [previously] selling for pennies on the dollar."

Berry asked his early customers for testimonials, which he posted on the website. He began calling other towns and telling them about their success stories. That was back in 2006. Today, Municibid serves 4,000 state and local governments. With a team of ten people and several contractors, it has made the Inc. 5000 list, which requires that companies must have a minimum revenue of $2 million.

Berry, now 41, also loves the opportunity to make a difference. For many governments, selling surplus goods is a great way to raise much-needed cash. "They always needed money, even before the coronavirus pandemic," says Berry. "COVID really hurt a lot of local and state governments. They are not getting as much tax money from local businesses."

WHAT BUSINESS IS RIGHT FOR YOU?

Looking for a tiny business that makes big money is different from finding one that you can run solo or turn into the next hot startup. These are lifestyle businesses powered by the owner's resources. Unlike solo ventures, though, they depend heavily on employees, a regular network of outside contractors, or a combination, meaning people-related costs are higher. The tradeoff is that tiny businesses tend to have more growth potential than a business where one person does most of the work.

To find the right business for you, it helps to look for opportunities where (1) you're genuinely interested in what the business does, (2) there is significant market demand, and (3) you can run the business with very low overhead, very high profits, or a high enough sales volume to make money even if profits are on the lower end. Without these three things, it will be hard, as an individual, to build a tiny business that brings in substantial revenue and profits. Fortunately, there are more opportunities where you can have fun and earn a great living than ever before, thanks to the digital revolution.

For Berry and many of the entrepreneurs you'll read about in this book, finding the right tiny business took some time and experimenting, often in several ventures. Municibid wasn't Berry's first business. He'd started his IT services company right out of high school and then tried launching an online hockey supply store, but, in those early days of e-commerce, hit a big obstacle: "It was way too expensive," he recalls. Once he started winning customers for Municibid, he went all-in on his auction site in 2010 and sold the IT services firm. By that point, he says, "It needed my full-time attention." By experimenting and staying open to what these experiments were teaching him, he was able to find his ideal seven-figure business.

Finding the right tiny business starts with research. Simply living your life and paying attention to what's going on in your workplace, industry, or outside activities (family, friends, recreation, fitness activities, worship, charitable work, etc.) is often the best source of clues. You'll be in an ideal position to spot opportunities—and develop an intuitive understanding of the financial realities of your field. I'm not planning to start a yoga school anytime soon, but I'm a very passionate hot yoga student. Simply observing how my hot yoga studio navigated the pandemic—holding online and outdoor group classes during the peak in 2020 and then transitioning to socially distanced, masked-up, twelve-person in-studio classes and later operating at 40-percent capacity—taught me a lot about surviving in this industry. Once you start looking for opportunities to learn about tiny businesses in your daily life, you'll find they are all around you.

It's also important to determine if you can do business successfully in a tiny operation before you make a substantial investment of time and money. In some industries, tiny businesses can be competitive. In others, large or midsize companies dominate to the extent that it will be hard to coexist with them. You may have to find a creative way to find a niche for yourself. For instance, it would be hard for a tiny business to become an automaker, but many small manufacturers make components for automakers.

Look at the process of educating yourself as similar to the research you'd do before accepting a job offer. Before you gave up a job to accept an offer at a new one, you might read up on the new company, talk to colleagues and connections who work there or work with the company, and review the benefits package carefully. Fortunately, it doesn't take very long to do this detective work when it comes to a new business—usually not more than two or three months.

Your work might also give you clues. At age fifty-two, Sonsoles Gonzalez started the brand Better Not Younger, which sells shampoo, hair care formulations, and nutritional products designed for older women, after twenty-eight years in senior roles at corporations such as P&G and L'Oréal. She had sat through meetings for years where almost every new product targeted women aged twenty-five to forty. She would often joke ruefully, "What happens to women forty-five-plus? Do they die?" But it was those meetings that showed her there was a gap in the marketplace for products aimed at women who were over forty, who often have to deal with challenges such as hair thinning and dryness related to coloring their hair. "It's the perfect storm for everything that's happening with your head," says her business partner and chief operations officer (COO) Augusto Moronto.

Gonzalez started her business, based in Miami, Florida, after being retired for six months but getting bored. Armed with the extensive knowledge she'd built up during her career, she felt confident enough to start the company in January 2018, with her savings and funds raised from friends and family. She went on to raise $2 million from private investors known as angel investors. The first year in business, Better Not Younger brought in $1 million in revenue through its website and stores. In 2020, revenue hit $2 million, and in 2021, the company projected $10–12 million in revenue from its fourteen core products. It only had six employees and fifteen freelancers. "The key for me," she says, "is never losing sight of the longer-term vision for where I want to take this business, as every short-term decision needs to be a building block toward that."

If you don't have your big idea yet, take a close look at the charts in Appendix I. To identify the main categories of tiny businesses where you have the best shot of breaking seven-figure revenue, my team and I sorted

Streetfighter Strategy
FAST-TRACK YOUR RESEARCH

Most people have different learning styles—some people prefer reading, some watching videos, and some listening to audio. You'll speed your due diligence on any industry and niche within it if you consume the information in *your* ideal format. If you prefer learning by video, try searching YouTube. If you prefer audio, go to Listen Notes, a search engine for podcasts. Also search for long-tail keywords such as "market research e-commerce" on Slideshare, where many market research firms publish their findings. Focus your research on the key players in the industry, the size of the businesses they run, their approximate revenues, their locations, key trends affecting the industry, and the industry outlook.

Here are some other sources to try:

The US Small Business Administration: The "Market Research and Competitive Analysis" page is a great place to start your research, with several free reports.*

The International Trade Administration: If you are looking to branch out into the international market, this agency's free reports may be helpful. (legacy.trade.gov)

The NAICS Association: In Appendix I: Tiny Businesses That Make Big Money, you'll see the North American Industry Classification System (NAICS) codes for just about every industry that might interest you. The NAICS Association publishes free reports that will help you get a quick understanding of the competition in a particular niche. (naics.com)

The Bureau of Labor Statistics. This government agency provides *Industry at a Glance* reports. These will tell you what the average wages are in a given industry—something that's important to know if you're planning to hire people—and whether employees in that field tend to be union-

---

* "Plan Your Business: Market Research and Competitive Analysis," Business Guide, US Small Business Administration, https://www.sba.gov/business-guide/plan-your-business/market-research-competitive-analysis#section-header-5.

ized, which may impact how you must set up the business in certain states. (bls.gov)

Research reports: Once you get clarity on whether you want to move ahead, it may be worthwhile to invest in a research report by one of the major players, such as Gale Business Insights (gale.com), Gartner (gartner. com), IBISWorld (ibisworld.com), or Euromonitor (euromonitor.com).

Some companies sell market reports for each NAICS code. These reports can help you learn about which companies already do business in this industry and how many competitors there are. D&B (dnb.com), Mergent Online (mergentonline.com), and Statista (statista.com) have robust offerings.

pretty much every industry in the United States, using the North American Industry Classification System (NAICS) code. We calculated the average revenue and the average payroll for businesses that use each code, and then ranked them according to how much money they have left over after we subtracted payroll. (This list uses US data, but these industries operate globally. If you plan to do business outside the United States, look for similar, country-specific data, as market realities could be different.)

Studying the industries near the top of the list will point you toward niches where you'll have a better chance of generating high revenue and, depending on how you manage the business, decent profits. Profit is, to put it in very basic terms, the money you have left over after paying your expenses. Bear in mind that the methodology I used—subtracting the average payroll for each industry from the average revenue—is a blunt instrument. It'll give you a broad idea of which businesses are profitable to get you started in your research. Because I could not gather and include data on the overhead for every industry in America without writing an encyclopedia, it will not give you the complete picture. For any industry, you'll need to do more homework on the overhead to make an educated decision. You can do this by reading market research reports, attending industry events, talking with people who work in that field, etc. (More on that later!) For insights into how much profit businesses generate, check out the data compiled by New York University's Stern School of Business, as well as trade magazines' benchmarking reports.[11]

As you'll see, we sorted our list into businesses with fewer than five employees, five to nine employees, and ten to nineteen employees. That way, you'll be able to see how many small-scale businesses already operate in a niche successfully. If there are only a handful in a category, it's important to research why that is before you plunge ahead. There might be some barrier to entry to smaller businesses. If your ideal business is fewer than five employees, you'll want to focus on the list that provides details on that size, as there are some industries where you'll need more people to do business.

As you look at the options, don't ignore the businesses at the middle or even the bottom of the list. Although most businesses in a given category may not be bringing in much money, there may be outliers who earn more than everyone else because they have a very different business model. One example is hair salons. While some people run tiny salons from their homes or small storefronts that make very little money, other salons are high-end operations with multiple stylists that sell their own products through their salons and online, bringing in considerably more money. (It's also possible that the numbers for payroll minus expenses are depressed in categories with a large number of "cash" businesses that are not claiming all of their income on their taxes!).

If you're thinking about entering an industry that is new to you, also speak with people running businesses like the one you want to own in that industry. To make connections, start attending industry events, whether by showing up for the many free webinars that have proliferated since the COVID-19 pandemic, going to in-person events, or joining a trade association and taking part in its gatherings. You'll have to pay a membership fee to join most trade associations, but there's no substitute for getting on-the-ground information

---

11 "Operating and Net Margins by Sector," Stern School of Business, New York University, updated January 2021, http://pages.stern.nyu.edu/~adamodar/New_Home_Page/datafile/margin.html.

Streetfighter Strategy
FIND A DISASTER-PROOF BUSINESS

If you choose a brick-and-mortar business, make sure it has potential online revenue streams you can unlock if a crisis shuts down or limits how in-person businesses can operate. Also, make sure you can accept digital payments. Yes, the processing fees cost money but you'll pay a bigger price if no one can pay you at all. The good news is, once you invest the time in preparing, you'll know that you're well positioned to make it through a major business interruption with your income more or less intact.

from people who already work in that field. Attend a few meetings and pay close attention to what's on everyone's minds, the industry trends they're concerned with—and excited about—how technology is changing the industry, and any clues you can get about how everyone is doing financially in their businesses. It's also helpful to join industry groups on LinkedIn and Facebook and discussions on Clubhouse. Pay attention to the overall mood and how you feel being around the people you're meeting. You'll feel a very different vibe when you're surrounded by people who are hanging on for dear life in a dying, dated, or troubled industry than in one where everyone is pumped up about the opportunities ahead. Listen to your gut instincts. They are powerful.

Another great source of ideas for businesses you could start are the online marketplaces where people buy and sell businesses, such as BizBuy-Sell (bizbuysell.com), BizQuest (bizquest.com), and Flippa (flippa.com). Even if you are mainly thinking about starting a business from scratch, the listings will give you an idea of which types of small businesses people are running right now. You'll also learn the level of investment they might take, which type of facility is required, how many people usually work in them, and other practical details that will help you assess whether you have the necessary startup cash lined up or would enjoy running the day-to-day. It will also give you a sense of which businesses are not doing well right now.

If many people in a particular industry are selling, you'll want to do some digging into what's going on. You don't want to start a type of business that sounds great on paper but is a dud.

If you want to join an industry that's brand new to you, you'll need to do more legwork to read about it. Fortunately, that's gotten easier than ever before, given the explosion of YouTube channels, podcasts, and online summits on just about every area of entrepreneurship, as well as blogs, newsletters, and other publications. To keep your research costs down, start by looking for free material, such as blogs and videos, by entrepreneurs who are doing *exactly* what you want to do. (Steer clear of heavily advertised, pricey programs that promise you five steps to getting rich and owning a Maserati while you're lying on the couch watching football.) Pay close attention both to what the entrepreneurs say and how interesting their message is to you. If you start a similar type of business, you're going to have to immerse yourself in the details, so it's best to figure out now if you do want to think about it seven days a week. Don't worry about whether other people think it is interesting. What matters is how you feel about it.

Also take time to understand the financial side of the ventures you're considering. There are many ways to determine a business's true potential, as we'll explore in this chapter. The more varied the opportunities to take in revenue, the more income security you will have. Speaking with an accountant or banker who serves small and midsize businesses can be a great way to get insight. Professionals who serve many types of businesses will have the true picture of what the financials look like in the options you're considering and can save you days of research.

MEANING, INC.

No matter how great your desire to make money, you'll be happier if you find an industry in which you can also do meaningful work, find fulfillment, get control over your workday, interact with people you enjoy, and have a positive impact. Berry saw a chance to make money with Municibid, but he also loved the technical aspects of building the site, was genuinely interested in serving local governments, and wanted to make a difference.

If there are few rewards for you other than money, it will be hard to stay interested in the business.

Kenric Hwang learned how important it was to make a difference through his business after building an e-commerce store that sold camouflage clothing to $1 million in annual revenue. Hwang, 49, who lives in Scottsdale, Arizona, had a job as a program manager at an insurance company when he decided to start the store selling camouflage styles. He'd done a lot of market research and discovered that the niche wasn't heavily saturated. He was good at running the store and made a nice living through it from 2007 to 2018, socking away plenty of money for retirement.

There was one problem: He wasn't entirely happy running the store. He enjoyed serving his customers, but he didn't have a particular passion for camouflage clothing. Once the initial buzz of launching the store and building it to $1 million started to fade, he found himself considering his next act.

Rather than resign himself to the situation, he started another business called Max and Neo in 2015. It tapped in to Hwang's passion for dogs, as a pet parent to a Belgian Malinois named Shara and foster parent to a menagerie of rescue dogs. He ran both businesses for a while, but as Max and Neo picked up traction, decided to sell the camouflage store. "I had a passion for one. I didn't have a passion for the other," he explains. "I thought I was hindering the growth of both."

As a foster pet parent, Hwang noticed that adopters often showed up to pick up their dogs without a collar and leash. They left with the dog in the collar and leash it was wearing. That meant that rescue organizations ran out of both items quickly. Max and Neo's business model addresses this situation. If someone buys an item, the store donates the same one to a rescue operation. This past Christmas, the three-person company and its volunteers packed up 4,000 boxes of dog supplies as gifts for foster pet parents.

The idea caught on. Today, Max and Neo has three employees and $5 million in annual revenue. Profits are lower than at the camouflage store because of all the donations, Hwang says, and he is fine with that: "I started the business knowing that the profit margins would be low. I'm okay with it because of our roots. We were trying to decide how to donate to dog rescues and built the business around that model."

WHICH TINY BUSINESSES OFFER THE MOST POTENTIAL?

In studying census data, I identified seven broad categories of businesses where an average person can get a toehold with a tiny business and generate seven-figure revenue and beyond. Some of the industries below are "fun" ones that you may have fantasized about and can imagine chatting about at cocktail parties, while others are about as unsexy as a business could be. There are many businesses that you might never notice as you drive through your community every day because they're tucked away in nondescript office buildings, industrial parks, or in warehouses—or inside someone's home. But within these industries are creative entrepreneurs who are finding ways to make them exciting for themselves and their customers. As Augusto Moronto at Better Not Younger put it, "What I love is to grow a business—putting things together, structuring things, even tackling the challenges and growing pains. I love the process and being part of a team. I find joy in that."

You'll notice that I drew on both census data and my research as a journalist. Simply cherry-picking from the top of the list didn't make sense, because certain businesses required very specialized skills or have barriers to entry that are too hard for most of us to break through. Others just didn't seem like they had enough appeal to most people. Here are the categories I believe will have the greatest interest to the average smart person.

E-Commerce

Selling online, whether to businesses or governments, as Berry does, or to consumers, can be an ideal route to a seven-figure tiny business. As you probably know, e-commerce has accelerated dramatically in both the consumer and business to business (B2B) markets since the pandemic. Now that more buyers—both consumers and businesses—have adapted to purchasing online, that trend is only going to accelerate.

It's next to impossible to compete with Amazon, so virtually every tiny business that succeeds in this space is a niche player. "E-commerce has gotten much more competitive the last two to three years, and advertising costs rise year after year," explains Andrew Youderian, founder of e-commerceFuel, an online community for high-revenue online merchants. "To compete, you need to either be incredibly good at marketing, have a differentiated product, or, ideally, both." You also need to allow time to experiment and find that perfect niche. "I know hundreds of successful e-commerce entrepreneur stories, but most of them have taken years of hard, patient work to come to fruition," says Youderian.

Nicole Brown embodies what he is saying. She built an e-commerce store called Izzy & Liv that brings in more than $7 million in annual revenue—while raising four children. The online store, based in Matawan, New Jersey, sells clothing and housewares with inspirational and empowering themes, designed by and for women of color.

Brown, who spent much of her career working in corporate marketing, didn't expect to find herself running an e-commerce store. "I call myself an accidental entrepreneur," she says. "I never set out thinking I was going to own my own business."

Without knowing it at the time, the opportunity to run the store *found her* back in 2003, when she started Mahogany Butterfly (MaBu), a free online community featuring content aimed at Black women. She ran the site as a hobby for five years, tapping into what she'd learned working at the women's community iVillage during the dot-com boom. As her family grew to three children, however, she didn't have time to keep running the community while working full time, and closed it.

Entrepreneurship started to beckon after she had her youngest child in 2013. When Brown experienced a health emergency during the pregnancy, her daughter, Olivia, was born four months prematurely at one pound, five ounces. The fragile infant had to spend her first four months in the neonatal intensive care unit at the hospital and went through multiple surgeries and therapies during her first year. Brown left her work-at-home job at a creative agency, where she was a digital marketing manager for brands selling consumer packaged goods, to take care of her baby. "I was not going to let anyone else do that," she says. "I had to make sure I was giving her the best care and giving her the chance to have the best life."

Traveling back and forth forty-five minutes each way to the hospital to see Olivia in between taking care of the rest of her family, Brown started looking for something to distract her from the stress. She looked back at the online community she'd started—but had discontinued. "I regretted it," she says. "I thought about what would have happened if I had treated it more like a business."

Brown decided to channel all of the emotion she was feeling into building a new community. "There were not a lot of sites that spoke to Black women," she says.

By 2014, she had started up Izzy & Liv—named for her daughters Isabel, "Izzy," and Olivia, "Liv" (a healthy seven-year-old as of this writing)—attracting visitors with inspiring content focused on themes like feeling beautiful and loving the skin you're in. After doing outreach on Facebook, where she spent about $1,000 on paid advertisements, in 2015, Brown created a store on the e-commerce platform Shopify and began offering T-shirts she created through a print-on-demand company. One advantage of using such a company is that very little startup capital is necessary. The print-on-demand firm charges the customers for the products and takes a cut in each sale, passing on the rest to the entrepreneur. Customers started flocking, and that year the business hit $50,000 in sales.

Then Brown branched out into accessories, like hats, and home décor products, such as pillows and shower curtains. As she added to her offerings and expanded her sourcing, annual revenue grew to $550,000 by 2016. Brown funded more growth by reinvesting her earnings in the business, breaking $1 million in revenue and growing it to $2.7 million while she was still a solo entrepreneur.

Her biggest win was launching the Brown Sugar Box in February 2017. Now one of her bestsellers, it's a subscription box that includes themed T-shirts, accessories, and decorative items that she sells for $39.95 a month.

"Because I had spent the first couple of years building my audience, once I launched my box, I didn't really have to promote it," she says. "I sent an email out—a teaser. There were a lot of people interested. The next week I launched it."

She knew she'd made the right call when 1,000 subscribers signed up in two weeks. "They were people who were already my customers," she says.

By the end of the first year, there were nearly 10,000 subscribers. Izzy & Liv reached $3 million in annual revenue in 2017. Today, the business has grown to ten employees and has over $7 million in annual revenue, up from $6 million last year, according to Brown. She uses a fulfillment center to ship her wares.

One thing that made the Brown Sugar Box so popular was that it was more than a surprise in people's mailboxes. It became a way to make friends. Members of Brown's 20,000-member Facebook group started reaching out to other members in their cities to get together to "unbox" their monthly deliveries when they arrived. Fans of the boxes started calling themselves "Brown Sugar Babes."

"It was something completely organic," says Brown. "It was not something I can say was my strategy. It came naturally from my wanting to serve my audience and make sure I am adding value to their lives and delighting them."

As the company has grown, Brown has learned to manage a team, which now includes an assistant buyer to help her with sourcing and a brand manager. She works with a business coach she met in a mastermind group in 2018 to develop her leadership skills. "The business coach has her own business and works with other entrepreneurs," explains Brown. "She understands the challenges unique to entrepreneurs and women entrepreneurs. That's very helpful."

As the mother of four children, Brown leads a full life, but she never has to imagine what might have happened if she'd continued her efforts at building a community online. She's following that passion every day.

Brown's community-driven approach to e-commerce is one route to success, but it's not the only one. If you have the financial ability and risk tolerance, Andrew Youderian says that, for some potential owners, it may be better to buy a business. "Trying to figure out a product line and/or marketing strategy that works well is a very imperfect science that can sometimes elude even the sharpest of entrepreneurs," he says. "By buying a business that has cash flowing and has a proven model, you're jumping past what is often the hardest part of the process."

CAN YOU BE TOO OLD FOR E-COMMERCE?

Some people think that only digital natives in their twenties and thirties can master e-commerce, but Max and Neo's founder Hwang doesn't buy into that. "There are a lot of limiting beliefs people have because of age," says Hwang. Given that there's no physical stamina required, he doesn't see any reason why people of any age can't succeed. "It's just a computer and you," he says. "Almost anybody can type and move a mouse."

And running a successful e-commerce business can be a great way to make up for lost time in saving for retirement, he finds. "Someone who's been working a job their whole life thinks about saving a little money every year," he says. "The world talks about how you have to save for twenty years for retirement. Someone at fifty who feels they are too late could fund their nest egg in two or three years. It's crazy how fast it can grow."

Johan Hattingh, 71, runs a thriving e-commerce business called Ain't It Nice with his son Eugene, which brought in $2.5 million in annual revenue in 2020. Hattingh was a fee-based financial planner in his earlier career, until a life-changing medical crisis forced him to find a new line of work. In 2005, when he was driving seventy miles per hour on a freeway in Utah, where his family resided, his vision suddenly went black. Taking his foot off the gas, he was able to steer the car for five or 10 seconds until his sight came back. "I couldn't see, but I could still think straight," he says.

After that close call, Hattingh went to the doctor, where he was diagnosed with epilepsy. With his blackouts continuing, he had to go on disability at age fifty-five. By 2008, his disability insurance had run out, and he and his wife Drienie, a freelance writer, had to live mostly on their investments. Suddenly, his best-laid plans seemed to be for naught, as the value of their portfolio dropped during the global financial crisis that began in 2008. "In many ways, it was like the perfect storm," he says. It turned out later that he was misdiagnosed and he had heart trouble, but the impact on his career was the same: He had to make a change.

Initially, Hattingh tried selling cruise tickets and later took a job on the night shift at the IRS, but neither was ideal for him. Finally, while looking online for a home-based business that didn't require a lot of phone work due to a chronic cough he suffered, Hattingh found his answer. Coming across a wholesaler of garden and home ornaments online, he decided to try selling a few of the company's products on Amazon, where he would have quick exposure to a big audience, and started his store, Ain't It Nice, in July 2011. He set what he thought was an ambitious goal: Bring in $100,000 in sales, with a $20,000 profit the first year.

Investing about $700 in inventory, Hattingh bought a small number of products and put them up for sale. Although his wholesaler offered 2,000 items, he selected only 100 initially. He stocked only products with high reviews on Amazon, to avoid returns. "I wouldn't sell a product that was three stars," he says. To his great surprise, he ended up doing better than expected and brought in $540,000 in revenue in 2012. The store broke $1 million the following year.

One of Hattingh's secrets to success was rigorously tracking the performance of each product on spreadsheets he created and eliminating the duds. He also programmed his spreadsheets to tell him when to change prices because, for instance, inventory was low. To eliminate a lot of the tedious work of running the business, he used Fulfillment by Amazon to pack and ship orders.

With the business thriving, Hattingh invited Eugene, who had left the navy, to join him in 2014—and they have no intention of slowing down. "We have a philosophy of continuous small improvements—kaizen," he says. "We want to keep growing it. If you can grow a business 10 percent, you are doubling the size every seven years."

Souped-Up Service Businesses

Running professional services firms, such as small law firms, marketing firms, and engineering consultancies, can be lucrative. The same holds for medical and wellness practices. However, because it costs a lot to bring talented professionals on staff, it can be hard to run such firms as profitably as other industries. To build a tiny business that makes big money, you will need to think creatively and, for instance, tap in to expert contractors to extend what you can do. "It's not about your labor," Gene Zaino of MBO Partners says. "It's not just about billing your own time by the hour. It's building your 'IP of relationships' on both the supply side and the demand side so you can deliver value. It's all about leverage."

No matter what rates you charge, however, you are inherently limited in growing your business by how much service work you and your team can do. And if you run a firm that requires a brick-and-mortar office, you may face high overhead for commercial real estate. The same holds in personal services businesses, such as nutritionist practices, fitness training services, and massage therapy.

So how can you run a tiny service business that generates both high revenue and profit? One promising way to do that is to use your professional knowledge to create products. These could be actual consumer products. Steven Sudell, 35, whose fundraising story you'll read in Chapter 5, created a physical product. He runs a physical therapy practice in Venice Beach, California, and when he found that he couldn't find a good at-home neck traction device to offer his patients, he invented his own: the Neck Hammock. He sold the Neck Hammock online while working with his patients for thirty-two hours a week, generating $3 million in annual revenue from that pursuit—far more than his practice would ever generate on its own—before he sold the business in early 2021.

For many professionals and experts running services businesses, another profitable route is creating informational products—such as paid online webinars and courses—either as your main service or in addition to it. While online education is an increasingly crowded field, people who have something very unique to teach, or who teach it better than everyone else, can still do very well in this space. And with more people familiar with online learning than ever before, thanks to the pandemic, there are many more potential customers, as long as you can break through the noise and present something that people feel is worth their time and attention.

Jenna Kutcher tapped what she learned in running a one-woman wedding photography business to build a mini-empire where she teaches people how to build creative businesses through online courses and her podcast,

The Goal Digger Podcast. She covers topics that include email list building, online marketing, social media strategies, team building, finance, and podcasting. Her businesses bring in more than $6 million in sales annually.

Kutcher's journey into entrepreneurship started when she got what should've been good news from her boss: She was up for a better job. At the time, she worked as an executive human resources team lead at a major retail chain headquartered in Minnesota. And as she thought of how her parents had done the same work for thirty years, and how she felt her soul was being sucked from her every day, she saw that it would be a mistake to say yes to the opportunity. "I didn't want a promotion," she says. "I'd be working more hours. I'd be trading my life away for this job."

So, rather than go the "safe route," Kutcher decided to change her career. Buying a camera on Craigslist for $300, she taught herself photography and started a business shooting weddings as a side hustle in 2011. "I told myself if I can figure out a way to book twenty-five weddings, I can match my salary," she says. It turned out she was good at photography, and she built a thriving business that generated enough revenue to allow her to leave her job behind in 2012.

But events in Kutcher's personal life made her rethink the business. She and her husband were trying to start a family and had experienced two miscarriages. "I was planning our family around wedding seasons, which isn't fun when you're struggling with loss," she says. Working all the time in the photography business was also wearing her out. "I quickly realized I had built a business where I was trading time for money," she says.

So, Kutcher decided to try creating an online product. First, she developed an online five-week course on photography. She marketed it to an email list of several hundred people she'd built at the photography business. She attracted twenty-five students. In teaching the course and working one-on-one with the students, Kutcher realized there was room for improvement and continually tweaked and tailored the course. To learn even more, she invested several hundred dollars in taking a course by online marketer Amy Porterfield on . . . how to build a course. Over the next few years, she used what she learned to create online courses teaching students how to set up a photography business, market a small business via email and on social media, and create a podcast. This when she started her own pod-cast, *The Goal Digger Podcast.*

While she was developing her products, Kutcher began posting her photos on Instagram, getting more serious and consistent about styling the photos and writing captions in 2015. "I was getting more thoughtful with what I was sharing," she says. Gradually she built up her following to 100,000.

It was at that point when an online mean gal who saw her Instagram feed sent her a nasty message marveling that Kutcher's buff husband had married a curvy girl like her—shortly after Kutcher had lost a preg-nancy and was trying to get pregnant for the third time. When Kutcher's heartfelt response went viral, her following shot up to 500,000 almost overnight—and her troll inadvertently propelled her business to a new level of visibility and sales. "I said the way we love does not depend on what we look like," says Kutcher.

Now Kutcher has 915,000 followers and gets paid $10,000 for a spon-sored post, in addition to revenue from her courses. Kutcher says she loves being an influencer but only promotes products she truly supports. "I have so many products and things I've created, I'd rather promote my own busi-ness," she says. To make sure her business does not depend on Instagram, her posts lead followers to a website that feeds into her email list. "Insta-gram is a handshake, not a sales pitch," she says.

Kutcher's business broke $1 million in revenue in 2016. By 2018 it brought in $3.5 million, and in 2020, she brought in more than $6 million. When we last spoke, her team had grown to five full-time employees, as well as five contractors.

She loves being able to run her company in a way that's best for her team—stay-at-home women and moms who work remotely. "It's super flex-ible," she says. "We want to be present for our families and walk the walk, not just talk the talk," says Kutcher.

Manufacturing

When most people think of manufacturing, they envision giant corpora-tions such as General Motors. That's because, until the recent past, the behemoths were the only ones who had a shot at it. "Thirty years ago, if you were going to start a small business in manufacturing, you almost had to figure out a way to build your own manufacturing facility," says Emergent Research's Steve King. "Today, even the biggest companies outsource their manufacturing."

Many of the tiny businesses thriving in this industry today achieve the results you'd expect from a much bigger company by outsourcing different aspects of the manufacturing process. "If they want to manufacture a widget, they can find a manufacturer online to help them with a prototype or production of that product," explains Curt Anderson, founder of B2Btail, a manufacturing and e-commerce consultancy based in Lakewood, New York. "You can take advantage of their machinery, their supply chain, their inventory. You could be working out of your living room, coordinating it all." Other tiny businesses serve more as distributors, says Dani Kaplan, owner of SMC Data Systems, which provides software to help middle-market companies automate their supply chain. "They go to the Far East and buy components and assemble them in their warehouse," he says. "They bypass the manufacturer and go straight to retail stores."

Geoffrey Stern, 64, has run a tiny manufacturing business since 1997. His company, Voice Express Corporation, based in Fairfield, Connecticut, makes interactive print media—relying on small devices that play audio or video on demand, using an internal battery source. One client is Build-A-Bear Workshop, where he makes the gadgets that let the teddy bears talk. Stern has alternated between running the business with two employees and relying on a team of regular vendors and contractors instead; currently, he has twelve contractors. The business brings in about $4 million in annual revenue.

Stern, who spent the early part of his career as a researcher for a brokerage firm, made his first foray into entrepreneurship when he started a business that made fire-suppression systems for companies' computer rooms. He'd met someone who made similar systems for the defense industry and was looking for new markets.

Stern had a good run with that business, but it dried up in the early '90s after it was discovered that freon, a gas used in the fire-suppressing chemicals, was hurting the ozone layer. Brainstorming new ideas to make a living, he dreamed up a greeting card for florists that included a gift-giver's recorded voice.

Stern ran the idea past several florists, whom he met through his father, who ran a business that supplied florists with ribbon. When they seemed receptive to the idea, he found a chip company in San Jose, California, that helped him design the voice-recording component of the greeting cards. Then, he traveled to China and found a factory, one of the chip maker's qualified manufacturers. "I had to jump on a plane and put on my Sherlock Holmes hat and do a lot of footwork to find the company," he says. He used some of his $500,000 in startup capital to finance Voice Express Corp's pilot manufacturing runs.

Working with a team of contractors he found online and through networking—including graphic artists, package designers, and videographers—Stern designed several products with voice devices: a gift tag for wine bottles that he sells on Amazon, direct-mailing cards that pharma companies use when marketing to doctors to address their frequently asked questions in recording, and voice boxes for crafters to use in their projects, sold at stores like Michaels and JOANN. "You are not going to come across any opportunities unless you are active and engaged," he says. "You have to have your eyes open and your antenna up to look for friction points and opportunities."

One of his biggest victories was landing Build-A-Bear Workshop as a client. "For my first pilot, I wanted to show how the voice recorder could enhance a gift or toy, and thought that in addition to the sound, it should be tactile and visual and thus trigger the sense of touch and sight, in addition to auditory," he recalls. "I sourced a teddy bear with a pouch for the sound module and then started looking to source a tiny T-shirt that could be printed with an image. I found a supplier of tiny T-shirts in Saint Louis, and he asked if he could share my sound device with another customer. The other customer was Maxine Clark, the founder of Build-A-Bear Workshop, who, at the time, had four stores. They now have over 350 stores worldwide, and we have sold them over 50 million 'sounds.'"

Upon landing Build-A-Bear Workshop and other big brands, such as

FTD and Snapfish, as clients, Stern took their purchase orders to friends and family. They provided the funds up front in exchange for repayment with interest later.

One thing that has surprised Stern, after many years in business, is how much easier it is to run a manufacturing company than it ever was before. Now he can find all of the resources he needs online. "It's an amazing time to start a company," he says.

Wholesaling

When you analyze the chart of tiny businesses that make big money in Appendix I, you'll notice that many businesses at the top are wholesalers. Wholesaling entails selling food or goods—grain and beans, writing paper, auto parts, you name it—to retailers and industrial, commercial, institutional, and other business clients, either independently or through a platform like Amazon Business Services. Many of these enterprise clients place very big orders, so successful wholesalers often have very high revenue. However, they also have high costs. Profit margins vary quite a bit by industry, ranging from 3 to 20 percent, according to Steve King. Checking out trade magazines' benchmarking reports can help you determine a business's potential upside.

Apurva Batra, 31, started out in a tiny niche of wholesaling—selling plastic pouches for food, pharmaceuticals, and other products—and gradually ventured into custom manufacturing for his clients. Batra was working for Chevron in Houston when he dreamed up the idea for his company FlexiblePouches, a B2B e-commerce company, launched in 2016.

Batra was doing very well in corporate life when he began toying with the idea of starting his business. He enjoyed the camaraderie in the office, but felt something was missing in his life. Often, he'd find himself muttering, "I'm going to spend the rest of my life going into someone else's office, at a time someone else prescribed, and do meetings for someone else. At the end of the day, the reward is going to go to the boss."

Though he was impatient to leave, he knew that breaking away would require a plan. Gradually, he began putting money into his savings account regularly so he could quit someday and become an entrepreneur. Although he was in his twenties with no dependents, he still needed to pay the bills. "Everyone cares about security," he says. "But I think it's something you make for yourself."

After work, Batra threw himself into researching potential businesses he could pursue. He set several criteria: His startup would have to be in the well-paying B2B space, a field he knew offered a lot of opportunities. It would need to be based on repeatable processes, so he could automate some of it. And it would need to have an opportunity to scale. "I wanted to create something of value that is a cash flow–generating asset," he says.

As he conducted his research, he was drawn to the idea of a product-service hybrid, where he would not only sell a product but offer useful expertise. "Service businesses are easier to start. Product businesses are easier to scale," he explains. "Being a hybrid offers the advantages of both."

Ultimately, Batra's digging led him to decide to offer attractive, retail-ready packaging for consumer goods at a price point affordable to small and midsize brands. Moving back in with his parents, he tapped $25,000 he had saved during his five years as an engineer to get started. Initially, he flew to China to research his sourcing options. He then invested $10,000 in inventory, printed some business cards, and headed to the trade show circuit to pick up clients.

Although Batra started making sales at trade shows, he discovered that promoting his company's website using Google Ads and other online advertising, which he taught himself how to do using YouTube videos, was one of the most fruitful ways to win customers. Small and midsize companies were especially receptive. Batra dove into serving them. He quickly built a reputation for being willing to do ultra-small print runs, by working with outsourced manufacturing partners who had a high-end digital printing tool needed for the task. "The advent of high-quality digital print technology for flexible packaging changed the game," he says.

In 2020, Batra hired his first three full-time employees. Having other people on board full time to help him allowed him to enjoy his passion for world travel (one trip took him to Antarctica) before COVID shut everything down. He never regrets trading his engineering job for his B2B e-commerce store. "I get up every morning and see the traffic outside and am not envious," says Batra. He hit annualized revenue of $1 million his first year, and when we last spoke was bringing in $3–3.5 million in revenue per year at the profitable company.

As Dani Kaplan notes, becoming a distributor is another route to joining the manufacturing industry. That's what Sean Kelly, 24, did. When the United States got hit with the coronavirus, he was running Jersey Champs, an online store he founded in his dorm room at Rutgers University in 2016 that sells sports- and rapper-themed jerseys and that he had grown into a million-dollar, one-person business.

As hospitals and nursing homes searched for the PPE they needed in the early days of the crisis and faced price gouging, he sprang into action to use his skills to help get N-95 masks, nitrile gloves, and other needed supplies that have been approved by the Food and Drug Administration (FDA) or National Institute for Occupational Safety and Health (NIOSH) into their hands at reasonable prices.

Teaming up with a silent partner who had relevant experience, he formed PPE of America, a distributor based in Delaware, and began looking for hospitals and other healthcare providers that needed help. "I would either get a warm intro or send cold emails. We tried cold calls, but they didn't work," says Kelly.

The company built a network of procurement professionals at major hospitals, healthcare and government organizations, and first responders, such as police, firefighters, and emergency medical services, for whom it fills orders. In some cases, it donates the PPE. PPE of America also sells items such as the Orbel personal hand sanitizing device.

One reason the business grew so quickly was that Kelly was able to help hospitals find a way around challenging supply-chain issues, as shipping from Asia got backed up. "A lot of big hospitals and states never got products they paid for," he says.

Kelly hired two employees to help out, a website developer and someone who handles customer relationships. Everyone worked remotely. "None of our deals are in-person deals," he says.

In 2020, PPE of America generated $15 million in sales. Although many people jumped into selling PPE during the pandemic, it's not a high-profit business. The margins for products like this are thin, Kelly says, but sell-ing them allows him to help institutions that have been on the front lines of fighting the coronavirus. He was able to keep the cost of these products down by sourcing them directly from manufacturers and distributors.

With more Americans vaccinated, a business like this is likely to see some changes in its sales patterns in the future. However, Kelly was well positioned. He never stopped selling his sports jerseys. He had also moved into a new opportunity, supplying a shop that musician Steve Aoki runs in Los Angeles with sports trading cards—hotly sought after by investors at the time we spoke. "[Entrepreneur] Gary Vaynerchuk was pushing it really hard on social media," says Kelly.

Financial Services and Technology

Not everyone has the professional background and contacts to enter the financial services or fintech arena, but for those who do, this is an area with a lot of potential to build a tiny business that makes big money. As you'll notice from the chart in Appendix I, businesses such as accounting, book-keeping and financial management firms, and reinsurance carriers are well represented among tiny businesses that are doing well. So are financial technology firms.

Greg Pesci has found there is a lot of opportunity in this space. Pesci, an attorney by trade whom I've gotten to know by providing editorial services to him, worked for years as president of a company in the payments indus-try. When he flew to Mexico for a blockchain conference in January 2018 while working on another startup—a freelance community—he suddenly had an idea: Wouldn't it be helpful for a financial institution to be able to invoice clients by SMS text message and to take their payments? He decided to turn the idea into a business. While on his trip, he called a friend in tech to help him line up two software developers. "I went back to something I knew, where I had plenty of contacts and some credibility," he recalls.

The developers got started quickly on creating the technology that would become MessagePay, working on it from late March until early Sep-tember of 2018. Meanwhile, Pesci, who had worked in the space for years, raised $2.1 million in funding from three private, accredited investors and one institutional investor, a subsidiary of Overstock.com. "It likes to invest in companies that use blockchain, which we do," he explains.

By October, Pesci had already made his first sale, with Alpine Credit Union coming on board to use the technology, and, by July 2019, MessagePay was fully up and running and processing payments. Pesci signed up three more financial institutions in 2019. Then deals fell off during the early months of the pandemic. That was disappointing, but by May and June 2020, as business opened up somewhat, he had signed on twenty more financial institutions. In 2020, MessagePay had annual revenue just shy of $1 million, with six employees. "We're hoping we can grow this," he says.

Creating fintech products such as MessagePay is just one type of business where it's possible to make the most of the financial services skills you've developed in a previous career. Gene Zaino, chairman of MBO partners, which provides back-office services for independent workers, says many of his clients are doing quite well in specialized financial service businesses. One, for instance, runs a successful business as a turnaround specialist, generating $10–13 million a year in a tiny commission-based business. This client calls upon a network of accountants and attorneys when she needs their expertise.

Transportation

Another area in which tiny businesses shine is transportation. While the transportation industry suffered during the pandemic, as vaccines rolled out, it started making a comeback. Although it may take a while for public transit to recover, as you'll see from the charts in the appendices, there has historically been a lot of opportunity in providing services like private air transportation, freight transportation, last-mile trucking, and equipment for this industry.

Janine Iannarelli, 60, has created an exciting entrepreneurial career for herself at Par Avion, the international business aircraft marketing firm she founded in Houston, Texas, in 1997 to sell used private jets, primarily to corporations and private individuals. "A lot of my referrals come from wealth managers and attorneys they've worked with—trusted partners," she says.

Iannarelli got her start in aviation after graduating from Montclair State

University in New Jersey with a BA in business administration. Working at a market research firm that focused on aviation immediately after graduation, she recalls, "I found a window into a very exciting, dynamic industry."

Inspired to take her interest further, she took a job in sales and marketing at an international business aircraft dealer that specialized in the sale and acquisition of corporate jets. After rising to vice president of sales and marketing, she decided to go out on her own and founded Par Avion. Like many other entrepreneurs who build high-revenue, ultra-lean businesses, Iannarelli specialized in a specific area of aviation marketing—selling pre-owned jets—and she is known for her expertise in a complex area of selling them: cross-border transactions. This isn't always easy and, in addition to financial smarts, requires creative logistical thinking. One of her early projects involved moving a Falcon 10 and 100 aircraft from the tip of South Africa to Texas. The airplanes needed to make several stops in Africa, due to their range, which meant she had to travel within war-torn countries and negotiate with local ground support in French, which she had studied at Alliance Française de Houston.

A big part of succeeding in her niche has been marketing. When you're selling a big-ticket item like a jet, clients expect an elaborate sales presentation. Iannarelli, who has always loved marketing, goes all out on this front, investing considerable time in developing promotional materials, both print and online versions, that convey the value of owning each jet. "I understand the power of advertising," she says.

Many of Iannarelli's customers are CEOs and entrepreneurs who have one thing in common: very busy schedules. For these customers, she emphasizes that a private airplane is a "time machine," enabling them to arrive and depart from their destinations at the most convenient times possible. "There is no other way to buy back time," she explains. "There is one way to save time: through a business or private jet."

Iannarelli doesn't sell every jet alone. She sometimes teams up with marketing partners—primarily industry contracts she has known for decades—to co-brand advertising for her jets in markets such as Europe. It helps that she is active in her industry and has formed many longstanding relationships with colleagues. She is a member of the National Business

Aviation Association (NBAA), European Business Aviation Association (EBAA), Women in Aviation International, and the American Marketing Association.

Iannarelli has been self-funded since her first day and never borrowed money to grow the business. She has kept overhead lean by working from home, operating as a solopreneur for many years and, when she began hiring employees, building a fully outfitted office on the second story of her garage; currently, she employs one person, who works from that office. Building a brain trust of contracted professional advisors helped her to grow the business. "My accountant is the same one I used when I started my business," she says.

In recent years, the solopreneur has typically brought in revenue in the range of six figures to $1 million, with some wild swings in an industry that is very sensitive to economic conditions. Her commissions are based on the net sale price of the planes and range from $50,000 to $500,000 per sale. "In a really good year, I generate seven-figure revenue," she says. When many businesses were hurting in the pandemic, she took steps like relocating aircraft to Houston from all over the world, so she could be ready to sell them once the market opened back up. "There is no better time to be a small business in the aircraft brokerage industry," she told me.

Construction and Real Estate

Construction of new housing, multifamily housing, and nonresidential and commercial buildings is another area in which very small businesses can have a big impact. Many owners of tiny businesses that make big money have worked in this field for years and teamed up with connections they've made along the way.

That's the case for Wade Hiner, 49. Hiner spent much of his career on the sales and business development side of the commercial real estate industry before he became a partner in Destiny Homes, a company in Waukee, Iowa, that builds residential homes at all price points. That company was founded by his partners in 2008, with one managing construction and operations, and the other handling operations, such as securing bank financing. They invited him to come on board in 2017 after he had left his last job. They needed someone to help them with sales and knew he had the right skills. Hiner negotiated a partnership, where he got sweat equity in exchange for his contributions. "We're a good three-legged stool," says Hiner.

Hiner and his partners initially distinguished the company by creating attractive homes for $200,000 (now $280,000, amid a boom in housing prices), which they market in their "Smart Series," aimed at budget-conscious buyers. There weren't many builders in Iowa who could create new homes in that price range at the time they introduced the series. They had to talk with both local governments and subcontractors to pull it off. "We rolled up our sleeves and got everyone involved around the table," recalls Hiner. "We convinced a couple of municipalities to look at their regulations on how many houses per acre they would allow in a different light, which allowed us to create the Smart Series. Normal development is about 2.5 homes per acre. We convinced them to do 7.5 homes per acre." Consumers who'd been priced out of the market in the past flocked. "We sold fifty-two before we could dig a hole," he says. "It just went crazy."

That worked for a while, and the company, which was building 370 houses per year at the time we spoke, now employs twenty people. Eventually, though, copycats appeared. "Now we've got a bunch of competition doing it," says Hiner. "That motivates us to move on to the next thing." Right now, he and his partners are trying to figure out how to deliver a brand-new home for $135,000–$175,000. He is optimistic that they can get both municipalities and subcontractors to work with them to enable the building of what his firm calls "essential" housing, for people such as first responders, teachers, and retail workers, needed in every community. "The municipalities that have said yes to this concept are loving the additional revenue they are getting through taxes that they wouldn't normally get," he explains. The subcontractors also stand to earn additional revenue.

His advice if you want to get into home building is to network. "I got into this opportunity because of my past experiences and relationships," he says. "To me, it's really about leveraging your relationships. They don't necessarily have to be within the industry you are trying to get into. Some people whispered in the ears of people I am working with right now: 'You need to go after this guy. You built a great house. You don't tell the story. You don't know how to sell yourself. You need someone to help you tell the story and help you expand.' I wasn't looking for them. They were looking for me."

Suzanne Zahr, an architect, has run her homebuilding firm, Suzanne Zahr, Inc., in Mercer Island, Washington, since 2015. Zahr's first foray into entrepreneurship was in 2002, when she teamed up with an interior designer to start a boutique firm. But not long after they opened their doors, a recession hit. "The industry fell off a cliff," she recalls. "It was like someone turned off the faucet and the money stopped flowing. After two years of struggle, she took a corporate job, where she worked with large iconic brands like Amazon and Starbucks. One project entailed rolling out thousands of square feet of Amazon's workspace in Europe.

Still, she never lost her desire to run an independent business. "I was gainfully employed for some pretty incredible architects and learned a lot until I felt my learning curve plateaued," she says. "I decided it was time for me to take the plunge and launch my practice." By 2015, the timing felt right to leave the corporate scene once again, and she partnered with two real estate attorneys to start her current firm. She'd worked with them on a 300-unit multifamily development, and after enjoying the collaboration, they invited her to partner with them. "This time, I diversified my efforts," she says. "I got into not just design, but also construction management and real estate."

It took some investment to get the firm going. "For me, the biggest expense to start up was building out my office space," says Zahr. She took out a loan to cover the cost of building out the 1,200-square-foot retail space. She started with one employee, an intern she trained to become a project manager. Today, there are four employees, and the firm brings in about $2 million in annual revenue.

In running her firm, Zahr gets a chance to focus on developing the "organic modern" style of homes she likes, though what's more important is understanding what customers want. "We actively listen to what our clients are looking for," she says. When she is not doing her architectural work, she devotes a lot of time to marketing and was in the process of hiring a public relations firm to help her when we spoke. "Trying to connect with clients and bringing in work is my primary role as a business owner," she says.

Even if you are certain you are choosing the right business, things don't always go as planned. If life happens and your efforts go awry, that doesn't mean you'll never run a successful business. Fortunately, there are many ways to test the waters before you go all in. In the next chapter, we'll look at how to take educated risks as you first get started, so you'll know what you're getting into with your tiny business and can fine-tune as you go along.

CHAPTER 4

TAKE EDUCATED RISKS

Ana Gavia, 28, founder of the bathing suit brand Pinkolada, didn't plan on becoming an entrepreneur. She was looking to earn some extra money while studying podiatric medicine at La Trobe University in Australia when she started her e-commerce business in 2017. When she wasn't study-ing, she enjoyed sketching and design—"I get inspiration everywhere for the colors and hues," she says—so she decided to try her hand at designing a bikini and selling it on the internet. Growing up in a beach community, she'd long searched for a suit that was both stylish and durable. And, with just $200 to invest in a sample, she was glad swimsuits didn't require her to buy as much fabric as a dress would.

With no experience or connections in manufacturing, Gavia searched Google to find a plant to make the swimsuits and eventually traveled to China to a fair where she met a group of suppliers. She quickly discovered that most factories don't want to do small runs, which are not cost-effective. After reaching out to some of the factories she found online, she connected with a small plant in China that was open to filling orders that totaled less than $1,000. "I went there and met him before we started filling orders," she says. "I wanted to make sure everything was ethical." Once the factory passed muster, Gavia used some of her minuscule budget to order a single, medium-sized sample, put up a photo of it on her website, and to run a few ads promoting it on Facebook. "I think my Facebook budget was $5," she says. She also posted the image on Instagram.

A week later, Gavia had made her first sale through an e-commerce store she put up on the platform Shopify. "I was so excited," she says. She used the money that came in to manufacture her first batch of about 100 bikinis. She soon ran more ads, offering the swimsuit for preorder through Instagram. She planned to use the money from the orders to pay for the manufacturing run.

Fortunately, the bikinis sold out quickly, and the design became one of her perennial bestsellers. Empowered by her early sales success, Gavia designed three more styles and again posted photos of the samples on her website. Each time, Gavia advertised the suits on Facebook to gauge the response of her target customers, as measured in comments and "likes." For consistency in her comparisons, she targeted the same audience with each ad. This method was an easy way to avoid investing in products no one wanted. "Especially when you are starting small, you would not want to put your money into something that was not going to sell," she says. "It's trial and error. It mitigates the risk when you ask the customer what they want."

Gavia built the brand's following by running contests, such as free give-aways of her bikinis, where entrants would have to follow her Facebook page and tag three friends. Although Gavia targeted teens initially, women from ages eighteen to forty-five turned out to be her main customers. Armed with that knowledge, she expanded the styles she offered to take a slightly older demographic into account and began sharing pictures of real women wearing her designs on Instagram. As she sold more suits, she quickly discovered she'd underpriced them and needed to charge more to turn a profit. She soon raised prices a bit, making the business more sustainable.

Once she figured out how to run the business profitably, Gavia put her studies on hold to work on it full time. About three years into running the business, she found she couldn't keep up with demand on her own and gradually hired five employees to handle customer service and warehouse work. She hired another six team members, who work remotely, for her back office, along with about ten contractors she found on LinkedIn and other sites to help with tasks such as content marketing, design, and financial work. Building her team enabled the business to keep growing. Today, the profitable business Pinkolada brings in the equivalent of more than USD $2.5 million annually, with Gavia communicating with everyone through Microsoft Teams and email. The Melbourne, Australia–based business has also expanded into the US market, with a country-specific e-commerce site. "We're growing exponentially," she says. "We're investing everything back into the business."

Many people see entrepreneurs as gamblers, but successful founders of tiny businesses that make big money usually aren't impulsive high rollers. They're more like Gavia: They want to make money, not burn through it, so they take time to test the appeal of their products and details such as pricing in small experiments, pivot quickly if their initial hunches don't work out, and improve on what's working. "Entrepreneurs are not risk-takers. They are risk-averse," as one of my mentors and clients Verne Harnish, founder of Entrepreneurs' Organization and author of *Scaling Up: Mastering the Rockefeller Habits 2.0*, put it at the ScaleUp Virtual Summit in February 2021. "They have a plan B, C, D, and E."

There's no way to entirely de-risk the process of starting a business. Just as when you take a new job, things may not work out for reasons you could never have anticipated. At the same time, by testing a new business idea on the smallest possible scale, you can move ahead from a position of knowledge, conserve any money you invest, and form your plan B, C, D, and E as you go along. Here are some ideas on how to do that.

DO ON-THE-GROUND TESTING

Jason Vander Griendt, 40, didn't start out planning to be an entrepreneur. He studied engineering at Fanshawe College in Ontario, then began working his way up in his field at big companies that include Gerdau Long Steel North America, Hatch, Siemens, and SNC-Lavalin.

But today, he runs a fast-growing product-design firm, J-CAD Inc., in

Toronto. It brings in revenue of CAD $1.5 million—the equivalent of USD $1.2 million—annually. He runs the business with the help of forty expert contractors, such as engineers, around the world.

Vander Griendt didn't have a grand plan for finding the right business. He tried starting an app to help people buy sunglasses—he loves collecting them—at one point investing about $25,000, but closed the business soon after opening it when he realized there was too much competition in the marketplace.

Vander Griendt stumbled into running J-CAD Inc., in 2006, while working at SNC-Lavalin. To supplement his CAD $60,000 annual salary, Vander Griendt began doing freelance design in engineering. Digital marketing hadn't really taken off at that point, so he offered his expertise in developing conceptual designs to welding and fabrication shops in Toronto by handing out flyers.

To his surprise, he started getting calls right away, many from busy shops that needed him to stop by the same night to help them. Seeing that he did a nice job with the work, many came back to him repeatedly. As the business grew, he was able to bring in about CAD $25,000 extra a year.

By 2011, Vander Griendt decided to get more serious about growing revenue in his side business. He set a goal of bringing in CAD $20,000 a month and gradually expanded the work he took on. "I realized I could really crank it out and push the limit," he says. He eventually reached his benchmark. Unfortunately, he had no life away from his laptop. "All I did was work that month," he says. "I could *only* work."

As Vander Griendt looked for ways to regain control of his schedule, it hit him: He had to start outsourcing. There was no way he could complete all of the projects he was bringing in himself without working around the clock. He gradually built up a stable of talented freelancers he found on oDesk, a freelance platform that has since been absorbed into Upwork. He tested each contractor with a simple project before trusting them with more advanced assignments. Eventually, he built up so much business that he went part time at his job until a project he was working on ended, then took J-CAD full time.

Vander Griendt took J-CAD's business model a step further after he began advertising it on Google, with the help of a Google Ads contractor he hired. The added visibility helped J-CAD Inc. attract new clients, from manufacturing facilities looking to make new products to inventors working from their garages and kitchens.

Vander Griendt eventually expanded to another 3D printing plant in Los Angeles, which reached out after noticing how much traffic his website was getting. Because he was sending so much business to the plant, he was able to negotiate a volume discount and to offer his services at better prices than individual clients could get on their own. And he was able to protect his lifestyle even as he doubled his revenue, thanks to the outsourced services he used. "Their businesses are already set up," he says. "If the printer breaks down, I let them worry about it."

With that part of his business humming, Vander Griendt decided to tweak his business model again. Often, when he created prototypes of a product, customers would say, "I'd like to order $50,000 worth." At first, he told them he didn't offer that service. Finally, he asked himself the same question as he did with prototyping: "Why not?" He was already getting emails every day from manufacturing plants in China that wanted to work with him, after finding him online. By 2015, he had flown to China and visited fifty factories. After he found one he liked and started 3D printing, he was able to "5x" his revenue.

As his business has grown, Vander Griendt finds himself coming up with new ideas constantly. He's had to be disciplined about testing them so he's not running off in all directions. Now, when he has new ideas, he'll launch them within the hour. "I want to test them as cheaply and quickly as possible," he says.

To do that, he uses GoDaddy, the domain registration service. It has a program where, if you buy a domain, you get a free website for a month. "In that month, I'll buy the domain, make the website in 30 minutes, and spend another 30 minutes driving traffic to that website." He'll typically run online ads promoting the idea for a week or two. "If I get a good response, I'll continue it," he says. "If not, I'll shut it down. All I paid was $10 for the domain. That's business. People think their one idea is going to be a home run. It's rarely the case."

The result is that he knows any business he starts will make money right away. "I'm not taking out a loan for $50,000," he says. Why borrow when you can let paying customers finance the business for you?

PUT MARKETPLACES TO WORK FOR YOU

If you're thinking of running a tiny business in professional or personal services, online freelance platforms such as Upwork, Freelancer, and PeoplePerHour—or industry-specific ones such as 99designs for creative professionals or Contently for content marketers—can give you a low-risk way to test your business concept, even if you ultimately decide to market to customers another way, such as through word of mouth.

That's how Evan Fisher, 34, found a niche for his business plan–writing agency, Unicorn Business Plans, in Atlanta, and tested his business concept. Fisher, who studied finance and international business at Villanova University, discovered through his initial career in finance that there was an ever-expanding number of startups that needed to have business plans written. Working at a boutique investment banking firm in Geneva, Switzerland, after college graduation, he wrote business plans and pitch decks as part of his job. He developed his business-writing skills further when, in 2015, a client invited him to come on board to help raise capital, a role in which he wrote similar documents.

As he was doing this, Fisher learned that a great business plan needed certain elements. "It was always about telling a very clear story in a specific manner for a specific audience," he says. That story needed to address three questions for investors: Does the business model make sense? Can this business sell its products or services and make money? Is there an opportunity to finance the business? "If those three things are true, you have a very strong chance of raising capital," he says. Fisher also learned another valuable lesson: busy investors liked these plans to be concise; they didn't have time to sift through a 100-page plan. "Distilling is exactly that—cutting out things that are not relevant and making the plan exceptionally clear, so it cannot be misinterpreted," Fisher says.

After he got inspired by reading Tim Ferriss's book, *The 4-Hour Work-*

week, Fisher felt the itch to go out on his own about two years into his last job. He wanted to start a business where he could use his business-writing skills, but was not sure which were in the most demand. So, before he started his business, he spent a lot of time studying the giant freelance marketplace Upwork to look for a niche where he had a real shot of standing out and to see which services potential clients needed. "You're going to see a good, average mix of what people are looking for," he says.

At the same time, Fisher knew there was a lot of competition that could lead to frenetic bidding on projects—driving some freelancers' rates down to the point they were unsustainable. This was when he came to an important conclusion that's relevant for anyone who wants to run a tiny business that makes big money: "**You need to pick a niche you want to be number one in**," he says. "If you're not actively working every single day to be the best, you are going to have to play the pricing game." For instance, he says, if you want to do Google ad management, it's better to market yourself as a specialist in Google ad management for cosmetics brands (assuming you are) than as a provider of Google ad management, in general.

After poring over the many categories where freelancers marketed themselves on Upwork, Fisher decided to focus on business-plan writing, even though he could have applied his business-writing skills elsewhere. There was high and consistent demand for business plans, and he already knew how to write them, so there was not much of a learning curve. "I always look for something that I will be able to make into a repeatable process, where I will be able to deliver better results than anyone else," he says. "Where can I be number one by niching down?"

Fisher started Unicorn Business Plans in September 2017, posting his profile on Upwork. He soon started winning projects—de-risking his business by getting valuable proof of concept and his ability to sell his services before he went further with it. He also learned how to execute projects efficiently and to create systems for getting them done. "It was not like it was an instantaneous process, where the first one we did was perfect," he says. "The first one we did was nerve-racking and almost turned into a disaster along the way. We didn't have our processes down yet." But he persisted in fine-tuning those processes until he smoothed the speed bumps that

Streetfighter Strategy
BE CHOOSY ABOUT CUSTOMERS

Client selection was one of the most important areas where Evan Fisher reduced risk in his business. When he first set up his profile on Upwork, Fisher received between one and three invitations a week to talk about projects with potential clients, but as his firm's reputation grew, that number hit about fifteen. At first, he talked with everyone but, finding that these calls took time away from writing plans for paying customers, he gradually started asking more questions during his initial email dialogue with prospects to weed out those who weren't a good fit. He learned after several projects that his service best suited companies that are looking to raise $10 million to $50 million, an area where he is very experienced. As a result, he'd ask clients about their fundraising goals early in the discussions to eliminate entrepreneurs outside that range. When we spoke, he was mainly working with founders who'd launched multiple startups and had raised money successfully in earlier rounds. "When you make sure you are only working with people you can crush it for, that's what makes for a great working relationship," he says.

In his initial calls, Fisher learned to listen closely to how potential clients present their business concepts—another factor that determines how successful he can be for them. "You may have the most wonderful idea on paper, but if you can't talk me through your business and have me understand it, you've lost me already," he says. Ultimately, he knows that when he creates a business plan, the client has to sell investors on the ideas behind it. Industry regulations prevent him from phoning an investor on a client's behalf. Selecting clients who can make a positive impression on their own gives him confidence that his business plans will make it into the right hands and contribute to a successful financing round.

Fisher also learned to pay attention to prospects' attitudes and soft skills, which could make or break a project. He only took on clients who seemed to have a positive attitude and a willingness to learn—qualities that will allow them to succeed in raising capital. "Ultimately, it's about

'Can you work with other people?'" he says. "If you can't, how are you going to be perceived if you are asking for millions of dollars?" He treated any signs that potential clients liked to create drama—something that could disrupt the flow of a project—as red flags. "It slows everything and everybody down," he says. When a potential client needs something far too quickly, he also proceeds very carefully. He is very protective of his team and does not want to subject them to undue stress. "If they don't want to wait, they won't be our client much longer," he says.

When he engages clients, Fisher shares a set of house rules at the outset to set expectations with them. **"If you don't make the rules, someone will make them for you,"** he says. One rule is that family time is sacred. Fisher, who is married with two children, makes it clear that he and his team are not available to respond to emails, texts, and calls after hours. "If any client has that expectation, we're not working together," he says.

slowed him on the first ones. As he won and completed more projects, he focused on doing the best job he could so he would get great reviews and attract other customers. He was also willing to tweak the mix of services he was selling. When we spoke most recently, his team was mostly working on pitch decks for series A fundraising rounds, because demand for them was high. "We should be called Unicorn Pitch Decks," he joked.

His focus on continuous improvement worked well for him, and Unicorn Business Plans brought in $107,000 its first year, according to Fisher. It hit $438,000 in year two and $1.2 million in year three, he says. As the business grew and he built a track record of success, with multiple pitches going in front of investors such as SoftBank, he attracted even more business.

At the same time Fisher was fine-tuning his client selection process, he experimented with his pricing model. He needed to make sure he was charging enough to run a sustainable business—but not more than the market could bear. When Fisher first got started, he charged $2,500 for a business plan but soon concluded he was undercharging. "It is a lot of work to put together a financial model and a plan around that," he says. "I quickly realized I would burn out." To give clients the time each plan required, he raised his prices gradually, and today clients pay more than $10,000 for a plan. He does not accept equity as payment for his services or negotiate prices with clients. "The moment price starts to become really important to someone, we're not a good fit," he says. "You can dine on steak at Sizzler or Kobe beef. We're not Sizzler."

Fisher also tried new approaches to marketing. Although his company's positive reviews on Upwork helped attract clients, he wanted to cast a wider net and needed to find a low-cost way to do it. He and his team began interviewing satisfied customers who raised capital using his agency's business plans on recorded Zoom calls to create video case studies. He posted them on his company's website. His company rolled out the videos during COVID-19—prompting an 80-percent increase in sales, he says. "Some of the things the entrepreneurs have done are absolutely mind-boggling," says Fisher. "It turned into a piece of referral business for us." He also gets a lot of business through organic word of mouth. "When people raise $10 million, the next question is, 'Who did the deck for you?'" he says. "We realized word of mouth is incredibly powerful." As a result, less than half of his business now comes through Upwork.

Fisher started as a one-man shop but to keep delivering the "Kobe beef" as his business grew, he realized he needed a team. Although he has no employees on payroll, he now relies on fifteen freelancers from Upwork with complementary skills who work with him regularly. "The first person on the team was a designer," he says. "I would write, and she would design." Finding that collaborating with the designer made his life easier, he later expanded to hiring providers who did accounting and back-office support work. Eventually, he hired someone to help him with writing. "It grew from there," he says. Fisher still serves as the final editor on every project, to make sure they all have the right flair. "You do have to commit time to every project," he says. "You have to make sure you are personally involved. That is a challenge from the perspective of scalability."

Fisher has organized the business so his team members can tackle projects remotely from wherever they happen to be. "If you work your best on a beach in Fiji and you have a reliable Wi-Fi connection and can deliver super-high-quality work, go for it," he says. "I want you working your best in the best place for you." When we last spoke, Fisher wasn't capping the size of the business, but for the moment planned to keep it to boutique size, to make sure he had control of the client experience. "We tried to keep it as tight-knit as possible," he says. He also wanted to have time to enjoy with his two children, then ages two and a half and nearly four, while they were little. "You don't want to miss it," he says.

MAKE THE MOST OF ONLINE COMMUNITIES

Some entrepreneurs find that starting an online community can give them an ideal laboratory for testing their tiny business ideas. That's the approach that helped Tiffany Williams, 40, when she realized her days as a senior sales consultant at a daily-deals website were numbered. She had heard rumors that the company planned to lay off team members in smaller territories, like the one where she worked. Having earned a BA in business management and marketing from Dillard University and an MBA in technology management from the University of Phoenix, she decided to put what she'd learned to work in a side hustle. It was an online, print-on-demand T-shirt business she launched in 2012 through Teespring (teespring.com), a platform that lets entrepreneurs create and sell products online. Inspired by her pet—an adorable Yorkie named Prada—Williams hired graphic designers on freelance platforms such as Upwork and Fiverr to design Yorkie-themed T-shirts for her to sell. She didn't know it then, but it was to be two weeks before the layoffs hit her company and she would plunge into the business full time.

Fortunately, the business she chose had a low cost of entry. "There was no money up front," she says. That was because, in a print-on-demand model, the entrepreneur does not have to stock inventory. When she uploads a T-shirt design to Teespring, or a similar site, and selects a selling price, customers pay the site and then the T-shirt is printed. The site takes a cut of each sale, then mails her a check or direct deposits a payment. "A lot of people think that they need to borrow money from the bank or write a 100-page business plan to get started," says Williams. "A lot of times you don't. You can start where you are. As your business grows, you invest more."

Creating the T-shirts and finding a place to sell them was just the first step to building a successful business, though. Williams also needed to find a way to let dog lovers know the T-shirts were for sale. She had always enjoyed social media, so she started a free Facebook group for fellow Yorkie owners to chat with each other, investing about $150 in Facebook ads to attract people who shared this interest. Whenever she had a new design ready, she would present it to the Yorkie group for sale.

Although many Yorkie group members bought her shirts, Williams did not replace her corporate salary right away. Still, she continued to show up at her laptop, day after day, to keep moving the business forward. She knew her experiments on Teespring were an important part of her education as an entrepreneur. "I was in business, but I was learning," she recalls. Eventually, by popular request, she branched out into totes and aprons.

To bring in additional income, she tapped what she had learned in her past corporate life and through her experiments to start an agency, Buzz Social Media, in 2013. Between her business ventures, she built her revenue to the high five figures over two years. "I don't want to go back and work for anybody else," Williams said to herself. "I have to make this work."

Then, in 2014, Williams experienced a breakthrough. She began experimenting with new revenue streams, such as running an online Kindle store where she sold e-books, and began purchasing household items on sale at Target and Walmart and selling them at a markup on Amazon. By using this approach, she grew the business to the point that, once she subtracted her expenses from her revenue, her profits hit $350,000 that year. "That was my breakout year," she says.

As her business grew, Williams began hearing from other women who learned about her success and were interested in launching a business of their own. First, she heard from a woman who wanted to leave her job at an insurance company to stay home and raise her children. She wanted to know how Williams pulled it off. Two weeks later, Williams got another similar inquiry. Soon, the questions were snowballing.

Williams was excited to help, but realized that speaking with each woman one by one wasn't practical as a solopreneur. "It started to take up time when I was running a business to answer everybody's questions," she says. Her solution was to start her free Facebook group, Rich Girl Collective, to support other women who wanted to start businesses. That would allow her to give back to the entrepreneurial community while still staying focused on her own business. "I could answer everyone's questions one at a time in a group," she says.

Williams chose the group's name carefully to reinforce her view that wealth isn't about buying material things but rather building a better quality of life. "For me, the 'rich' in Rich Girl Collective stands for more than money," she says. "It is an acronym: *R* stands for relationships and family. *I* means 'invest' in entrepreneurship. *C* is for community, and *H* is for health and wellness."

Williams kept her group very active by posting three times a day, Monday through Saturday. She also livestreamed Q&A events where members could ask her questions about starting a business. Over several years, the group grew to 15,000 members, as members wrote to her to ask if their friends could join. To keep the discussions focused on business and to keep out spammers, Williams set ground rules. Potential members had to apply, answering questions that showed whether they were serious about starting a business. She also checked out their Facebook pages to make sure the profiles looked legit. "If they have no profile picture, they can't get in," she says.

Over time, Williams noticed common themes in the conversations on the site and tailored her messaging to her community's concerns. One was that perfectionism was holding some women back from starting their businesses. "They try to have the perfect logo, the perfect website," she says. She developed messaging that urged followers to let perfectionism go. "I tell them branding is important," says Williams. "However, don't try to be so perfect you're taking months to get started. Learn as you go."

Many of the women in the community were percolating with business ideas, and they often struggled with focus. Williams encouraged them to master one business before moving on to the next. "We have so many passions, so many businesses we want to start," she says. "I encourage them to start with one thing. Get that one thing flowing, and then if you want to think about branching out to another business, do that. If you've never been a business owner before, you don't know how much work it is. You are going to spread yourself way too thin if you start out doing too many things."

Just as Williams's life as an entrepreneur was humming, her life changed overnight when she was thirty-seven. When she went to the doctor, she learned she had very early-stage ovarian cancer. "It was a shock," she recalls. "I don't have a history in my family. It was a tough time in my life." She opted not to share the news with her community at first, as she went through four months of chemotherapy, preferring to keep her focus on the business. "I wanted people to treat me the same way," she says.

She kept up business operations throughout her treatment, maintaining her regular livestreams. She didn't tell her followers about her diagnosis until the last day of her treatment. "I wanted them to see the entire time that I still pushed through, that I got work done," she says. "I wanted that to be a lesson: Whatever comes to you, you can push through." Six months after completing her chemo treatment, Williams held her first Rich Girl Live conference, a two-day event in New Orleans. "I wanted to test the waters," she says. "I was determined to do it."

Williams's business plateaued in 2016 and 2017 while she coped with her illness. During that period, she experimented with offering more digital products that would enable her to scale back her hours and to focus on getting well. "I wanted to work, but I didn't want to do as much work," she says. To that end, she started introducing online classes on topics where she had the expertise, such as starting a T-shirt business, launching an online boutique, and selling products on Amazon. "I only teach what I've done and have gotten results with," she says. As her digital products took off, she de-emphasized the physical products, including her T-shirts.

To host her online classes, she uses the platform Podia. For a set price per year, Podia allows her to offer classes, downloads, and monthly membership groups. Podia's capabilities came in handy when, in response to requests from her followers, Williams introduced a live training class in 2018 called Rich Girl Academy, for which she charges $37 a month through the platform. In addition to providing personalized support to the women business owners who join, such as an analysis of their websites, she invites monthly guest speakers to talk about topics such as business finance, credit, and mental health. "I realized a lot of people need additional help—accountability," she says. "They need the push. They need the camaraderie to see that if other people are doing it, they can do it, too."

With her classes growing, Williams formalized her business even more. She registered the trademark Rich Girl Collective and introduced live chapters for members of the academy, which meet quarterly in seven cities, intending to turn it into something akin to a sorority. In 2021, in response to her community, she offered a free masterclass on how to write an e-book. These have been valuable selling tools for her. When more than 1,300 women signed up, she saw there was real demand. She began building a mailing list of women who had requested an alert when she introduced a new product, Easy eBooks, a digital planner to help women map out their e-books before they write them. "My audience loves planners," she adds.

Williams experimented further with how she got her work done as she was growing her business. She was fortunate that her mother was available to help her with a wide variety of projects during the first few years she grew the business, working as a contractor. "She knows all of the ins and outs of the business," says Williams. "She is my biggest supporter and helper."

As she could afford more help, Williams enlisted a recurring team of contractors so she could stay focused on strategy and business development. She grew her team to six contractors who help her regularly, including a graphic designer, a personal assistant, someone who handles membership enrollment and email support for customers, an attorney, a publicist, and a video producer. Because everyone works virtually, she needs no physical office space. Williams's willingness to delegate enabled her to grow the Facebook group to 39,000 women and her email list to 30,000. To stretch her capabilities and to help her team get more done in the time available to them, Williams uses free and low-cost apps and software programs, spending about $1,500 a month on her subscriptions to these platforms. The cost of hiring people to do the kind of work these tools do for her would be far higher. Today, her annual revenue is more than $1 million.

Ultimately, Williams sees all of her experiments as essential to building a successful company. When someone says, "I want to start a business.

Streetfighter Strategy
AUTOMATE EVERYTHING YOU CAN

One of the best ways to stretch what you can do in a tiny business is to use automation. Here are Tiffany Williams's favorite tools.

Adobe Stock (stock.adobe.com): This is her go-to source of high-quality stock photos for use on her website, Facebook, and other digital properties.

Canva (canva.com): "I love, love, love Canva," says Williams. "All of my graphics are done by my designer in Canva."

ClickFunnels (clickfunnels.com): Williams uses this online marketing tool to convert prospects into leads. "You can buy templates or have someone do ClickFunnels for you," she says. "My virtual assistant knows it better than I do, and she does it for me."

ConvertKit (convertkit.com): This is an email marketing platform aimed at helping creative professionals deepen their relationships with their fans.

Podia (podia.com): Williams uses this platform, aimed at non-techies, to host her courses. You can use it for selling webinars, downloads, and memberships.

TXT180 (txt180.com): This marketing service uses text messaging to stay in touch with customers.

I need help with my marketing," she wants Rich Girl Collective to be the first thing that comes to mind. That's a tall order, given all the competition in the space, but following her illness, she says, she became very clear on how important it was to her to focus her life on helping women. "My mission now is, I want to impact as many people as possible," she says.

Fortunately, Williams says her health is now excellent—"I'm back and better than ever," she says—but she makes sure her life is balanced. She spends much of her free time outside the business involved in community activities, at the gym, or with her family, which includes her baby daughter,

TEST THE NAME OF YOUR BUSINESS

One of the most important decisions you'll make as an entrepreneur is naming your company and your products or services. A great name can instantly help you bond with potential customers—while the wrong one can leave you feeling lonely and ignored.

So how do you know if the name you love is a winner? If you already have an existing website where traffic is flowing, traditional A/B testing services will let you compare "option A" with "option B." However, to be meaningful these do require you to have some traffic to the site and sometimes to make coding changes to your site.

One alternative I have heard about from several entrepreneurs who used it is PickFu (pickfu.com). This platform allows users to set up instant polls of 50 to 500 people to test brand names, book titles, book covers, ad banners, email templates, and the like. The polls can be private or public, depending on your preference.

PickFu allows you to ask a simple question such as, "Which brand of dog food would you buy?" and to post two or more alternatives side by side. Responses—which, based on two polls I conducted, tend to arrive in about fifteen minutes—allow you to see respondents' demographic information, such as their age, sex, income level, and level of education. The panelists, all paid, are supplied by panel companies or recruited by PickFu. The company uses human and AI audits to ensure quality, according to John Li, a cofounder of PickFu.

Polls start at $50, and the cost depends on how many options you choose. When I recently used the site to test titles for a writing project (well, actually the title of this book!), it cost me about $200 to test four options among 100 people. I opted to ask for detailed information relevant to the project, which raised the price a bit.

PickFu started as a weekend project in 2008, but took off around 2013, after Gabriel Weinberg, a user and founder of search engine DuckDuckGo, shared the tool with his network. "People were realizing that getting validation for ideas before committing work and time was useful," says Li.

Soon self-published authors, game developers, product managers, and e-commerce store owners were showing up, looking to narrow down ideas they were considering. "Generally, business people and authors suffer not from a lack of ideas, but from too many," says Li.

Li shared with me some of his best practices for entrepreneurs who are testing names and titles used in their businesses. They're relevant whether you use PickFu, or another service like it.

1. **Check your feelings at the door.** You may be in love with your concept, but if your target customers aren't, it's better to know sooner rather than later. "Don't be insulted," Li advises. "Let it make you more aware."

2. **Only test one thing per test.** Trying to test both a company's name and logo design at one time will distort your results because readers tend to react to whatever is most meaningful to them. "First test the business name, then test the logo," advises Li.

3. **Pay close attention to comments.** The most valuable aspect of testing a name—whether on a survey platform or in person, in a focus group—is reading the comments poll-takers make. "Your name may bring up certain connotations you never thought of," says Li.

4. **Don't lock yourself into a single audience.** Although you may have an inkling of who will buy your product or service, you'll be leaving money on the table if you limit yourself to the prospects you expect to purchase it. Asking the general population if they would spend money to buy a product in a poll may point you to new demographic groups you might target. "See if there are patterns of people who respond to your idea," says Li.

5. **Use testing to save money on digital ads.** Experimenting with pay-per-click ads can get costly. Testing out an individual ad before you pay for it can help you conserve cash. "We've seen people test Google and Facebook ads before running them on the ad platforms," says Li. "They get the gist of how the audience interprets the offer they are trying to make." Once they know how the ads are perceived, they can either fine-tune them or invest in the ads with greater confidence. Entrepreneurs may be natural risk-takers, but taking measured risks is always better than the shotgun approach.

whom she adopted in 2020. "You don't want to be so focused on your business you're not spending time with family," she says.

PIVOT LIKE ELVIS

We've looked at businesses that have gotten their product and service right. But many people don't do that on the first try. What if your product isn't working? You may have to pivot until you find success. That approach worked for Jeff Sadowsky. He's the founder of Party Innovations, an internet store he runs from his home in Brooklyn, New York. When Sadowsky, a former computer consultant, went into online retail, he started selling decorative ribbons but didn't get as far as he'd hoped. Then a visit to a stationery company changed his life. The owners casually mentioned that their bread-and-butter product was napkins that they drop-shipped to customers.

Sadowsky decided to give selling napkins a try and began advertising them using Google Adwords. His experiment bore fruit from day one. "I never had such an immediate response," he says. That was about thirteen years ago. After some experimenting with his product mix and marketing, and bringing on a contractor who manages his paid advertising on an ongoing basis, he estimates that he built the business to $1.3–1.4 million in revenue five or six years ago. Other than during the COVID-19 pandemic, which hit his business hard, since then, he says the firm has maintained revenue in that range, which is profitable. This year he expects sales to be back up, thanks to efforts like amping up his customer service and seeking reviews on Shopper Approved, a site that provides reviews from verified customers. "I realized if I can treat every customer like my only customer, that's how I can differentiate myself," he says.

PERFECT YOUR PRICING

Another big part of taking the risk out of your business is testing your pricing. Either overcharging or undercharging can send a message to customers that drives them away from an otherwise appealing product. Because pricing taps into people's emotions, it's not an entirely logical process. It's important to try small experiments so you're able to build recurring sales and a sustainable business.

The difference between a tiny business that makes big money and one that makes average money for that industry is often in finding a way to charge premium prices by delivering unusual value. Dana Derricks, 30, a freelance copywriter who also runs a small goat farm in Wisconsin, is a good example. He did a series of gradual experiments with pricing to see what the market would bear—and built a seven-figure business along the way. Tired of scrambling from one freelance project to the next, Derricks wrote and self-published a book using Amazon Kindle Direct Publishing print on demand called *Conversion Secrets: Optimize Your Business for Sales*, to teach his customers who were Amazon sellers how to do their own copywriting. He marketed it for a mind-blowing $400 a copy. His premise was that books aren't priced based on the value of the knowledge they impart, and his book was worth all $400. Many people felt the same way. He sold about 1,600 copies in nearly seventy-one countries. Frequent speaking engagements helped him generate those sales.

Following that success, he introduced other books at higher prices that targeted Amazon sellers, his initial market. His next book, *Ascension Secrets, Back-End Mastery Guide: Maximize Your Reviews & Profits*, focused on how to get positive online reviews. He priced that book at $1,000 a copy. He sold 243.

Another of his books—*High-Ticket Book Secrets*—came out in 2017. He initially priced it at $2,500 a copy and sold four copies. He later changed the business model for that one and charged $25, selling about 500 copies. "It has done a really good job of fueling sales for my other products," he says. One of them is a course for writing and self-publishing books.

Book number four, *The Dream 100 Book*—which explains how to connect with 100 key influencers in your field—initially sold nine copies at $2,000 a copy on preorder. Derricks revised his strategy for that book, as well, repricing it at $20 and selling 5,500.

Derricks ran his business, the Derricks Group, as a one-man show from 2010 to 2017, but with his book-related activities and speaking engagements picking up, he was able to expand it to seven employees and to grow it to seven-figure revenue, according to Derricks. However, he later found it stressful to manage traditional employees and hard to find the talent he needed locally—he lives in a town of 1,000 people—so he revised his business model to make it contractor-based. Now he has no employees, with four contractors handling design, copywriting for campaigns, and building websites, click funnels, and Facebook ads on an ongoing basis. "I've found people all over the world," he says.

It's just as important to experiment with how you discuss pricing with your clients. Emily Tryon, RN, has perfected this. Tryon, 46, is the founder and CEO of Esthetic Solutions, a Scottsdale, Arizona–based medical spa where her team never even quotes prices over the phone. Like Fisher, she caters to people looking for quality, not price shoppers. She has trained her team to tell bargain hunters, "If you want cheaper prices, go to Groupon. If you are looking to be well cared for and love your look, we are the place for you." Clients have flocked, with some flying in from around the world, drawn by her reputation for creating a natural look as she uses Botox and fillers to slow the aging process. "We've all seen people who look overfilled and artificial," says Tryon. "Those are not my patients. My patients have subtle, gentle enhancement."

By the business's fifth year, Tryon, who now teaches physicians and nurses her techniques, grew her single-chair spa, founded in 2013, to $1 million in annual revenue by word of mouth, with the help of one assistant. Today she has a team of five to ten employees, depending on demand. When we last spoke, she was working toward a goal of extending Esthetic Solutions "from Scottsdale to Singapore" with fifty locations by 2024 and was on the hunt for single-chair spas to acquire.

Before starting Esthetic Solutions, Tryon spent many years as a nurse, clocking twelve-hour night shifts in the intensive care unit. Although she was making a difference, she reached the point of emotional burnout. She knew she needed to make a change after a woman came in to thank the ICU team for saving her husband's life. As the woman teared up, Tryon was alarmed to realize she was thinking about the next to-dos on her busy shift: " 'I have to take out the trash and fill out the paperwork.' That was a wake-up call," she says. She knew she needed to get out of the ICU and to pursue a less stressful career tied to her passions.

Although Tryon was a registered nurse, she had no training in the aesthetic techniques she wanted to perform, so she invested in educating herself at workshops by successful practitioners. "I got on planes on my own dime, flying all over to be trained by the top injectors the world," she says. In 2013, she rented a 150-square-foot space and opened her spa. Tryon was still working at the hospital, which allowed her to fund the business and still pay her bills. "I was working eighty hours a week between my twelve-hour shifts at the hospital and getting my tiny business started," she recalls.

To spread the word that she was open for business, Tryon went to free business networking events. "I talked to strangers, and I asked the tiny trickle of patients coming in the door to refer their friends and family," she says. She often mentioned at these gatherings that she had fifteen years of vascular and cardiac experience as a nurse. "I used my past to be able to sell myself," she says. What she found was that clients didn't care about her medical experience as much as she thought. What interested them more was her genuine passion for helping people look more youthful. "We're living longer and having a better quality of life," she says. "It was easy to say yes to my services."

Even so, there were some tough years, like 2015, when cash flow was tight. "There were two months that year I couldn't pay myself," recalls Tryon. "Any other person would have closed their doors if they only looked at 2015." She was determined to make the business work, and instead of giving up, looked closely at all of her processes and procedures, including those related to pricing, to make sure she was doing enough to generate new business and referrals.

One change she made that helped the business grow was qualifying patients by charging an initial consultation fee, so she did not end up spending an hour of chair time with people who were not serious about working with her. She now requests a credit card number when someone books a consultation and waives the fee if they proceed with treatment. "It's a way to weed out the people who aren't serious," she says. "If they are not willing to pay a consultation fee, they will never take action on the advice you are giving them."

She also creates scripts to guide her team through conversations such as requesting a credit card when customers book appointments. She puts the scripts into a handbook for new hires and role-plays with her team, so there is consistency in their communications. "It's not that we want to be parrots and say the same thing all the time," she says. "We do want to add the human element."

In adopting approaches like this, Tryon is an avid student of companies that are known for high-end customer service, such as BMW, Nordstrom, and The Ritz-Carlton. "You would never call a Louis Vuitton store and say, 'How much is a purse?' What would they say to you? 'Which purse?'" she asks. "It's no different in this industry. We can't diagnose you over the phone."

Over the years, Tryon has become so proficient in the techniques she uses that she spent 2019 traveling across the country training physicians and nurses in them. "I've immersed myself so much in the industry that I'm familiar with all of the latest products and techniques," she says. Fellow medical professionals like her "Safety first, beauty second," approach, she finds. She ceased travel during COVID-19 and used the time to upgrade the spa's technology, redo its retail display area, and repair broken equipment. "This has been stressful," she told me at the time. "There are dark days for all. But one of the questions I constantly ask myself is, 'Emily, what has you seeing this situation as anything other than an opportunity?'"

With the economy opening up, Tryon was looking to acquire other salons. She also focused on reaching new clients early, in their teens. "It is much easier to prevent than correct," she says. To that end, she maintains an active Instagram presence, which she bolstered during the pandemic. "It's not what you put on your social media platform—it's what you don't," says Tryon. "I don't have thousands of 'before' and 'after' pictures. I have real people talking about their real lives."

Although the work Tryon does helps people look better, her ultimate goal is to help them enjoy their lives more. "I worked with a sixteen-year-old gal who suffered severe cystic acne," recalls Tryon. A deep laser resurfacing "completely changed her life," she says. Beauty may be only skin deep, but for many people, looking their best makes a difference. Tryon finds it rewarding to help them.

Once you've built confidence that you're selling what you should be selling and that you've found the right branding and pricing, there's another critical piece of the puzzle: finding the money to launch and grow your business. In the next chapter, we'll look at how the average person who doesn't hang out with millionaires can do that.

CHAPTER 5

FIND THE MONEY YOU NEED

Steven Sudell, 37, didn't start out expecting to become an inventor. Happily running his physical therapy practice in Venice Beach, California, he was frustrated that he could not find an effective at-home surgical neck traction device. Having played football for a while in college, he'd suffered from neck pain himself and knew how difficult it was to find relief.

One day, after hurting his neck while working out, he said, "Enough is enough." Using materials he had on hand, he'd soon created a makeshift prototype of a small sling-like device that hooks up to a doorknob or railing. After using this rough prototype of the invention for ten minutes, he says, he got a break from his neck pain.

That was in early 2016. Working on the idea with an industrial designer for a year and a half, Sudell brought his product, the Neck Hammock, to market in October 2017. Between that time and 2021, he sold 300,000 units, bringing in $5–7 million in annual revenue. He did it while still running his two-employee physical therapy practice—which he founded in 2013, focusing on outpatient orthopedic treatment for people who play sports and do CrossFit—for 32 hours a week. "It's one of those things I really enjoy," he says. "It's also a huge source of ideas." He sold the Neck Hammock for a seven-figure amount in January 2021. "I knew there were a lot of buyers in the market for e-commerce businesses," he says. "I had eight offers the first day."

Previously, Sudell had started StretchLab, an "assisted stretching" studio, with two clients in 2015, and grew it from one location to more than 220 nationwide with the help of a franchisor. "You're lying down, and someone is taking you through all the stretches," he says. "It's much more passive. They may be getting you into areas you can't reach in yoga." He and his partners sold that business in a seven-figure exit, as well, in 2019.

It wasn't easy to find the time to launch the Neck Hammock while maintaining a full patient load. However, Sudell was motivated by a family crisis: His younger sister had recently suffered a recurrence of leukemia. Working on the invention gave him a way to alleviate the feelings of helplessness he had.

"I remember her sitting in a hospital room," he says, "going through pain I could do nothing about—but there were others I could help." And through inventions like the Neck Hammock, he says, "I can do it on a much larger scale than seeing them individually in my clinic."

That business took off so quickly on Amazon that he grew his team from himself and two contractors to approximately ten employees before he sold it and began thinking about his next venture. And fortunately, when we spoke, his sister had been in remission for four years.

Although it's easier to start a business with fewer people and less cash than ever before, entrepreneurs do need some money to realize their vision. Like many people who start product-related businesses, Sudell needed some money to create and test his prototype and to bring it to market. He didn't have a wealthy family member to bankroll his business, and he wasn't raking in enough income from his physical therapy practice to pay for it all out of pocket. The only way to keep moving forward with his idea was to find another source of cash.

Fortunately, there are many fast-evolving options for financing a business—and, by the time this book comes out, there will probably be even more. "There's a ton of money out there right now that's being deployed," says Scottsdale, Arizona–based venture capitalist Dave McLurg. "I don't know if I've ever seen such a frenzy to deploy capital, which is sort of staggering and interesting, given what we went through in 2020." In addition to traditional forms of funding and financing, which usually depend on the personal credit profile of the entrepreneur, the digital era is ushering in new ones, for example, credit cards for startups that don't require a personal guarantee.

That said, it takes some creativity to go after any kind of financing. To get the medical device he invented registered with the FDA, Sudell needed to test his product for safety and durability—a pricey proposition. Armed with his prototype, Sudell started a campaign on the crowdfunding site Kickstarter in October 2017. With crowdfunding, in case you're not familiar, people who want to buy a product you would like to manufacture place preorders for it, essentially financing the costs for you.

In doing his research about Kickstarter, Sudell learned about Katherine Krug. She had invented a back-support product called BetterBack and run a successful campaign for it on the crowdfunding site. "If you have a real-life hero, she's mine," he says. When a client mentioned knowing Krug and offered to introduce them, Sudell took him up on it. She gave him advice on how to make sure his campaign would be successful.

Reaching out to everyone he knew on social media to share the news of his campaign, Sudell raised $901,058 from 12,354 backers who placed preorders for the device on Kickstarter. But that still wasn't enough to take his product to market, so he did another campaign on another crowdfunding site, Indiegogo, raising a total of $1.64 million through the two crowdfunding sites.

To make sure his product took off, Sudell invested some of the money he raised into digital advertising on sites such as Facebook, to drive people to an e-commerce store he set up. At one point, he brought in $500,000 in sales in 30 days. "Awesome," he thought. "This is going to be a $1 million company by the end of the year."

Then Facebook changed its algorithm—and sales went off a cliff. Even worse, he'd just placed what was for him a massive order with his factory: 50,000 units, for which he'd spent close to $300,000.

"Panic set in," he recalls. He didn't know how he would sell his inventory, and needed to shore up his financial reserves.

Fortunately, he was able to get a $100,000 short-term loan through

Shopify, the platform he used for his store, at 10-percent interest. He followed that with a second short-term loan of 3.5 percent, at about $75,000, from BlueVine, an FDIC-registered provider of banking services to small businesses. "I didn't necessarily need it all," he says, "but I know that when you don't have money, it's a lot harder to get money."

Armed with the financing he needed, he was able to keep growing the business. Before he sold the Neck Hammock business, he marketed on his website and Amazon.

In interviewing thousands of entrepreneurs over the years, I've found that no two businesses' financing stories are exactly alike. But one thing that almost all new businesses have in common is depending on the owners' resources. Sudell managed to start his physical therapy practice with less than $10,000 by partnering with a CrossFit gym and working from a table in an extra room upstairs in the beginning. "I basically used most of their equipment in the gym," he recalls. "That really helped me cut down on overall startup costs. I slowly added things I needed as the business grew."

If you're starting a professional-services business, you might only need to spring for a computer and a DIY website. You'll need more funds for a product-based business or one that requires real estate. That might mean tapping your paycheck, your savings or an inheritance, or a spouse or partner's income.

Once you make the business "real" and take it beyond the idea stage, it will be easier to get other people involved in backing you, whether by lending you money or investing. And you'll likely discover that there's plenty of money out there to help you start your business. You just need to know where it is and how to go after it. Let's look at some common avenues of financing that high-revenue tiny businesses have used.

CROWDFUNDING

Many people don't have the luxury to save up for months to start a business. If that's the case for you, the route Sudell took—taking preorders from customers through a crowdfunding site—is one way to start on a shoestring. Pebble Time Smartwatch, the Coolest Cooler (which has a built-in

Bluetooth speaker and ice-crushing blender), and the Canary smart home security device are some high-profile startups that raised money through crowdfunding.

In addition to Kickstarter and Indiegogo, consider other "rewards-based" sites, such as Fundable (fundable.com), Pozible (pozible.com, Australia), and Ulule (ulule.com, Europe). There are also industry-specific sites, such as Good Shepherd Entertainment (formerly Gambitious) for game developers, which you may be able to uncover through some targeted web searching. Some entrepreneurs don't even use the platforms, but instead put up a simple website themselves to take preorders for their products.

Typically, with what's called donation-based crowdfunding or rewards-based crowdfunding, customers will pay you in advance for a product you're going to make; in exchange, they'll expect you to send them the product when it's ready. That may sound simple, but it takes advance planning. Building up your following on social media and creating an email list will help you get better results. You're going to have to tell people about the campaign for them to invest—and can't assume that every person you invite to support you will be inclined to do so. You may also want to reach out to influencers to spread the word, and the time to do that is way before you launch.

Some entrepreneurs hire a professional marketing agency that specializes in crowdfunding campaigns to help get their messaging right. Finding the right way to ask supporters to place their orders or donate is critical. Many people like to know they are helping someone, so consider phrasing like, "Your contribution of any size is bringing us a step closer to helping middle school girls learn coding through our new game."

Try to build as much momentum as early as you can. Raising a significant percentage of your goal in the first two or three days will improve your visibility on some sites. One way to make that happen is by asking your friends and family to contribute as early as possible. Some entrepreneurs try to build excitement around their campaign by hosting an event, like a backyard barbecue, where they let supporters know how much they are appreciated.

If you crowdfund, you'll also need to stay in touch with supporters.

Streetfighter Strategy
ACCOMPLISH YOUR STRATEGIC GOALS— EVEN WHEN YOU'RE JUGGLING

When you're raising money, you'll win backers' confidence if you show you can reach the goals you are setting for the business, such as hitting a production date. That means managing your time carefully, even if you have other commitments, like Sudell's physical therapy practice.

Sudell says his most effective means of doing this is to have a whiteboard on the mirror in his bathroom where he writes down his goals every day. He adds a to-do list below them. "I find that staying consistent about this and constantly knocking off that to-do list helps me get there over time, rather than me obsessing and trying to sprint there," he says. "Achieving goals is easier when you are consistent. One of my favorite quotes is 'The harder I work, the luckier I get.' So many things that have fallen into my lap, I believe, have manifested from my working really hard and talking to the right people consistently."

Make sure to build an email list you can use to communicate with them and to let them know about your progress—even if it's to let them know you're changing factories because of a snafu and the product will arrive late. Otherwise, some supporters may post negative comments on your crowdfunding pages or social media.

There are other hybrid crowdfunding platforms worth investigating, too. Quirky (quirky.com) is a site for inventors where you can get help from the community with projects in the business, in exchange for giving the helpers a percentage of your royalties. At Patreon (patreon.com), supporters can buy a monthly subscription to contribute to your efforts, as we'll discuss further in Chapter 7. Beyond this, there is equity crowdfunding, where investors on the platform can buy an ownership stake in your business. Some of the major equity crowdfunding platforms include AngelList (angellist.com), EquityNet (equitynet.com), Fundable (fundable.com), MicroVentures (microventures.com), SeedInvest (seeinvest.com), and

Wefunder (wefunder.com). With equity crowdfunding, you will be giving away some of your ownership to other people in exchange for their cash, so be sure to get legal advice. You don't want to give away so much equity that you'll have little left if you decide to raise more funding.

Many entrepreneurs who try crowdfunding use it in combination with other types of funding. Tim Swindle, 41, a Chicago-based entrepreneur, is one of them. In July 2011, Swindle left a corporate job in commercial real estate to help launch the software startup PointDrive. By January 2014, he and a friend had dreamed up a board game, Utter Nonsense, a card game in which players read phrases in funny accents, and launched it as a side project on the crowdfunding site Kickstarter that August. They raised a little more than $16,000. "It was our first win and got our momentum going," he recalls.

Although Swindle had experience as an entrepreneur, when it came time to create Utter Nonsense, he had to turn to Google searches for keywords such as "how to manufacture a card game." "We didn't know how to do that," he says. But he didn't let that stop him. He learned how step by step.

Rather than try to teach themselves game design, Swindle and a former business partner he bought out hired professionals to create a prototype. Swindle reached out to his professional network to find a graphic designer for the game and packaging, and located a husband-and-wife team to assist with this. Through other referrals from friends at the Second City, a comedy improv venue, he found comedy writers who were staffers at the club's late-night show to write the content for the game. "It was all of these gig economies coming together," he says. They also hired a manufacturer, Delano Games, to design the prototype, including the box, and to eventually manufacture the game. "With any product you are going to build, rarely are you going to do all of the manufacturing yourself," says Swindle. Making games in the United States is not common, he says. More often, entrepreneurs turn to manufacturers in China, but he and his partner were nervous about working with a factory so far away.

All told, getting started took $40,000, with each partner putting in $20,000 from his own savings before the Kickstarter campaign. "What I've said to myself is that, if I lose money, at least I'm going to have fun doing it," he says. Fortunately, he turned out to be very good at earning it. When Swindle and his partner launched Utter Nonsense on Kickstarter and started pulling in preorders, interest caught fire; local and industry media started writing about the game. After his sister, then an independent public relations and marketing consultant, pitched a trade magazine that covered toys and games, a buyer at Target discovered Utter Nonsense and reached out with an offer to carry it. As exciting as that sounded to Swindle and his partner, it posed a massive challenge: Ramping up production. "It was hundreds of thousands of units," he says. "That's serious volume."

Swindle decided to be open with Target about his concerns. The retailer's internal team stepped up with valuable guidance. "To their credit," he recalls, "they were listening to every single objection we brought to them and would come back and say, 'Meet this distributor. They will work with you to get games to sell in our stores.'" Following the retailer's suggestions made it easier to get up and running. Target stores nationwide began stocking Utter Nonsense by March 2015.

With full-time day jobs, the cofounders set up everything to be outsourced, taking inspiration from the lifestyle Tim Ferriss described in *The 4-Hour Workweek*, the same book that inspired business-plan writer Evan Fisher. Because Swindle and his partner had outsourced most of the work of making the game, they had the freedom to do other things they enjoyed, even while running a fast-growing startup. At one point, Swindle and his now-wife spent six months traveling the world. "I did everything from my laptop," he says. "It gave me the freedom to work from wherever."

One thing that made it all possible was hiring a reliable distributor to manage the relationship with Target. "You are paying them for their fulfillment skills," explains Swindle. Having distribution nailed down also held a lot of weight with other retailers. Amazon, Barnes & Noble, and Books-A-Million soon began carrying the game. About three years into the project, the company's annual revenue hit $1 million. By year four, 2017, Utter Nonsense was operating as a three-person team, with Swindle's sister now on board regularly. Then the toy company PlayMonster got interested and acquired the company. In the meantime, LinkedIn had acquired PointDrive, Swindle's software startup, in August 2016. Swindle started

Streetfighter Strategy
ADOPT THE BOOTSTRAPPING MINDSET
(EVEN IF YOU PLAN TO RAISE MONEY LATER)

Tim Swindle finds that Nick Jonas, a Chicago restaurant owner and tech entrepreneur, has had a powerful influence on this thinking about financing. Jonas has talked about learning from his dad that money goes into three shoeboxes: "The money comes in, the money goes out, the rest goes for college." Swindle has learned not to spend more money than he has and to finance as much growth as possible through bootstrapping. That means being diligent about spending the money he's raised on Kickstarter. "I want to be operating at a profit year-round," he says. That's the secret, he's found, to building a business that's not only sustainable, but an attractive acquisition target.

an early-stage venture capital firm, Hubbard Street Capital, after Point-Drive sold.

Tapping what he had learned with the launch of Utter Nonsense, Swindle moved on to his next venture, Playtacular, an independent toy and game publisher, in 2018, with entrepreneur Brady Peterson. Finding that Playtacular was a better fit for smaller markets and specialty and hobby stores, they licensed it to a smaller publisher. Swindle missed running a game company, so after completing that transaction, he moved on to the Root Beer Float Challenge, another family game he launched in July 2019, where players compete to build a root beer float. The game now sells at Target, Amazon, and Walmart.com. In 2019, he also launched Cheeky, a company selling naughty holiday ornaments that brought in about $350,000 a year in revenue, and which he was in the process of rebranding when we spoke.

His latest project, with Peterson, is Alley Hoopster, a kit that helps people perform basketball trick shots like their partner, twenty-one-year-old YouTuber TJass, from Kenosha, Wisconsin, who had five million followers between TikTok and Instagram at the time of our interview. Swindle, with his new business partner, again turned to crowdfunding. They raised $20,125 in funding on Kickstarter, exceeding their goal by 35 percent.

He and his wife also had a baby along the way. That makes Swindle's life very full. He wouldn't have it any other way. "I wake up every day and decide what I want to do for that day," he says. "I'm working really hard—but it's 'choose your own adventure.'" And his entrepreneurial lifestyle, enabled by the products he fueled with crowdfunding, helps him live a more interesting life. "I'm trying to avoid a desk job," says Swindle. "Deep down, everyone wants to be their own boss."

SUPPLIER FINANCING

For some entrepreneurs, getting funding from suppliers makes more sense initially than turning to customers. If you make a product, you may be able to negotiate payment terms with manufacturers where you can collect from customers first and pay your factory later. That is the case for Bryce William Monkivitch, 30. When he was twenty-five, his family sent him to China to work in his uncle's factory. That adventure didn't turn out as planned. "He thought I was too immature and said, 'Go home and get an education,'" Monkivitch recalls.

Although this bruised his ego, Monkivitch, who lives in Queensland, Australia, realized his uncle meant to help him, so he decided to get practical. He enrolled in accounting classes at TAFE Queensland. Six months into studying, however, he gave in to the temptation to start an e-commerce business and began selling cute dog hats online through Facebook and Instagram. He had found a supplier through the online marketplace Alibaba.

Sales took off, thanks to the photos he posted of adorable pooches wearing their headgear. He'd soon ventured into selling trendy clothing to teens and young women, creating an online store called Sincere Sally on the e-commerce platform Shopify, using $5,000 he had saved from doing freelance concrete work. That was in March 2018. Monkivitch, who learned to code growing up, built an app—similar to a bot—that starts conversations with people on Facebook and Instagram. It "chats" with them about what styles they like and gives them offers and discount codes to attract them to Sincere Sally's store. Once he started using the app, sales took off. Today, the store sells its apparel in both the Australian market and the United States, competing with brands such as Nasty Gal, Fashion Nova, and Princess Polly.

With no track record, Monkivitch initially had to work with a factory that required payments up front. That lasted about a year and a half. Then, a friend introduced him to a new supplier. This factory agreed to make clothing samples for him that he could photograph and post online to attract orders from customers. He was free to pay the supplier after receiving customers' payments. This arrangement, which improved his cash flow, was only possible because he had a history of paying the supplier on time. When you treat suppliers well, he found, "everyone is almost fighting over your business in the end." The give-and-take in the relationship extends beyond payment terms. If, for instance, a product he orders turns out to have a flaw, he can discuss it with the supplier and come to an agreement about how to handle it. "They take a little loss, we take a little loss, and we work together to make it better the next time," says Monkivitch.

As the store started bringing in money, Monkivitch invested some of his earnings in paid Facebook ads to spread the word about the store. Knowing his way around the platform has come in handy, with ads getting more expensive. "You have to learn pretty quickly," he says. To expand his knowledge, Monkivitch traveled around the globe in 2019 with other young e-commerce entrepreneurs and influencers. "Hanging out with them and people who are really engaged in marketing has helped me to become much better," he says. "I'm pretty much obsessed with marketing. It's pretty much all I do every day—figuring out more effective marketing techniques."

Through his app, Monkivitch attracts "micro-influencers," who are just building their followings. They start conversations on Instagram with potential customers. When we spoke in 2021, his network of micro-influencers had grown to about 450,000. He gives the micro-influencers a discount code they can place on their own Instagram account, so the company can track sales they bring in and pay them a commission. With many micro-influencers based in the Philippines, Monkivitch has traveled there to offer on-site training in skills such as building a following and taking product shots. "We're building communities there," he says. "That's also why we're getting rapid growth."

For the first two years, Monkivitch ran the business solo. Then he joined forces with his sister Joy and the small army of influencers. When COVID hit, Monkivitch expected business to fall off. To his great surprise, when stimulus money started flowing, many customers spent it on new clothes at his store. "Our sales went through the roof," he says. Fortunately, his accounting skills helped him to keep track of it all. Sincere Sally now brings in the equivalent of more than USD $1 million annually.

FRIENDS AND FAMILY FINANCING

For many entrepreneurs, friends and family financing is the first place to turn for startup cash—and their loved ones and inner circle are happy to support them. "They feel, 'Well, it's higher risk but at least it's someone I know, and I can see where my money is going,'" says venture capitalist Dave McLurg.

The plus side of working with friends and family is that they will be rooting for you. The downside is you have personal relationships with them, which may change somewhat because of your business relationship.

After interviewing many entrepreneurs over the years, the one piece of advice I'd give any entrepreneur is to accept friends and family funding only if individual backers can afford to lose all of it without anger or resentment. No matter how great an entrepreneur you are, events like the COVID-19 pandemic can arise out of nowhere and cause steep financial losses in a business. You never want to be in a position where you've used up an elderly parent's savings or the money your best friend needs to send her child to college next year. If you're not sure how much risk someone can bear—financially and emotionally—ask a few other people who know both of you for a second opinion or even ask to speak with that person's financial planner or advisor together. Particularly with people who "can't say no," be very, very careful. Close personal relationships are irreplaceable—and worth far more than any startup cash.

That said, if you do have very risk-tolerant friends and family who have spare money they'd like to park somewhere, and they're well positioned for any financial emergency that comes along, they can be ideal backers. For one thing, they're not as likely to put the squeeze on you for quick results as professional investors might be, and, when your business finally does take off, they'll be able to share in your success.

That approach worked for Jan Jens, 29. He turned to his father for the startup capital he needed for his Miami-based business, the Jatina Group, which rents multimillion-dollar luxury villas. When he moved to the United States from Germany at age twenty-two, he didn't know how he was going to make a living, but he was determined to move to Miami, where his family had gone on vacations while he was growing up. Jens had worked in his family's construction business but wasn't keen on the nine-to-five routine. "That's not how I wanted to live my life," he recalls.

So he decided to become an entrepreneur and to start a business that sublet vacation properties. After doing online research to determine which ones were in hot demand, he persuaded his dad to loan him $39,000 so he could rent a high-end, five-bedroom villa in Miami and start renting it out. That was the start of his business. Some entrepreneurs might view financing from their dad as a gift, but he did not, and fully intended to pay back every penny, ASAP. "I was scared, to be honest," he recalls. "That was a lot of money for me at that point."

Eager to start generating money from the property right away, Jens quickly advertised the villa on sites such as Airbnb and HomeAway. Within six days he had booked his first guest. As a rookie property manager, he now realizes he had underpriced the rental, but that didn't matter: he was off and running. With the property filling up and guests staying an average of four to five days, Jens recalls, "I saw this was going to work within the first month." He was able to repay his father within three months.

That was in 2015. As a solopreneur, he broke $1 million in revenue within a year and a half after starting Jatina Group, he says. He added his first two employees in 2017. Today the business manages twenty-two properties and has fourteen employees, eleven of whom are full time. The Jatina Group brought in $15.5 million in revenue in 2020, up from $10.3 million in 2019. One thing that helped the business was the exodus of people during the pandemic from locked-down states, such as New York, to Miami. "It's crazy how much we've grown the business in Miami right now," Jens told me when we chatted in early 2021. "I had to stop a little at one point because I couldn't find the right people to run the properties. The people I had were maxed out. I can't give a property manager more than three houses. It's too much work."

One reason Jens was able to pay his dad back so quickly was his perfectionism. In Miami's laid-back business culture, Jens made sure he stood out by delivering concierge-level customer service that went beyond the highest levels he was observing in the market—even if that meant working fifteen hours, seven days a week at first to meet customers' requests and to answer their questions. "I'm always on top of everything," says the self-described "control freak." "I want to make sure everything is 110 percent."

His meticulous approach helped him build word of mouth quickly, and he soon found himself serving a client roster of wealthy vacationers that includes professional athletes and celebrities. Although he now has a team, he handles high-priority clients personally. "My name is more important to me than money," says Jens. "If it's super important, I take it on myself."

When Jens realized he had priced his first property too low, he started increasing prices, step by step. By the same token, if rentals were slow during the week, he adjusted prices in the opposite direction, to make sure they were rented, as well. "My goal is to reach 90-percent occupancy," says Jens. "On average, if a house costs you $10,000 a month, you need to be sure you reach break-even within twelve days, with all of your costs—like electric and gas—factored in. Then, after that, you start making money."

Instead of spending all of the money he was making from his rental, which could be tempting for a successful entrepreneur living in a sunny, beachfront city full of exciting diversions, Jens began saving money to lease a second property. In the meantime, he built up a website to showcase the property with dramatic photos and learned how to use Google advertising to spread the word. "I invested the money back into the business to get more guests and build a brand," he says. He started out investing $1,000 a month in his advertising and, finding it paid off, now spends $3,500 a month for ads and search engine optimization. To bolster his online presence, he has asked his many happy customers to post reviews of his company on the sites where they book the properties. That has been essential to building trust among affluent clients, as well as property owners, who value a high level of service and privacy.

With cash flowing steadily into the business, Jens rented a second villa and started subletting that one, too. Gradually, he built his portfolio of homes that he rented from the owners. Continually reinvesting in the business, Jens now owns four of the twenty-two properties he manages, subleasing the others on behalf of other owners. Currently, the villas rent from $950 a night for a four-bedroom villa in Fort Lauderdale, to $7,500 a night and up for a six-bedroom villa on San Marco Island.

The expansion into renting villas for other owners happened organically. As neighbors in Miami got to know him and learned about his business, some started coming to him to rent out their properties. When a neighbor first asked Jens to rent out his residence, Jens offered to do so for 25 percent of the rental fees. It worked out so well that the neighbor moved out of the house and now rents it year-round while living in another similar-style house in town. "He still makes more money," says Jens.

In expanding the portfolio of properties he manages, Jens learned a great deal about how to keep cash flowing into the business. He initially leaned toward larger properties with five bedrooms or more, which he found very marketable. "You have groups spreading the costs, and it's cheaper than a hotel," he told me initially. But when we reconnected a couple of years later, his thinking had evolved and he was focused on four- and five-bedroom villas, maximum. With bigger villas, he found, there was a high risk of groups of partiers coming in and disturbing the neighbors. "If you have a ten-bedroom home, you sometimes have eighteen people," he says. "We want to keep it as calm as possible for the neighbors and the community."

To lower the risk of renting to someone who might do costly damage to a villa, Jens doesn't make it possible for people to rent villas directly from his website. Potential customers must speak with him or his team before they make a reservation. "I like to talk with the guests and see what they are looking for, to ensure everything goes well," he says.

Streetfighter Strategy
KEEP DISTRACTION AT A DISTANCE

When you're looking to build a sustainable business, tackle one project at a time, even if you're tempted to veer off in other directions simultaneously. "That's how I run my business—I do it step by step," says Jens. "I'm not trying to dance at four parties at the same time. If I have a new house, I finish that house from A to Z and then move on to the next one. I don't do two houses at the same time. You get too distracted."

Through sites such as Airbnb, Jens has insurance, but so far, he's been lucky. His guests have been considerate, and there have been only minor accidents, like stains on the wall from a suitcase or broken drinking glasses. "Most of the time, if the client breaks something, they pay for it directly," he says.

On a continual quest to add new properties, Jens works with Visio Lending, a lender in Austin, Texas, specializing in financing for the rental-home market. It bases loans on the monthly revenue the property makes. "My options are unlimited, as long as I have a 20- to 25-percent down payment," he says.

Jens enjoys his business so much that he doesn't take long vacations, though he will go away for two or three days at a time. For now, he's focused on taking his vision as far as he can. He was expanding his operations into Los Angeles through a new venture called Villa Pads when we spoke. "My goal is to keep building Villa Pads to big, big yearly revenue and then one day try to sell everything to someone like Airbnb," he says.

Although there's a lot of temptation to join the perpetual party in Miami—"You get very easily blindsided by the nightlife," says Jens—he resists the temptation. "You need to be hungry, wake up early, get up, and work," he says. "Some people ask me, 'What is your trick?' I don't have any tricks. I just get my ass up and work."

BANK LOANS

Generally, it is hard to get a bank loan for a startup. However, if you can build a strong credit profile, you may have a shot at it. That's the approach Shakil Prasla, 35, has taken since 2013, as he's built his Austin, Texas–based company, Pro Click Ventures. He's gradually built a portfolio of thirteen e-commerce businesses, mostly solo operations, all of which have hit revenue in the seven-figure range and have a net profit of at least a quarter of that, for the most part by using bank loans.

Prasla didn't start his career as an investor. After getting a bachelor's degree in economics from the University of Texas at Austin and an MBA from the Acton School of Business, Prasla—who previously worked as a financial consultant—realized he wanted to be an entrepreneur but faced a common dilemma. He was not sure which kind of business to launch. Researching business ideas on the internet, he came across a blog on how to start an e-commerce company and got intrigued. After learning about Alibaba, a giant marketplace through which e-commerce stores often import goods from China, he traveled to China to research his options firsthand. Over the course of about a year, he educated himself on topics including search engine optimization, marketing, and pricing and, once he knew the basics, dived in to his startup. "I learned by doing and by researching what other people are doing," he says.

Prasla's first business was ProCuffs, an online seller of cufflinks and other accessories that he financed with his savings. "After about a year of learning the ins and outs of the business, I finally made it profitable," he says. Then Prasla had a stroke of luck. He came across a broker, called Quiet Light Brokerage, that was selling a business called MisterCold.com, which sells beverage coolers. When he inquired about the business, the broker sent him a prospectus. As he pored over the prospectus, he realized that the cooler company was not investing heavily in marketing, and thought that by giving it more TLC, he could grow it. He bought the business in 2015 for $52,000, using money he'd saved while working.

With that business growing, Prasla soon decided to acquire more e-commerce businesses. He focused on an area many investors overlook: one-person businesses and others with very small teams that are not dependent on Amazon for sales. To Prasla, they had lots of untapped potential. "If you look at any kind of business that's just being run by one person, they're doing everything," says Prasla. "They're working seventy to eighty hours a week. They're not delegating. They're getting burned out. They may not be investing time in themselves to learn new skill sets. Those are the types of businesses I like to buy. I can take over the business and delegate the tasks to multiple people."

After using his savings for his first acquisition, Prasla turned to bank loans, frequently those backed by the US Small Business Administration, though on one bigger-ticket deal, he brought in a group of investors. Banks don't usually want to lend to e-commerce businesses, which don't often have real estate as an asset, but the SBA's guarantee took out some of the risks for them. "Why the banks like them is they are backed by the US government," says Prasla. And from Prasla's point of view as an entrepreneur, the loans were relatively inexpensive. Typically, the interest rate on his loans has been prime plus 2.75 percent, he says. At the time of our interview in 2021, he was paying 8.25 percent.

A critical part of securing bank financing has been making sure that the businesses he is acquiring have been operating for at least five years and have complete financial records, such as a profit-and-loss statement and a balance sheet, so he knows he'll be able to pay back his loans. He has also looked for deals where he would make one-third of the acquisition price in net profits each year. That has helped reduce the risk of making acquisitions. Even with loan financing, he found he could make money on an acquisition of a very profitable business. "If you buy something for $100,000, you should be making $33,000," he says. "You could borrow at 8.25 percent and your rate of return will be even higher."

There's another benefit to his approach: SBA-backed loans only require the borrower to put down 10 percent of the money to make a purchase. That is convenient, given that his priciest acquisition cost him an amount in the mid seven figures. (Its annual revenue was more than $10 million.) Even better, he had no risk of losing his home by borrowing to finance the acquisitions. In Texas, under state law, entrepreneurs don't have to put down their homes as collateral, he notes.

With his most recent acquisition Gloves.com, Prasla's stable of businesses now brings in total combined revenue of about $25 million per year. Each company pays Pro Click Ventures a management fee in return. This helps keep personnel costs in check. "We're able to spread those costs across the companies," says Prasla. Typically, an owner will stay on for three months and then a business manager Prasla employs will take over. Ultimately, Prasla plans to cash out. "At the end of the day, I hope to sell the whole portfolio to a private equity group," he says.

How does he keep everything organized? "At the beginning of the year we come up with three goals," he says. "We focus on these three goals only and break them down into micro actionable items we can do weekly. We track them on a project management system to see how things are going along." Beyond that, the company relies on a dashboard that tracks each brand's financials and customer reviews. "I think data is very important," he says.

Prasla used to handle all of the financials on his own, given his strong background in this area. As keeping up with this became more complicated, he brought in a CPA to maintain QuickBooks for all of them. "He does it even better than I did," says Prasla. "That saves me five hours a month." The company shares information with its employees on each brand's revenue and profits, providing a summary for each team member. That way, they know how each site is progressing and can see the results of their work.

Although he's built a team, Prasla is very much involved in the day-to-day, and the income he gets from Pro Click Ventures isn't passive. "There's no way my business would run if I was sitting on my couch watching TV," he says. "I'm a very active operator." Then again, he enjoys his involvement. "We're all lucky to be alive in this era," says Prasla. "It's pretty easy to start a business with a low amount of money." Staying active ensures that the businesses' performance will enable him to pay back his bank loans.

His advice to others who want to start or acquire e-commerce businesses? Don't just follow the money. Make sure they're a good fit for your interests, skills, and knowledge. "If you're good at finance, find a company that's not doing a good job with inventory that you can help," he says. "Don't just buy it because it's making money."

GRANT FUNDING

A grant is a type of cash award that you don't have to pay back, like a loan, and that doesn't require you to give up equity in your company to investors. Often, grants are available in scientific and technical areas, but during the COVID-19 pandemic, more organizations began offering them to small businesses of all sizes, particularly to those run by founders from underrepresented groups or in communities hard hit by the recession that followed. Typically, if you apply for a grant, you'll have to fill out an application. This can require a lot of work, so it's important to familiarize yourself with the rules before you start, to make sure you are truly eligible.

If you do qualify, grants can be one of the best sources of funding. Jessica Ochoa Hendrix, 40, an entrepreneur, and two of her friends initially funded their children's game company, Killer Snails, a three-employee business founded in New York City in 2016, by securing more than $1 million in funding from the National Science Foundation, the US government's Small Business Innovation Research (SBIR) program, and crowdfunding on Kickstarter. Since then, they have raised $3.1 million in total, with their funding sources now also including two additional SBIR grants, one grant from the Institute of Educational Sciences, two grants from the National Institutes of Health, and a second Kickstarter campaign.

When you're seeking grant funding, your funding providers will want to know you will put the money to good use, so it helps if you have strong credentials in your field that you can detail on your application. All three cofounders did in this case. Ochoa Hendrix, the CEO and cofounder, has worked in K–12 education since 2003 and was previously director of organizational learning at Uncommon Schools, a network of nonprofit charter public schools. Cofounder Mandë Holford is an associate professor of chemistry at Hunter College and the CUNY Graduate Center, with scientific appointments at the American Museum of Natural History and Weill Cornell Medicine (mollusk research is one of her specialties). And cofounder Lindsay Portnoy, the firm's former chief learning officer and now an associate teaching professor at Northwestern University, is a cognitive psychologist and scientist who has spent nearly two decades studying human development and learning.

The trio decided to start a business together after discovering their passion for spreading their love of science. Holford and Portnoy got to know each other because they had each won fellowships for faculty who were using technology in innovative ways in the classroom. Holford later met Ochoa Hendrix, an MBA, after doing a Secret Science Club talk in Brooklyn, on venomous snails, that Ochoa Hendrix attended. The Secret Science Club is a nonprofit lecture, arts, and performance series on science.

When they came together, they were particularly interested in reaching middle school girls, whom they knew from their professional experience often like marine biology. "We saw that kids were dropping out of science in middle school, especially girls," says Portnoy. After doing 130 interviews with parents, teachers, and museum educators, they realized something was missing in the available science games. The existing offerings were not engaging middle school girls who might potentially pursue science as a career. "Being a scientist is open to everyone," says Holford.

That led to their decision to create a game about killer snails. Many people think of snails as harmless, slow-moving creatures—but the marine cone snail doesn't fit the stereotype. This predator dines on fish, worms, and fellow mollusks, delivering a deadly venom cocktail through a very sharp tooth used to attack its victims. The marine cone snail is the star of their card and video game, Assassins of the Sea.

Given that the world of game design was new to them, the cofounders knew they needed outside input on the concept they were creating. When Holford and Portnoy were teaching in the mornings at a camp at the American Museum of Natural History in New York City, they got valuable feedback from the students and worked in the afternoons with a game designer who was also teaching at the camp. "The kids took it to a whole other level," says Holford. "This is complex material. They gave us insight into things they grasped right away and did not grasp. They gave us cool cards to put in the decks."

The team fueled this activity with a relatively small amount of grant funding. A $50,000 I-Corps grant from the National Science Foundation that Holford won in 2014 provided critical early capital. That was followed in 2016 by a $150,000 six-month SBIR grant, for which Ochoa Hendrix was the primary investigator, and which they used for product development. Ochoa Hendrix has become a big fan of the SBIR program: "They are the largest source of seed funding in the country, and you still keep 100 percent of the company."

After six months of testing Assassins of the Sea anywhere they could, they created a prototype that could be boxed, and they sold the game through the American Museum of Natural History. They also supplemented their grants with a Kickstarter campaign in March 2016, in which they raised about $25,000 for the game.

When they were ready to create their next game, Biome Builder, they turned to Kickstarter again, raising $19,313, and greatly exceeding their $6,000 goal. To make sure both campaigns succeeded, they turned to the community managers on Kickstarter frequently for advice. "They played our games and gave us feedback on our videos," says Ochoa Hendrix.

During the Kickstarter campaigns, the Killer Snails team appeared frequently at live events. "We would be at the New York Hall of Science one day, the New York Botanical Garden the next, and the Brooklyn Children's Museum the next," says Ochoa Hendrix. "We tried to make sure we were in very public places." That gave them a talking point for the Kickstarter campaign updates they sent to followers—and an opportunity to say, "You can preorder it right here."

They went on to win a second SBIR Phase II grant for $750,000 for which Hendrix was also the primary investigator, as well as a $150,000 Technology Enhancement for Commercial Partnerships (TISA) grant.

Although Killer Snails has been very successful in applying for funding, the cofounders stretched their budget by building the business as much as they could on their own. When they needed interns, they turned to the New York City Tech Talent Pipeline, a program in which the city connects local businesses with interns, and paid them $15 an hour. They also turned to the Brooklyn Tech Triangle's internship program, led by the Brooklyn Navy Yard Development Corporation and the New York City Department of Small Business Services.

After hitting the million-dollar mark in their funding on their own, the trio hired a developer and a UI/UX designer. Last year, they brought in close to $1 million in annual revenue.

With Assassins of the Sea going strong, the trio has introduced other games. One is their second game, Biome Builder, a card game in which players learn about creatures from different biomes, such as the Amazon rainforest and the American Prairie. They have also dreamed up two virtual-reality games: Scuba Adventure, in which players take on the identity of a marine biologist who is tagging creatures before an oxygen tank runs out, and BioDive, an ecology curriculum supplement in virtual reality; players act as marine biologists investigating the ecosystems of venomous killer snails and do digital journaling. The latter was piloted at middle schools in twenty-six states. "We wanted to meet the kids where they were," says Holford. "They were on screens and playing games. We wanted to give them content that could be engaging and scientifically accurate, to make them excited about the field of science."

During the COVID-19 pandemic, the Killer Snails team piloted a new augmented-reality and digital-journaling game, WaterWays, aimed at grades three through five. They did their first test of the game remotely with a group of English-language learners at a school in the Bronx, New York; 100 percent of the students said they were interested in playing WaterWays when surveyed after the pilot.

Ochoa Hendrix's advice for anyone who wants to apply for government grants like the ones this group did, particularly if you are not a scientist? Form a strong team. You will need someone with a strong academic or research background to find research papers supporting your approach. "They look for you to have a strong pedagogical framework," she says.

Streetfighter Strategy
GET FREE MONEY TO GROW YOUR BUSINESS

Small-business grants are competitive and often come with strict rules, but if you have a great idea, it can't hurt to look in to this type of funding. In addition to government grant programs, private grant programs are springing up constantly, and some run out of funds, so it's worth doing a thorough online search every quarter to make sure you're not missing out on any sources of funding that could help your business grow. Bear in mind you will have to account for how you spend the funds, so you will need to keep accurate books if you receive a grant.

Here are some sources of information on the latest grant news to check out.

Hello Alice (helloalice.com)
This site offers frequent updates on public and private sources of funding, available through its e-newsletter.

Small Business Grants*
This compilation of public sources of grants is updated frequently. Subscribe to weekly grant alerts to stay on top of the latest opportunities.

The US Small Business Administration**
Find out about grants for research and development, exporting, and winners of the SBA's award programs.

The Chamber of Commerce***
The chamber has compiled a robust list of government grants available in 2021.

---

* "Small Business Grants," USGrants.org, https://www.usgrants.org/small
-business-grants.htm.
** "Grants," Funding Programs, US Small Business Administration, https://www
.sba.gov/funding-programs/grants.
*** "Government Grants for Small Businesses in 2021," Chamber of Commerce,
https://www.chamberofcommerce.org/government-grants-for-small-businesses.

PURCHASE-ORDER FINANCING

For businesses that have orders coming in from clients, purchase-order financing can be a helpful way to cover the cost of manufacturing. Often, purchase-order financing comes in handy when a business has received a much bigger order than usual and needs to pay for inventory. With purchase-order financing, a lender will use the value of your orders as collateral for a traditional loan or line of credit. This method has some downsides: When you convert the fees you are charged to an annualized interest rate, it may be very high, sometimes more than 25 percent. And some companies don't want customers to know they had to secure financing to fill an order. In some cases, customers must pay the lender for the purchase order, not your company.

Raquel Graham, a former analyst at JPMorgan Chase, needed financing quickly at her business Roq Innovation in Chicago when she won a big order for her NEKZ wraps, a scarf alternative, after showing them at a trade show. When she came away with $50,000 in orders to license the wraps in the colors of forty top NCAA colleges, she used her first purchase order to get financing through a program in Chicago to support the fashion industry, funded by the late philanthropist Richard Driehaus. This was a short-term measure. "It was paid back in three months," she recalls. "Once I delivered the goods, they got their money back."

Filling that order successfully helped her raise her visibility. She started getting orders from the Grommet, an e-commerce site that sells innovative products from small businesses, and HSN, where the wraps sold out within twenty minutes of her launch in 2016. Today, she sells other products, including cloth face masks and a line of rechargeable LED knit hats and headbands for running in the dark. Over the years, she's gotten funding from other sources, such as Accion, a microlender. She brought in $1.6 million in 2020, with the business expanding to nine to twelve temporary workers around the holidays. "When I look at the fact that I can do this and not even need an office, that's crazy," she says.

Once you've figured out financing for your business, you'll be ready to put the systems in place for success. In the next chapter, we'll look at how entrepreneurs in tiny businesses that make big money are doing just that.

EQUITY INVESTMENT CAPITAL

Many tiny businesses that make big money are owner financed, with some supplemental funding from banks and other lenders. But if you decide you want to put your growth on the fast track, you may need to bring in outside equity investors. This means providing them with an ownership stake in your company in exchange for the cash you need to grow.

If you're at a very early stage of business, where you're not earning anything or are earning very little, you may need to turn to private investors known as angels, whom you can find through local angel networks and often at events such as business-plan competitions, for what is known as "seed" financing. Once you've built a track record and are bringing in about $2 million in earnings before interest, taxes, depreciation, and amortization (EBITDA), says Dave McLurg, venture capitalists may become interested. "If you're earning less than that, it's tough to get any type of funding," he says.

Sadly, I must note that this route is more productive for some entrepreneurs than others. The venture capital community has not had a great track record of investing in women-owned businesses and diverse founders—despite the innovation we've seen in these communities. Fortunately, that has started to change, albeit very slowly, as a result of the racial justice movement, efforts to fund more women entrepreneurs, and other factors, so hopefully by the time this book comes out, the situation will be more promising. If you've written off this type of funding, it's worth doing some research to identify firms that are committed to supporting *all* entrepreneurs, because sometimes, there's no substitute for the vast amounts of financing they can provide.

Streetfighter Strategy
KNOW WHAT INVESTORS WANT TO SEE

Even if your business has a noble mission or a great story behind it, investors aren't looking to make a charitable donation when they back your company. They are investing to make money. If you can make a strong case showing they will bring in an attractive return on their investment, you may find yourself choosing from multiple offers.

So how do you do that? McLurg says you don't necessarily need to have a twenty-five-page business plan but you do need to have a plan—and be able to communicate it. "The more clarity you have in what your business is about and how you are going to execute your plans for the business, the more aligned [investors] will be to execute what you need and [the more] engaged they will be," he says. "Most businesses don't have that clarity. If you are going for capital, you have to have it. You have to show, 'Here is our path to profitability.'"

McLurg is a big believer in Peter Drucker's philosophy that the purpose of a business is to find and keep a customer. It's important to show that the marketplace will care about your product or service enough to spend money on it—particularly if it's brand new to the market—by validating it as quickly as you can. "Your biggest barrier is always the status quo," McLurg says.

With the COVID-19 crisis fresh in investors' minds, it's also important to show, in the present environment, how you will adapt to change. "I think that's the new norm," says McLurg. Investors will look closely at your overhead and ask themselves questions like, "Are you lean enough? Can you pivot or shift without a lot of overhead?" It doesn't matter if your plan A doesn't work out if you succeed with your plan B or C.

The more enterprising you are about operating on a shoestring, the more investors will appreciate your efforts. Once you have the money you need, you'll be able to do even more to grow your business. In the next chapter, we'll look at how you can set yourself up for success.

CHAPTER 6

SET YOURSELF UP FOR SUCCESS

When Kelly Cudworth, 43, joined his father's company, NuLeaf Office Solutions/PNWB Office Products, in 2005, it was an old-school office supply store in Seattle, Washington—complete with three or four salespeople who visited local businesses to make sales.

That high-overhead business model, which included up to ten people on payroll, made less and less sense to Cudworth over the years. It was hard for the store to weather crises like losing its credit lines during the Great Recession and seeing a big chunk of government business disappear overnight when the small company could not win "preferred supplier" status. There was also ongoing competition from both big box stores and mega websites.

But Cudworth still believed it was possible to make the business work—and thrive. By the time he bought out his dad in 2020, he was ready to try a new approach to selling office supplies: a high-volume, low-margin e-commerce model. Another fan of Tim Ferriss's book *The 4-Hour Work-week*, Cudworth believed that by using automation and outsourcing to keep overhead down, he could still make money, even if the markup on each product was low.

He says he embraced a new mantra: " 'If we can't automate it, we won't do it.' My goal is to have the business run without us doing any manual work for order processing or inventory."

Given that Cudworth was transitioning to an e-commerce model, he spent a lot of time researching which technologies he needed to make the transition. "There's not a playbook you can pull out," says Cudworth. He was happy to find that he didn't need anything "super fancy" to pull it off. To build the e-commerce store, for example, he invested in 7cart, a cloud-based technology. His IT team installed apps to tackle tasks such as transmitting orders to vendors, to make selling more efficient. And to reduce his team's labor, he programmed the site to send orders that customers placed directly to vendors, who would drop-ship the products to his customers; the vendors, in turn, would charge him upon shipping the orders.

Cudworth also streamlined his overhead. For instance, he got rid of the company's server and moved his data storage to the cloud, which allowed him to drop his managed IT services. He also upgraded the phone system to a digital one that cost a lot less. Those two changes alone saved him more than $2,000 a month.

It took time for Cudworth to get these changes in motion, but they allowed him to transition the company from doing a couple of hundred transactions a month to about 80,000. He let go of his sales force slowly, over time, as pipelines dried up. Today, he only needs two full-time employees, who help with catalog management and customer service, and a part-time bookkeeper. During COVID, the two employees began telecommuting, and it worked so well, Cudworth didn't plan to ask them to come back into the office, which moved to Issaquah, Washington, in 2019.

Cudworth's bet on an ultrastreamlined, e-commerce model paid off. Last year, his business—which had previously peaked at $5.5 million in annual revenue—hit $9.5 million and was profitable. When we last spoke, he was projecting $12–15 million in revenue for 2021. To keep his company's growth on track, he meets weekly with a "virtual CFO"—a freelance business consultant and coach rolled into one. They talk by phone daily and meet every Wednesday.

"The biggest thing for me is keeping the operation as lean as possible so I can maximize growth and pivot quickly," says Cudworth. "I'm a high-energy guy. I get excited. I can't stand waiting to implement my ideas. By working lean, we have the flexibility to make those moves really fast."

It's not just about making money. Cudworth also wants to have time for his passions. When we spoke, he was training for a fifty-mile trail run. He and his wife Melissa also cofounded a nonprofit called NuHope Street, which raises funds for various causes. One project that was especially meaningful to him was funding the construction of an orphanage in Congo, where his adopted daughter Marie was born. He has found that collaborating with the nonprofit's board members brings a new dimension to his life. "I find it brings me calmness," he says. "It's nice to have others you can connect with."

As Cudworth's story shows, building a tiny business that makes big money starts with setting a vision for where you're going (in his case, by converting to a high-volume e-commerce business). Then, it's a matter of setting up the business in a way that will get you there (as he did by automating many of his processes so he could make money operating at a low profit margin).

If you don't know exactly what your goal for the business is or what strategy you can use to get there, working with a coach or consultant, as Cudworth does, can be an excellent investment. Once you're clear on your vision and strategy, you can reverse-engineer things to figure out what steps to take.

In a very small business, you won't need an elaborate infrastructure to set yourself up for success. And you don't need to run things the way your old boss did. In fact, some of the ways you learned to work at past jobs will work against you if you want to build a tiny business that makes big money. As you've probably noticed, most of the businesses in this book run very lean. The entrepreneurs in this book generally use these five basic models to achieve their vision—and often, some hybrid of these:

1. **The automated approach:** These entrepreneurs rely on software, apps, and other tech tools to help them get more done. Often, automation is the first step entrepreneurs take toward offloading work

they might have done themselves. Once they exhaust opportunities to automate, they will move on to the other methods.

2. **The freelancer/contractor model:** If you can't use technology to do the work, it's time to think about bringing on freelancers, contractors, or consultants. It's a way to get things done without the commitment to keep everyone busy when you don't need the help. These independent workers will generally have other clients and won't expect you to keep them occupied all the time.

3. **The outsourced model:** In some industries, farming out work to an outside provider, such as Fulfillment by Amazon if you're in e-commerce, is a great way to travel light. In many fields, you can offload back-office services, such as a bookkeeping company or an agency that handles billing and collections.

4. **The traditional employer model:** Perhaps you need talent full time, and you want to make sure you are providing your team with a stable salary and benefits so they are there for you when you need them. Or maybe the government says the way you are working fits the legal definition of an employer/employee relationship and you need to stay compliant. In these cases, you may have to put people on payroll, even if they don't want to be W-2s.

5. **The partnership model:** Teaming up with other business partners can help you tap in to their resources to expand without adding employees or freelancers—or in addition to hiring them. For instance, you might give someone an ownership stake in your business if they will do some of the work of running your operations. Or you might provide another company with a cut in your sales if it promotes your service.

In this chapter, we'll look at how the five basic models look in "real life" for real entrepreneurs, and then how you can manage a team using any one of them. As you'll see, each business applies these models a little differently.

Beyond that, businesses don't follow a linear path in tapping into them. Some tiny businesses use all options simultaneously. Others use different methods at different times—for instance, using contractors to build a product, but then transitioning to an automated model, as tech entrepreneur Rajesh Srivastava did, whom you'll read about in this chapter. Or they may expand to an employer model when business is booming and contract to more of a contractor-driven approach when they need to keep costs lower, or out of personal preference, like copywriter/goat farmer Dana Derricks, whom you read about in Chapter 4.

It's worth experimenting with these models until you find the right one for you, to see if you will achieve better results if you get some help in doing the work, either from software and machines or from other human beings. Consider this: The average nonemployer business with no payroll brought in $47,000 a year, according to the US Small Business Administration Office of Advocacy.[12] The average employer brought in nearly $6 million. (By my calculations, the average employer had twenty-one employees—just slightly larger than the biggest companies in this book.) Nonemployer businesses that make extensive use of automation, freelancers, and outsourcing—the kind you've read about in my first book and this one—can often achieve much better financial results, because they are extending what their one or two owners can do.

THE AUTOMATED MODEL

So, let's look at how these models work and how you can put them to work for you. We'll start with the easiest, lowest-risk way to extend what you can do: finding software and apps to automate some of the work. Although technology and software cost money, they'll almost always cost you less than bringing on another person. That's worth considering, especially if you're operating on a shoestring and don't know how much money you will be taking in. Bear in mind that automation isn't free. It costs money to use technology, such as software as a service. But the right investments will save you money on labor costs. Similarly, if you're developing your own technol-

---

12 *A Look at Nonemployer Businesses* (Washington, DC: US Small Business Administration Office of Advocacy, August 2018), https://www.sba.gov/sites/default/files/advocacy/Nonemployer-Fact-Sheet.pdf.

ogy to automate your business, there will be development costs. However, in that case, you are probably developing valuable intellectual property. You may be able to license it to other businesses or to sell it at some point.

Rajesh Srivastava's company priceSeries is an almost exclusively automated business. Srivastava, a longtime Silicon Valley engineer, always loved trading stocks and options. After more than twenty-five years working in Big Tech, he decided to go out on his own and, with the help of a few contractors, developed an open-source, web-based trading-analysis software to help investors like himself. He now sells it through priceSeries, a business he launched from his home in Sunnyvale, California, in 2015. He also sells reports that help traders analyze and respond to the market. Although he could, conceivably, grow the company by building a staff, he does not want to go that route, as building a team would be costly and require him to raise outside capital. "This whole company, whatever lifetime it has, will be about automation," Srivastava says.

Tapping the skills he developed in his corporate career, Srivastava has done most of the technical work of the business himself. He built the price-Series platform with the help of a few contractors and has automated ways to use it to create and deliver his product. For instance, he programmed the software to create a chart showing what is going on in the market each day—and then to post this chart on his company's home page automatically. This new and frequently refreshed content helps raise his website's ranking in search engines. Once visitors come to the site, they can purchase monthly subscriptions to his platform. For instance, for $29.99 a month, they can subscribe to MACDVisor, a web-based trade-analysis platform providing hourly stock analysis for S&P 500 stocks. When subscribers complete the subscription form, they can access his platform from their desktop or mobile device. They are billed for their access automatically. "That's how you reduce the work," he says.

Srivastava doesn't try to reinvent the lightbulb in his business. If he can find an existing product to help him automate some of his work, he'll use it. For instance, he sends marketing messages via a customer management software called aMember—designed for subscription-based businesses. "When I started my business, I was doing everything on a shoestring

Streetfighter Strategy
FIND TECH NINJAS NOW

Even if you don't have the technical skills of Rajesh Srivastava, you can run an automated business. Hiring a programmer or developer through a freelance platform can help you tap in to the advantages of automation and may pay for itself in the long run. Here are some of the sites that entrepreneurs in this book have used to find technical talent:

- Fiverr (fiverr.com)
- Upwork (upwork.com)
- Toptal (toptal.com)
- Upstack (upstack.com).

budget," he says. "I tried a few but stuck with this one. It gives you all of the flexibility you need and integration with payment systems." Using PayPal and Stripe to accept payments saves him the hassle of building a secure payment processing system.

All of this automation allows him to stay focused on growing the business. "It gives me time to focus on marketing and trying to find new venues," he says. This approach has paid off for Srivastava, who now only relies on the occasional contractor. His business brings in about $1 million in annual revenue and is expanding worldwide.

AUTOMATION PLUS

Many tiny business owners who hit seven figures use automation in conjunction with outsourcing and/or hiring contractors or freelancers. That's what Anthony Martin, 38, has done at Choice Mutual, an insurance agency in Reno, Nevada, that specializes in a niche product: final-expense insurance. This type of insurance covers burial expenses, so someone's family doesn't have to pay the costs. The payout is typically in the range of $10,000 to $30,000. Martin started as a solo operator, but as demand grew, he started hiring people in 2020. He now has an office manager, three sales agents on payroll, and three freelance web developers, as well as other freelance agents. This year, he is on track for $5 million in annual revenue.

Martin discovered an opportunity to start his own business while he worked in a traditional job. Working as a manager at an insurance agency in Roseville, California, he wished he had more control over how he did his work. Seeing that there were many ways to improve on common processes in the industry, he left and started an agency in 2013 to sell final-expense insurance—a product he knew very well from his work—from his home. Not only was it an in-demand product, but there was not as much competition as there was for other types of insurance.

Although Martin knew his product well, he didn't have experience in marketing it, so he sought outside help. He hired a lead-generation company called SellTermLife.com to build a website that he hoped would rank well in Google and help him get leads through a customized marketing plan. He put up the website in June 2016. Unfortunately, his website didn't bear fruit immediately. "It took me six months before I got a single lead from Google," he says.

But Martin was committed to building the business, and he was willing to be patient. He kept showing up at his desk every day to build up his website, looking at it as a "long-term play." Martin had learned from the team at SellTermLife.com that it was important to publish high-quality, informative content to attract people to his site, so he stuck with it. Every weekday and for five to eight hours on the weekends, Martin would create articles that address frequently asked questions about final-expense insurance. His articles attracted visitors who were already seriously interested in his product and helped him "own" search-term keywords, including "long-tail" phrases—such as questions customers might type into a search engine.

As readers clicked on the articles he wrote on practical topics such as state-regulated life insurance, life insurance for eighty-nine-year-olds, and buying insurance for your parents, the site started to build its organic rank in Google. "You cannot find another website that sells this type of insurance that has anywhere near the level of in-depth, accurate information about this product," says Martin.

Martin paid careful attention to tagging his content. To figure out which keywords mattered most, he researched commonly used ones on tools such as SEM Rush (semrush.com) and Google's Keyword Planner (https://ads.google.com/home/tools/keyword-planner/). He also tapped his knowledge of the field. "After selling this type of insurance for so long, I know the words people use," says Martin. That helped him in pulling more people into the site.

About two months after Martin got his first lead through the site, they were flowing in daily thanks to his early investment in creating original, high-quality content. Now the site brings in even more leads per day. "It feeds me a never-ending flow of ready-to-buy customers," he says.

In recent years, Martin has also expanded into paid advertising. Through experimenting, he has found that for his industry, YouTube ads are the best investment. "There is a low cost per lead on Facebook, but in my industry, Facebook is saturated," he says. It is also harder to target the customers he wants. "You can't really narrow down the intent of the buyer," he says. "On YouTube, that is much easier, and the conversion rate is higher."

Martin uses outsourcing for his YouTube ads, hiring a marketing agency that specializes in creating them. "I am an expert in organic search marketing and Google," he says. "I don't employ anyone else to help me because I'm so good at that. Other people are experts at Facebook and YouTube advertising. I could become an expert in those but that requires time and experience. Instead of diverting my time away from something else, I'd rather pay someone else who has thought through that process."

Once people arrive at his website, Martin has automated the process of converting them into buyers. Choice Mutual's site enables visitors to "request to apply" for the insurance by filling out a form—an effort that signals they are serious about buying the product. Leads flow automatically to Martin's customer relationship management (CRM) system from VanillaSoft. This allows him to keep track of who has contacted him.

He has found that calling prospects is the best way to convert them into buyers. After customers complete their intake form and decide to buy, he has always guided them by phone through a remote application process that each insurance company has put in place. Sometimes customers sign documents using a program such as DocuSign, which automatically sends them a copy for their records. Other times, they use a voice signature on the phone. Although many insurance agents prefer to hold meetings like this in person, Martin finds driving around inefficient and unnecessary. "I've never met a person face to face to process the deals," he says. "It's all done remotely."

To make the most of his leads, Martin calls the newest ones first, assuming they're ready to buy. Using his CRM also helps him mine leads that don't pan out originally for various reasons. "If a lead comes in that doesn't result in a sale, it will go into a 'drip campaign,' and they will get a different email periodically," he says. (By "drip campaign," he means he has programmed the system to send them a series of emails he has drafted at set intervals.) He has also programmed VanillaSoft to send his existing customers notifications as their birthdays approach that they have opportunities to update their insurance plans—another way to keep his business growing.

Thanks to using this automated method of taking in leads, Martin never has to chase down anyone to get them to listen to a sales presentation. "I'm in a unique situation in the world of selling insurance," says Martin. "I don't really sell anymore. I'm more of a cashier. I just take orders."

Martin's approach put him in good stead when COVID-19 arrived. He didn't have to change the way he was doing business at all. "A lot of people in my industry were forced to shift their entire model," he says. "There are many people who got completely hammered. A lot of them didn't make it."

Some of Martin's contacts have recommended that he sell Medicare supplements or cancer plans, but he always says no, preferring to keep perfecting his approach to selling burial insurance. "The reason I'm successful in this space is I have been hyperfocused at being the most expert authority you can imagine on this type of insurance," says Martin. When he gets an inquiry from someone who wants to buy insurance outside of his niche, he refers the prospect to a trusted industry colleague.

Martin does not look for reciprocal referrals, finding that prospects that arrive this way are generally not as inclined to buy as the folks who come in through his own website. "Right now, if I had to choose between serving a customer who has said 'I'm ready to apply. Please sign me up,' or a referral who has a question, I'm not going to make as much money from a referral," he says. "That's why I tell people 'Don't refer people to me.' I allocate my working hours to people who are ready to sign up." One thing that helps Martin attract business is having many positive online reviews. He requests reviews from customers—you guessed it, automatically—using a digital review provider called Trustpilot.

In 2017, Martin moved his business from Roseville to Reno, where he now lives, because of its business-friendly climate. He rents an office there for $3,200 a month. In the meantime, Martin keeps the rest of his overhead, not including payroll, to about $2,000 a month. That covers his errors and omissions insurance, licensing fees, and CRM subscription.

Martin relied entirely on automation, outsourcing, and using freelancers until 2020, when it became clear that he could no longer optimize every lead on his own and needed to start building a sales team. His criteria for hiring someone is that doing so will pay for itself: "For me, the only question I have about hiring an individual is, 'Do I have the lead volume to support an additional sales agent?'"

All of the methods Martin uses to keep his business running smoothly give him time to pursue his personal passions. Before coming to the office every morning, he does strength training five or six days a week and plays basketball two or three times a week. Then he heads home for breakfast and starts making phone calls from his office around 7:30 a.m. On the weekends, Martin and his wife, Christelle, love to enjoy the outdoors with their German shepherds, Bear and Olive. "I could definitely sleep more," Martin says—but with his business growing rapidly, he's not inclined to hit the snooze button.

JUMPSTART YOUR AUTOMATED BUSINESS

Ready to dive into automating your business? Look for apps, software, and processes that will eliminate one or two tedious aspects of your daily work, and add new ones as you go along. Not sure where to start? Look for opportunities to do so through technologies you're already relying on—they may already be sending you prompts to do so. For instance, if you're manually entering transactions in your accounting software, consider attaching the software to your bank account, so those transactions are entered automatically. Or instead of emailing clients back and forth to set up appointments, try out a program like Calendly or ScheduleOnce or, if you book appointments in person, a general app such as Acuity Scheduling or one that targets your industry. Then look for a way to take this automation a step further. For instance, your scheduling app may also offer a service to confirm appointments by text message, or allow you to connect it to your email software.

To make sure you're getting the most out of automation, once a year list every activity in your business (or once a month if your business is growing rapidly). Your key tasks may include new idea generation and R&D, creating prototypes, market research, search engine optimization, testing ideas, marketing your products or services, pricing, upgrading your website, managing your social media, setting up sales calls with customers, placing orders with vendors, and taking payments, to name a few. Then, for each category, do some searching online to see if there is a tool to automate it. Trade magazines, associations, and industry-specific podcasts can be a good source of information on new time-saving products for your industry. Before signing up for an annual plan for software as a service, try it by the month for several months to make sure you will use it. If you're not getting around to installing an app, hiring a skilled freelancer from one of the online marketplaces to help get you set up could pay for itself quickly if the technology saves you several hours a week.

When you take inventory of processes you use, consider whether you should upgrade to the paid version of any software you use. Sometimes

(continued)

it can save you a lot of time and money. For instance, if you need to do a lot of transcriptions in your business and use Zoom for meetings, you might upgrade to the small and medium business subscription, which, at the time of this writing, comes with AI-powered transcriptions of meetings and costs $199.90 a year for an annual subscription. If you pay for transcriptions regularly, that might be a lot less than your usual transcription bill.

AUTOMATE YOUR WAY OUT OF "TRADING TIME FOR DOLLARS"

Many people in service businesses find that they can earn more money without simply working more hours by creating informational products. Using automated tools to help sell them can reduce the work that comes with this, especially if you get help from freelancers who know how to use the tools. That's what copywriter Laura Belgray, 51, has done to take her tiny business to seven figures.

For years, Belgray, a former TV promo writer, worked as a copywriter in New York City. She is exceptionally good at what she does—to the point that she was able to raise her rates from $250 an hour to $500, then $750, and, later, $950, in short succession. That didn't stop a small army of customers from flocking to her company Talking Shrimp, founded in 2009. "They were willing to pay if it will make them money, which good copy does," she says. Eventually, she raised her rates to $1,450 per hour.

One thing that helped was working with high-profile clients, who include entrepreneur and best-selling author Marie Forleo, whom Belgray met when Forleo was working as a life coach. "She and I made friends in a hip-hop class at Crunch," recalls Belgray. "Over the years, she became a kingpin of online courses."

When Forleo invited Belgray to speak about copywriting at a live event for entrepreneurs, more entrepreneurial clients started calling. Maybe it was her subject matter: "5 Secrets to Non-Sucky Copy." Some seemed to be attracted by her premium prices. "When they pay the money, it solidifies the idea they are getting the best," she says. "They place more value on what they paid for."

At first, Belgray was delighted that her business was taking off—"The more I got booked, the happier I was," she says—but eventually, she found herself feeling overwhelmed as she looked at her calendar. She specialized in writing copy in entrepreneurs' unique voices and loved her clients, but it was all getting exhausting. "When I looked at the calendar and saw appointments, it made me sad," she says.

To free up some time for herself and her husband, Belgray decided to block off Mondays and Fridays, scheduling her meetings the other days of the week. Then, as she raised her prices, she began toying with limiting her availability for appointments to Wednesdays alone.

But even with this pared-down schedule, Belgray got anxious when she thought of the appointments. Clients were expecting a lot when they paid her $1,450 for an hour. "Once I started charging higher prices, my emotional bandwidth started going down for taking on more clients," she recalls. "I couldn't take on the maximum. I would go crazy and be overwhelmed."

Belgray turned to her business coach, Ron Reich, for ideas on how she could replace her income while giving up one-on-one client meetings. Following his advice and trying some experiments of her own helped her break $1 million in revenue in the business and to stop meeting one-on-one with clients, for the most part. "Once in a while, one of my favorite clients will ask, 'Can you do an hour?' " she explains. "I don't take new clients."

One of Reich's most important pieces of advice was to sell more of her "mini-courses" —PDF products she had developed and "niced up" with the help of a designer, and had been quietly selling on her website since 2016. Belgray already offered a 60-Minute Makeovers Copywriting Mini-Course ($99), introduced in 2017, and "About Page and Professional Bio Builder" ($199), launched in 2018, but was not doing much to promote them.

To sell more of these products and others she introduced, Reich advised Belgray to put her copywriting talents to work by marketing more to her email list and on social media—a way to start automating her business.

Streetfighter Strategy
CLEAR TIME-WASTERS FROM YOUR CALENDAR

One of the best sources of ideas for what to automate is the software you already use. Providers of accounting and customer relationship management software often partner with app providers. The accounting software FreshBooks, for instance, has integrations with partners in:

- accounts receivable
- bookkeeping
- client scheduling
- customer relationship management
- customer support and education
- event management
- expenses
- file storage
- ground mail
- inventory management
- job boards
- lead tracking
- marketing
- payments
- payroll
- project management
- proposals
- getting online reviews
- shipping and tracking
- tax help
- team communication
- time tracking
- utilities like Zapier that can be used to connect FreshBooks to other online services
- website management

Even if you don't use a particular accounting software, check out its pages listing integrations or partners for ideas on what you can automate. In addition to FreshBooks, check out QuickBooks and Xero.

As a preliminary goal, aim to free one day a week through automation, then up the ante to one and a half days, and so on. If you have a team, make sure you're looking for apps that will help your team members save time, too. The technologies your customer service pros need may be a little different from the ones you use as an owner. The more efficiently you can help everyone work, the further your investment in hiring them will go.

"He advised me to step up my mailings from one to three days a week," she recalls. She doubled her revenue from her products when she took his advice.

Belgray later added another offering, Inbox Hero! Email Copywriting Course, in 2019—launching it on her fiftieth birthday. It features more than 100 pages of before-and-after makeovers. "It took time to create, but it was time I felt like putting in," she says. "It was something I felt I could do here and there, in bits and pieces."

As she moved to a more automated approach to growing her business, Belgray embraced a view of herself as an entrepreneur, not a freelancer. "I used to think that 'entrepreneur' meant someone with shapewear, like Sara Blakely," she jokes. In the online era, she realized, people who created digital products were just as much entrepreneurs as people like Blakely or Silicon Valley founders. "They don't need permission from anyone," she says.

Despite her success with her courses, Belgray could not replace all of her income through product sales. So, she took another crucial step: starting Shrimp Club, a six-month live mentoring "party" for twenty members, who must apply. They get access to her advice on two calls a week. Belgray offers them two live "hot seat" sessions, where she answers their question live on two Tuesdays a month, and Q&As, where, once a month, she records answers to questions they submit ahead of time. Current members pay

$15,000 to belong. She promotes Shrimp Club to her email list and through an occasional Instagram post.

Although many people assume the Shrimp Club is a copywriting mastermind group, Belgray keeps things unpredictable by including a mix of both professional copywriters and people from other fields, such as entrepreneurs and self-employed professionals in service businesses. Students have included a food blogger, someone who sources Japanese cars for import to Australia, therapists, and a graphic designer. "There's all kinds of collaboration—Shrimp on Shrimp action," she says.

Belgray doesn't rely on automation alone to get things done. She outsources administrative and strategic work to Sandra Booker, a contractor who has her own team at her company Any Old Task—and, when she's designing a new course, works with a designer and web developer. This lets her enjoy the benefits of tapping into other people's talents without the pressures of managing a staff.

It took some experimenting to figure out how to bring Booker into the mix. "She just helped me move around my client bookings," recalls Belgray. Booker quickly transitioned from acting as a virtual assistant to taking on other indispensable work, like customer service and email marketing tasks with her team—freeing up the time Belgray needed to reach $1 million. "I never would have hit that number without her there to help me execute," says Belgray.

Belgray's advice to other professionals in service businesses: Focus on adding a product and a program, along the lines of her Shrimp Club, and then find the most effective ways to promote them. "It's going to be really hard to make the kind of money you want doing one-on-one work," she says.

It's a good thing Belgray freed more of her time. She was in the middle of writing a memoir called *Tough Titties: On Living Your Best Life When You're the Fucking Worst* for Hachette when we last spoke. It was giving her a nice break from the how-to writing she does in her business. "It's not instructive. It's not prescriptive," she says. "I didn't want to write that kind of book. There will be meaning in these chapters, but there's no need for it to be instructive."

STAY CURRENT

Automation tools are changing all the time. Following a few productivity gurus who curate them can save you a lot of time. Here are some resources to check out:

The Tim Ferriss Show (tim.blog/podcast)
More than ten years after he wrote his best-selling book *The 4-Hour Workweek*, Ferriss continues to attract some of the world's leading thinkers on enhancing your productivity and performance to his podcast.

Automate and Grow (automategrow.biz)
This podcast is an up-to-the-moment source of new ideas on what to automate. Host Mike Devellano, a cloud and app consultant, interviews guests on topics like how to systematically build outreach campaigns, create marketing plans with AI, and monetize digital products with subscriptions.

Less Doing (lessdoing.com/podcast)
Ari Meisel is one of the most prolific experts on optimizing, automating, and outsourcing just about everything in your business. His *Less Doing* podcast will give you a constant stream of new ideas for offloading the work that's bogging you down to apps and software.

THE FREELANCER/CONTRACTOR MODEL

Almost every business in this book has tapped freelancers, contractors, and consultants for help, for the same reason: Even the most die-hard DIYers are going to discover there's some task they either (a) can't possibly learn how to do, (b) could learn how to do but not execute very well, or (c) put off because they dislike it or it takes too much time. Some owners go for years with an all-freelance model, while others eventually transition to more of an employer model, with a smattering of freelancers remaining. The beauty of hiring freelancers is that it's low risk. If a freelancer doesn't work out, you can always try someone else, without firing anyone. And it doesn't lock you into a fixed cost on your balance sheet unless you hire someone on retainer.

Streetfighter Strategy
KEEP IT LEGAL

If you use a freelancer model, make sure you understand both federal and state government rules on the classification of employees. Treating contractors or freelancers like employees could cause problems for you—and fines. The Society for Human Resource Management (shrm.com) offers some great resources to help you get the lay of the land, such as the document "Employee Classification Policy: Employment Categories." The Internal Revenue Service also provides a helpful guide called "Independent Contractor: (Self-Employed) or Employee?"* If you hire freelancers from outside the United States, you will be subject to the laws of that country, so make sure to consult an employment attorney or to hire them through a freelance platform that handles compliance for you.

Worker classification is a very hotly debated topic. How workers are classified tends to shift with the political winds, so it is not a bad idea to set a search engine alert for the term "worker classification" to help you plan for any changes. The issue is contentious in many countries, but the laws are different, so make sure to consult country-specific resources, such as your country's labor department, as well as local entities.

* "Small Business and Self-Employed: Independent Contractor: (Self-Employed) or Employee?," Businesses and Self-Employed, Internal Revenue Service, https://www.irs.gov/businesses/small-businesses-self-employed/independent-contractor-self-employed-or-employee.

THE ALL-FREELANCE TEAM

Let's look at a business that has relied on a team that is 100 percent freelance. Copywriter Brian Dean has done quite well with that approach in selling his online courses, allowing him to build a seven-figure business. Doing so has allowed the New Yorker to travel extensively in Berlin and, when we spoke, Lisbon, while running his business.

While backpacking around Europe about ten years ago, Dean—then a freelance copywriter—tried to think up a business where he could tap in to his talents but wouldn't have to hustle nonstop to make a living. Like Cudworth, he got inspired by reading *The 4-Hour Workweek.* "My dream was to build websites that would rank in Google and make money for me while I didn't have to do any work," he recalls.

Dean put up various sites to see which one would attract the most eyeballs. He finally hit his stride when he built one showing how people could make money by participating in focus groups and consumer research studies. The site—essentially a conduit between consumers and the research studies—took off rapidly. Dean shared what he learned about building search engine visibility for that site in a blog. One particular post—about the 200 factors Google considered in ranking a site—went viral. That taught him a powerful lesson: "I learned that everything I publish has to be that awesome."

In 2013, Dean formed a one-man business called Backlinko, which provides training in search engine optimization and link building. Backlinko sells several courses he has developed—his original one, SEO That Works, and two new ones, Create Profitable Courses and SEO for YouTube, that his team launched in 2020. The courses live on a platform a developer built for him about eight years ago. "At the time, there was no Teachable or Coursera," he says. The courses sell for $2,000 to $5,000, with his existing customers often buying his new releases.

While Dean writes every word of his courses in monthlong sprints, he relies on freelance writers to do things like creating a worksheet to go with a course. All told, it cost him $15,000 to $20,000 to create each program. "People think you can create a course in a weekend," he says with a chuckle. Not so.

To get everything done, Dean relies on eight to twelve contractors at any given time. They help him with writing, design, administration, and web development. He pays some freelancers by the project. For others he uses more regularly, he is shifting to a model where they get paid a flat rate for a certain number of deliverables every week. "That way they don't get punished for being efficient," he says.

Streetfighter Strategy
BREAK FREE FROM MEETINGS

Many people learn in the traditional workplace that meetings are mandatory for getting things done. Brian Dean is living proof that this isn't true in every business. Dean doesn't like meetings and has opted out of holding them. Instead, he and his team communicate on an app called Notion (notion.so). "It's like Asana and Slack had a baby," he says. He runs Backlinko and Exploding Topics in two different "rooms" on the platform. "It's been a game-changer," he says. The system in Notion allows his team to weigh in on creative materials, such as designs, as they have time, so no one has to check email constantly. One advantage of opting out of unnecessary meetings is that it saves your business money. You don't have to pay freelancers for the hours they might spend sitting on a Zoom call listening to everyone on the team do a check-in.

One reason Dean has been able to grow his business successfully with a small, fluid team is that he has built up an email list of 180,000 subscribers—a powerful engine for selling his courses. "Nothing even comes close," he says. "We've tried Facebook ads, Twitter, webinars. At the end of the day, it comes down to the email list and the quality of the emails." His rule for sending out email messages is to look at his relationships with subscribers as a bank account. Every time he offers free information that adds value, he's putting in a deposit. When he tries to sell something, he's making a withdrawal. For inspiration, Dean studies the approach the author of *Atomic Habits*, James Clear, has taken on his website. In late 2019, Dean branched out into a second business, Exploding Topics (explodingtopics .com), a website that focuses on new trends, with Josh Howarth, a business partner in the UK. When we last chatted, some of the "exploding topics" were portable bidets, reusable Q-tip alternatives, and decentralized finance.

Dean's freelance-driven approach has paid off for him. Backlinko brought in $1.2 million in annual revenue in 2020; meanwhile, Exploding Topics was starting to pick up traction. It had already attracted 400

Streetfighter Strategy
STREAMLINE YOUR FREELANCE TALENT SEARCH

Not sure which type of freelance talent you need to hire to put up a website, self-publish a book, or design your course? Most of the major platforms make it easy to identify the roles you need to fill and create teams. Some platforms, such as Upwork, let agencies put up profiles; hiring an agency can put you in touch with all the talent you need to accomplish a goal like putting up a website. Upwork recently introduced another option, the Project Catalog. You can shop on the platform for a curated collection of predefined projects with fixed prices. This can be a big help if you have no idea which kind of talent you need to hire to do something like self-publish an e-book.

After moving to Austin, Texas, from England in 2012, Alex Miller, 36, created Upgraded Points, a seven-figure business that shows people how to maximize their credit card points. One secret to the site's enduring appeal has been the quality of its writing. It's known for publishing 3,000-word articles up to three times a day, instead of the twelve to twenty-five shorter articles some competing sites produce. To produce articles of the depth and quality his readers expect, he relies on a team of fifteen to sixteen expert contractors, whom he communicates with through Slack and the project management software Trello. So how does he find these gems? "There's no magic trick" says Miller. "There's no place on the internet where you can find all of the wonderful people you want to find."

Instead, he looks for talent everywhere. There's a jobs and careers page on his site that brings in some inquiries. He met his director of special projects through Young Entrepreneur Council, where they're both members. "If you're looking for people who are passionate about your industry, the best place is the many Facebook groups for people who are passionate to talk about your industry," he says. Fortunately, there are lots of Facebook groups for people obsessed with travel. "If I need more writers, that's where I go," he says.

Although business slowed down during the decline in the travel industry in 2020, Miller held on to his extended team, keeping them busy on a
reduced basis as his budget allowed. He was getting set to launch a paid
membership site when we chatted in 2021, and to start introducing news
stories. "I was very proud the team kept together," he says. "We all knew
that travel was going to come back at some point."

subscribers to its newsletter for $47 a month. And running his business in
this hyper-efficient way gives Dean lots of time to enjoy his life and to pursue other interests, like traveling around Portugal and playing tennis. "The
weather here is great," he says. "It's like Southern California."

THE EMPLOYEE MODEL

Sometimes as a company grows and takes on more work, it makes sense
to add traditional employees. In some cases, it's more cost-effective than
working with contractors. It might make sense to pay a talented graphic
designer $150 an hour for a ten-hour project but if you need the same
designer for forty hours a week for an indefinite period, you'll probably be
able to negotiate a discount in exchange for giving the designer the cer-
tainty of a steady income.

More important, if you're going after big projects or orders or expanding your business, you need to know that you can deliver what you prom-
ised. Having staff can ensure that you do. "Going from solo entrepreneur to
building a team around you and scaling is heavily dependent on the ability
to hire more people and build out a sufficient team," says Tal Masica, 32,
cofounder of PAVOI, a Miami-based company that sells fast-fashion jewelry, mostly priced less than $15, on Amazon.

Masica and his childhood friend Zeke Araki, 33—both sons of
brick-and-mortar jewelry store owners, grew the business to $5 million in
revenue, without any employees, by becoming experts in optimizing their
Amazon listings, looking for ways to distinguish the brand on price and

quality, and automating and outsourcing every aspect of the business they could. But eventually, says Araki, "there are limits to what you can do as an individual. Especially during COVID, there was way too much work to be done. Two people can only know so many things."

So they started hiring traditional employees—first a data scientist and operations manager, then advertising managers. Today they have five full-timers. They were pleasantly surprised that many people they found through networking were open to working for a very small business. "Not everybody wants to work at Google," says Masica. "Some people are motivated by building something. You have so much more impact at a small company." To make sure their team wants to stay, they pay well and offer a lot of freedom to adjust their hours for work/life balance. Having the right people in place has now positioned the business to grow. "We've transitioned to two guys selling stuff to a business," says Araki.

Hiring an employee is a more formal process than engaging a contractor because there are a host of state and federal laws that govern employer/employee relationships. Many owners find it is easiest to onboard them through a payroll company, such as ADP Payroll, Gusto, or Paychex, because they handle many of the details, for example, how much tax to take out of their paychecks and how to handle unemployment insurance and workers' compensation. There is a cost to outsourcing payroll—typically between $50 and about $200 a month, depending on the size of your team—but it will probably save you a lot of time. If you want to use the DIY method, check the websites of your state and federal labor departments if you are in the United States, or similar agencies outside of the United States, and get advice from an accountant who is familiar with employment taxes. There can be steep fines if you make a mistake.

There are also a lot of decisions to make when you hire people, like how much to pay them and what benefits, if any, to offer. Set pay at a rate that strikes a balance between being competitive and being sustainable, in good times and bad. You are legally obligated to "make payroll" by cutting workers' paychecks on the day of the month or week you say you will, or you could run into problems with the tax authorities. If your wages are too high to be sustainable, you could end up having to lay off people or to furlough

HOW MUCH SHOULD YOU PAY PEOPLE?

Joining an industry association or networking among peers in your industry is often a good way to find out which types of compensation packages are typical in your part of the country. As an executive at a moving company once told me, a $75,000 salary in Manhattan, Kansas, is the equivalent of a $225,000 salary in Manhattan, New York. It can be hard for tiny businesses to compete with bigger companies on salary and benefits, but often they can still attract great people by offering other perks, like family-friendly hours or the ability to work remotely five days a week, on an ongoing basis. Now that many companies have found that their teams work well virtually, it may also be possible to find remote talent at affordable wages in parts of the country with a lower cost of living. Some small companies find that hiring team members through a professional employer organization (PEO), which acts as the official employer, is a way to offer them benefits that would otherwise be unaffordable to a small company at group rates. The National Association of Professional Employer Organizations (napeo.org) has a search tool you can use to find a PEO.

them—which can be a heartbreaking experience when employees and their families have been depending on you.

The good thing about hiring employees is you don't have to hire everyone at once. You can do it gradually by using a hybrid team, made up of both freelancers and employees, as you transition to becoming more of an employer firm. That's what Jason Martin, 40, and Patrick Falvey, 38, are doing at AppEvolve, based in Boise, Idaho. They started the business in late 2016 on the freelance platform Upwork, and built a team of twenty to twenty-five freelance tech professionals, all of whom work through Upwork, too. By 2020, they were ready to grow the business and hired their first employee, an office manager.

AppEvolve started as a two-man business. Martin and Falvey met while working together at a tech startup and discovered they both loved mountain biking. During many long rides together, they also discovered they shared a dream of running a business of their own—and had soon come up with an idea for it. At their last job, they'd noticed there weren't many web applications that integrated well with the customer relationship management software Salesforce. There was also significant demand for these apps, with customers requesting them frequently. Given that both Martin and Falvey were good at creating this type of technology, they decided to build a business doing app development for other companies. "We had all of the pieces that seemed to be needed for success," says Falvey.

By late 2016, the duo launched their software-development agency on the giant freelance platform Upwork. Both invested in professional headshots and videos, which they posted on the company's Upwork profile, to allow customers to get to know them better and convey the authenticity of their brand. "It's surprising how many people don't do that," says Martin. They also put up a simple website for their business, a step that gave the startup more visibility.

Soon prospects started reaching out and they began taking on projects. As orders began flowing in steadily, they gained the confidence to quit their jobs to start the business. Falvey did so first, in early 2016; Martin followed a couple of months later. Once they saw they could sell their applications successfully, they branched out to offer other types of web and mobile applications, along with hybrid applications that perform on all devices and machine learning projects, as well. They also offered consulting services where they assessed other customers' technology stacks and offered ideas for improving the tools they were using.

As their business grew, Martin and Falvey had more work than they could handle on their own. To lighten their load, they brought on contractors to do some of their development and project-management work. They gradually built a team of software developers they met on Upwork. Because everyone was on the same platform, it was easy to onboard them and pay them.

However, they still vetted everyone carefully. To make sure developers had the right combination of technical skills and soft skills to keep clients coming back, they created screening tests. For instance, for a back-end programmer role, they might ask an applicant to fill in gaps in code that was presented to them on an application they developed for testing potential hires. "It allows us to examine their thought process," says Falvey.

Today, on any given day, up to twenty-five developers may be working on their various projects. With competition for talent heating up around the globe, the founders make sure to pay these contractors competitively. "We want them to feel comfortable and get paid what they are worth," says Martin. They also provide benefits, even though this is not legally required. For instance, they were trying to figure out how to buy health insurance for a designer in Croatia when we spoke. "We want them to feel as secure as possible," says Martin.

Martin and Falvey have focused on building a strong culture in the virtual company, traveling around the world to meet team members. "We don't want to work with people we don't know," says Falvey. Those trips have helped them form personal bonds with their team. "We've had folks invite us to meet their family and cook us dinner," says Falvey. They have also flown remote team members to group gatherings in countries such as Nepal and India, so there is a feeling of cohesion. During COVID-19, they held the annual meetup on Zoom, sending out boxes in advance that included shirts, stickers, and a cocktail mixer. "We all had margaritas, even though for Pat and me it was 8:00 a.m.," chuckles Martin. In between the annual meetings, they have quarterly videoconferences. "We just talk about whatever comes up," says Martin. The gatherings help the group bond, says Falvey. "Teams of contractors never get to see each other," he says. "They may have been working together for months or years. The closer they can get and the better they can understand each other's communication styles, the more efficient they can be."

To maintain consistency on the team, AppEvolve has put some contractors who work regularly for the company on retainer, so they have a steady income and are available when the company needs them. "Some weeks are slow, some are heavy," says Martin. The company also invests in continuing education for its team in areas such as artificial intelligence and machine learning, paying for contractors to get certifications that will help AppEvolve serve customers better. They have also dreamed up perks like the "Amazon Book Club" to add to the company culture, which emphasizes continuous learning. "If we recommend a book, we pay for it," explains Martin.

When we chatted in early 2021, Martin and Falvey were working on building out the AppEvolve Network, an agency that would help clients work with talented programmers they have identified or enable them to expand the scope of existing projects—including both permanent employees they hope to hire and freelancers, if the scope of a project is large. As they laid the groundwork, they rented an 1,800-square-foot office in Boise, intending to bring on four in-house developers by the end of 2021. "We want to lock them down because they are exceptional," Martin told me. "They are extremely intelligent. The way they think through problems, interact with the rest of the team, and handle themselves with clients is really hard to find." Meanwhile, they had set up an extensive internal vetting process for the freelancers in the AppEvolve Network, one that includes working for at least 80 hours for the company. It was all part of making sure they could scale in a way that would keep customers happy.

Relying on a team, instead of doing all of the work of the business, enabled Martin and Falvey to grow the company to $1.5 million in annual revenue in 2020. It has also given the founders time to reboot. With hundreds of miles of trails around them, they were training for a thirty-mile ultramarathon together when we spoke. "We look at it as a method of mental training," says Martin. "Setting goals for yourself that you think are impossible and completing those goals is an incredible opportunity for growth."

They also enjoy going on backpacking trips in their spare time. "We take advantage of all of the things Boise and Idaho have to offer," says Falvey. Both have young families—Martin and his wife have three children and Falvey and his wife have a baby—and they make sure to make time for fun with them, too. "I think it's important to open up time for yourself," says Martin. "I love all of that. I love the freedom."

Some entrepreneurs dive right into hiring employees when they reach their capacity to get work done. They need someone to work specific hours and can only require that with traditional employees.

That's what happened in the case of Angie Lalla, 33, and Colin Raja, 35, a married couple from Queens, New York. The duo share a love of boxing—in which Raja was competitive in India—and CrossFit. But once Colin invited Angie to join him at the gym, she found that much of the gear for women came in drab colors and that she wasn't drawn to buying it. When Colin challenged her to come up with cross-training gloves that she would like to use, they found themselves working on an exciting project: developing a line of colorful sporting goods aimed at women. After researching how to get the goods manufactured, they eventually put their products on Amazon under the brand name RIMSports. "We understood the pain point that our customers were experiencing," explained Angie. "They're looking for appearance. They're looking for comfort."

At that time in 2015, both were working in the financial services industry—Angie in marketing and Colin in IT. To test their idea, they raised startup money through a side hustle where they resold water bottles they had bought for $1 for $20 on eBay. Then, through online and telephone research, they found a private-label manufacturer overseas who would make the gear, like cross-training gloves, in the colors they wanted. It didn't make sense for them to try to start their own factory when there was a multitude of factories to which they could outsource the production. In their first couple of months, they ordered a small amount of inventory they stored in their home, as well as at Angie's mother's house, and would pack up each order themselves. Colin would bring the packages to his job in Manhattan and race to the post office at lunchtime. "It was crazy," recalls Colin.

Then, about two months into the business, they decided to offload some of the work of starting the business when they discovered Fulfillment by Amazon. The service allowed them to store their inventory in one of Amazon's warehouses and to use Amazon employees to pack and ship the packages, in return for a fee. "We figured out Amazon is the best choice," Colin said. "I had a full-time job. Angie had a full-time job."

By advertising on social media, the couple attracted customers to their store. Their business took off, but keeping up with the fast growth, even with

Amazon doing the shipping, became an endurance challenge. They put in very long hours to make sure there was 24/7 customer service. Finally, the couple decided to hire a part-time, remote employee to help with customer service in 2016. "She was my neighbor in India," says Colin. Angie trained her by email in doing customer service. By that point, the company had reached $1 million in annual revenue.

After adding this customer service employee, Colin and Angie breathed a sigh of relief but continued working around the clock. With the company taking off, they decided to open an office in Chennai, India, where they could afford to add staff. To figure out which positions they needed to add, they analyzed the various roles that needed to be filled in the business, made a judgment call about whether they could use automation to do the work, and, if not, determined a dollar value for the job, based on how much it would bring into the business or how much hiring someone to do it would save the company.

As they created each job, Angie documented the requirements for it and how to do the actual work in a standard operating procedure (SOP) file. To do that, she or Colin would perform each task required for each job to set a standard for doing it well. Then they would break down the task into steps so they could teach it to an employee. Once they documented it, they would sit down with an employee one-on-one to show how to do the task. Finally, they would ask the employee to do the task independently. It took time to create these documents, but as they grew their team and needed to train more people, these SOPs saved a lot of time. The documents became so critical to their operations that they now store them in several secure locations.

As they looked for potential hires by placing advertisements and networking, they realized it would be hard to find people who had the exact skills needed for the type of business they were running. Instead, they looked for people who were open to picking up new skills, even if they seemed "un-hirable" on paper. "Whoever is coming on to our team should want to grow and learn," says Colin. "We try to inspire them if they are ready to get inspired."

During job interviews, the couple set up tests to see if someone had the aptitude to learn a particular job. For a customer service candidate, they might share a complaint a customer sent by email and ask how the candidate might respond to it. They would look for clues that applicants have strong emotional intelligence to the point they could pick up on issues the customer had not articulated clearly—and could solve those problems. They would also ask candidates to do some research into the type of work they would be doing, looking at the successful completion of this step as an indicator of their willingness to learn. "If they can't learn, we don't want to work with them," says Colin.

Gradually, RIMSports hired fifteen people. To create a strong culture, the couple formed a leadership team, currently made up of four people: an HR pro/general manager, their accountant, their account manager, and their sourcing manager. The leadership team, which meets weekly, came up with core values for the business: accountability, excellence, integrity, drive, and passion. Having these core values in mind helps the couple in selecting the right candidates to join the team.

Once team members come on board, they report to a member of the leadership team. The company uses Slack for communication and Asana for project management, asking each individual to provide an update on what they are working on in their Slack channel; if follow-up is required, the couple notes that in Asana. "We want them to be responsible for their work," says Angie. "It helps Colin and I are still involved and know exactly what is going on with anyone in the business. Sometimes they are waiting for things from us. They will tag us in these kinds of updates, and we will know we need to respond to them."

To make sure every team member has growth opportunities, the couple meets with one member of the leadership team each day. Their HR lead holds a performance and accountability meeting with each team member once a month.

RIMSports has focused on building a culture of loyalty by providing full-time salaries and benefits to employees. The couple tries to be understanding of their team's circumstances. One reason they started the business was a bad experience Angie had when an employer pressured her to come back to a job prematurely after a painful injury. "That was a big eye-opener," she recalls. Many of their employees are mothers, so they try to make sure everyone leaves work at a reasonable time, as well.

Having a great team in place has allowed the couple to focus on finding new opportunities. Colin has been able to travel around the world to make sure they have the best factories in place, along with backup manufacturers, in case one of them cannot deliver. Many of these factories, located in special economic zones, do not advertise, and Colin has had to do on-the-ground research once arriving there. These trips have enabled the company to shift their manufacturing from China to plants in Pakistan, and later India, that were closer to their offices. They also began working with some plants in Cambodia and Thailand that gave them supply-chain diversity. With many companies looking to spread their manufacturing among several factories as an insurance policy against supply-chain failures during COVID-19, Colin created a new venture called Indian Sourcing Co. The three-person company, still in startup mode, acts as an agent for companies that want to manufacture in India.

Today, all of this hard work to get set up has paid off. RIMSports had $3 million in annual revenue for 2020 and was on track for $5–6 million in early 2021. Their goal: to hit $10 million. But the couple said building their business is not just about achieving a monetary goal. Both find it very fulfilling to provide opportunities to work from home for their mostly female staffers, many of whom are part of families where it is uncommon for women to work. "We're allowing them to gain confidence so they can achieve something on their own," says Colin.

THE PARTNERSHIP MODEL

Automating your business and hiring people aren't the only ways to extend what the team in a tiny business can do. Many entrepreneurs discover that as their business picks up traction, partnerships can fuel their growth, as well. Some may want to get involved in managing or doing the work of the business in exchange for owning part of it. Others may want to get a cut of your sales in the form of a commission if they help you promote what you sell. Some potential partners may want more of a "silent" role, where they buy an ownership stake in your business, with the goal of profiting when you sell the business, or they eventually sell their stake back to you or someone else. There are many other variations on these relationships that are worth considering if you're looking to grow. Just make sure your lawyer reviews any partnership agreement you're considering, in case it doesn't work out.

As a newcomer to his field Patrick Murray, 33, founder of Noson, a San Francisco company that helps airport parking lots fill empty spots using specialized software, partnered with an industry veteran to get his business off the ground. "It's very old-school, mom-and-pop, and everyone knows each other," says Murray. Brett Harwood, chairman of Welcome Parking, a service that provides parking management services to owners of parking facilities in New York and New Jersey, was once president of the National Parking Association. As founder and principal of Park Equity, Harwood provided $200,000 in funding. With the help of a team of fifteen contractors, the business, founded in 2016, hit $1 million in revenue. Sales dipped during the pandemic, given the sharp decline in air travel, so Murray turned to another type of partner—the parking lots themselves. His company reached out to national parking providers that were previously too busy to talk with him to see if his technology could steer new business their way. "They're happy to try us out in markets I never thought they would have," he says. Today the business works with parking providers in fifty-six airports across the country and sales have come roaring back as business and leisure travel resumes.

Wes Johnson, 47, teamed up with a group of very hands-on partners to grow his business, Lawson Hammock, in Raleigh, North Carolina. Johnson started it in 2005 when he was working in home construction. At the time, many outdoor enthusiasts were buying rugged outdoor hammocks instead of sleeping bags. As an avid camper, he couldn't find a single hammock he found very comfortable. If he could come up with one, he reckoned, he could build a great business selling it.

Johnson kept his eye out for opportunities to start the business. When he met two brothers who were selling hand-sewn hammocks he liked at outdoor festivals, he offered to buy their inventory, getting a $30,000 loan from a friend. That was back in 2005. He soon found himself with a thriving side hustle selling the hammocks at Lawson Hammock—the brothers' last name is Lawson—and dove into creating the perfect prototype for a sleep hammock. To make the hammocks, he turned to local talent. "Literally, they were ladies out in the middle of nowhere who had a cut-and-sew facility," he says.

To sell the hammocks, Johnson put up a simple e-commerce site and began marketing them, all the while tweaking his designs and production methods. By the end of year one, he had brought in $10,000 in annual revenue, selling the hammocks at $139 each to a variety of customers, among them Boy Scouts, college students, and people who enjoyed lounging in them in their backyards.

As the business grew, Johnson found himself increasingly frustrated. "It was too time- and labor-intensive," he says. "If I got an order for a few units, I was excited but also overwhelmed." Each time an order came in, he'd remind himself, "It's going to take me hours to piece this together." Johnson became so frustrated he almost considered shutting down his store. "I had to make a call on, 'Hey, do I try to figure out a way to grow this and make it scalable—or do I just get out of it, pull the plug on the website, and get rid of the inventory I have?'" he recalls.

Although he had not yet figured out how to run the business efficiently, Johnson didn't want to give up on it. "I did enjoy it," he says. "I like the outdoor industry. I did think there was more potential for growth."

Johnson decided to stick with it and started pitching his hammock to retailers who might sell it for him. Signing on his first retailer, which had nine stores, inspired him to improve his processes. He knew the stores would order in larger quantities and that he needed a better way to keep up with demand.

Traveling to a trade show to find a manufacturer, he soon found one who made tents for large outdoor companies in the United States. He asked the firm to create a prototype for the hammocks (which can double as a tent). He outsourced warehousing and shipping to partners he found overseas, which was more efficient than handling these things himself.

By 2006, revenues were in the $20,000 to $30,000 range. The business grew gradually with each passing year. When the Great Recession hit in

2008, Johnson realized there was an opportunity to expand, as people cut back on pricey vacations and turned to camping instead. He began devoting more time to the business and, in 2010, left his former career in real estate development.

"It was good timing to get out of the building industry," he recalls. Although he was a little nervous about making the transition from traditional employment, he also recognized he'd taken some of the risks out of the equation. "At that point, there was cash flowing," he says. "I knew there was enough to get by and pay my bills."

Confident his design was up to snuff, Johnson decided to raise the profile of his business. He reached out to journalists in publications campers read and asked them to try the Blue Ridge Camping Hammock. He made sure to have great photos available so they could quickly run with the story. "A lot of writers want content if you make it easy for them," he says. *Backpacker* and *Outside* magazines rated his Blue Ridge Camping Hammock highly. His hammocks now sell in Bass Pro Shops, Cabela's, L.L.Bean, and DICK'S Sporting Goods. To make sure his business is profitable, he gradually raised the price to $199, to reflect his costs.

By 2015, Johnson hit $500,000 in revenue, and by 2018, he hit $1 million. To keep his budget lean, Johnson set up shop in a coworking space in Raleigh. He invested in getting a patent for the Blue Ridge Camping Hammock, to protect his idea.

Sales continued growing. By early 2020, Johnson realized it would be hard to bring the brand to its full potential on his own. "I knew there was more potential to scale, but to scale I needed help," he says. "I needed help on the funding side to ramp up marketing and to add new products. It's not cheap."

After talking with angel investors, he decided it would be best to find partners who had experience in the type of consumer goods he was selling. Johnson met the right partners when he had coffee with a local entrepreneur, Mark Saad, who started a company called Sherpa Collaborative, which invests in startups and provides help with sourcing, operations, pricing, brand strategy, and other services. "They now manage the daily operations," he says. This allowed Johnson to step back and focus his energy more on growth strategies and product development.

Johnson also found he missed being part of the commercial real estate world and had returned to a role in that field when we spoke, leasing commercial class A real estate and doing tenant representation. "It's very entrepreneurial," he says.

For Johnson, who was now the father of a new baby and a toddler at the time we spoke, the arrangement with Sherpa Collaborative was ideal. Although they purchased the majority of the company, he still has a substantial equity stake. "There's still upside for me," he says. "I didn't want to sell it outright and give all of that up."

Fortunately, in a tiny business, there's plenty of freedom to do things your way as you grow. In the next chapter, we'll look at how to accelerate your growth through the marketing methods that work best for you.

CHAPTER 7

GO VIRAL

Julian O'hayon, 30, didn't know he was planting the seeds for a business that would bring in nearly $5 million in annual revenue when he began posting images of iconic products—such as M&M candies and a can of Coke—that he'd colored black, on the Instagram page of his web design and development agency, Anckor. But when the images started going viral, he began to understand his potential to build a global streetwear brand—Blvck Paris, where all of the products are black.

Blvck Paris started small when O'hayon launched it with another entrepreneur he met on Instagram in 2017. They sold simple products, such as black MacBook cases, through an e-commerce store they built on the platform Shopify, using a manufacturing partner they found online to make the products and drop-ship their orders. The duo was fortunate to have $80,000 to invest in Blvck Paris that O'hayon had saved from other businesses, but they didn't want to blow through their startup cash on marketing alone. So, they turned to low-cost methods of spreading the word about what they were selling, for example, sharing their designs on Instagram and Facebook in organic posts. They also invested in paid ads on social media, spending $10,000 to $20,000 a month during the early months of the business to help the brand pick up traction.

O'hayon didn't realize at the time that he was embarking on a real-world crash course in grassroots marketing that would eventually help him build a business with multimillion revenue. Marketing is an essential part of building a tiny business that makes big money, but, as his business would soon demonstrate, creating a "viral" brand is not a one-step process. You've got to build your marketing program brick by brick, over time. It takes some experimenting to find the combination of marketing methods—and to create enough momentum for opportunities to flow to you, as other people notice what's happening and want to get in on it.

O'hayon and his partner learned a lot during their initial forays into paid Facebook and Instagram advertising, and later advertising on Google and Pinterest. One critical lesson was to pay close attention to the performance of each ad—and let data dictate whether they would double down on it or not. "We have a rule internally that the 'return on ads' (ROA) has to be at least two times for us to keep the ad on and be happy with the results," O'hayon says. "If we see a stronger ROA, then we will increase the budget and scale the ads to maximize the results, and also test various audiences on it. On the other hand, if an ad doesn't perform, then we will drop it."

That approach helped the company get off to a strong start. By early 2018, Blvck Paris had introduced a range of products, such as iPhone cases and tumblers, and was bringing in $40,000 to $50,000 a month in revenue. With many customers coming back to make new purchases, the company's average monthly revenue doubled by the end of the year.

But soon, the store's rapid success led to a problem: It was running out of inventory too quickly as orders flowed in. Although the founders had been inspired by trendy brands like Yeezy sneakers, which are made in limited quantities to keep the product exclusive, the partners realized that by focusing on low-profit, high-volume orders, they were bringing in more transactions than they could handle. They decided to add higher-ticket items, like $120 sweatshirts, where the profit per transaction was greater. Their all-black collection resonated with their audience, made up primarily of young men who liked the simplicity it brought to getting dressed in the morning. "What I like about all-black is that everything matches," says O'hayon. "That part of the morning routine goes away."

To inspire customers to buy more, Blvck Paris took a step beyond paid digital ads and turned to low-cost email marketing methods, sending coupons, free-shipping offers, discounts, and other incentives. The company used Klaviyo's customer relationship management software, which is designed specifically for online businesses, to automate this email marketing. As more business flowed in, O'hayon hired two freelancers trained in the customer support software Zendesk to help with customer service, well aware that if customers needed to return a purchase or had a disappointing experience, they might not come back.

By 2019, O'hayon's partner wanted to work on another business and left the company. To keep up with growing demand, O'hayon hired staff, including his two sisters, Steffi and Diorèle, who are in their late 20s, as full-time employees. Steffi, who had been a vice president at a global investment bank, serves as CFO and head of growth, with Diorèle, who had worked in digital marketing at a Paris-based AI startup, overseeing digital artwork and cofounding the company's new "Whte" collection. O'hayon also hired another employee to handle logistics and relationships with suppliers. He also hired public relations agencies in the United States and Paris to introduce celebrities to Blvck Paris's clothing, finding that if celebrities wore an item in photos on social media, it would help sales. To keep everyone on the remote team organized, O'hayon communicated with them virtually on Slack and WhatsApp.

O'hayon built such a strong foundation for Blvck Paris with his marketing efforts that with more people shopping at home during the COVID-19 pandemic, sales continued to climb. To bring in even more revenue to pay for its growth, Blvck Paris rolled out a series of digital icon templates for iPhones, as well as digital wallpaper. Although creating the templates and wallpaper required some up-front design work and technology help, there were no manufacturing costs, so these new products had a big, positive impact on the company's bottom line. "With digital products, you get paid instantly," says O'hayon. "There are no returns. All you make is profits."

The additional cash flowing into the business allowed O'hayon to start opening brick-and-mortar stores. Working with local partners who ran the stores and took a commission on sales, O'hayon opened two pop-up stores

AMPLIFY YOUR VOICE THROUGH PAID SEARCH

Most tiny businesses that make big money rely on as many free marketing methods as they can. However, there is intense competition for customers' attention in many fields. As O'hayon found, investing in paid advertising is often the quickest way to get noticed. For businesses that sell consumer products, advertising on Google, Bing, or Yahoo!, online platforms such as Amazon, or social media sites such as Facebook, Instagram, or YouTube can all be effective. If you're marketing to a B2B audience, you may want to look in to advertising on LinkedIn, Amazon, and search engines. There are many good books on pay-per-click advertising, but one overlooked way to learn about it is to study the online ads that have gotten your attention (without censoring yourself and editing down the list to the ones you would willingly tell the world you clicked on). What do they have in common, visually? What do you notice about their copywriting? The more pattern-matching you do, the more you'll learn.

Although Blvck Paris built a large presence on Instagram using "organic" posts, paid advertising has been a critical part of raising the brand's profile. Some of its ads show clothing, accessories, and digital goods. Others show aesthetic photos from the company's Instagram feed to convey the brand's vibe. O'hayon found that "unboxing" videos, showing delighted customers opening orders shipped in the mail, performed particularly well.

Some entrepreneurs find it's hard to stay on top of their paid advertising, resulting in unnecessary spending. If you are too busy to do this, it could be worth hiring an agency to manage it for you, like O'hayon, who outsources day-to-day ad management to an agency in New York. Otherwise, you may find that the tab runs up much more quickly than you expected, leaving your company unprofitable. It's not uncommon for a tiny business that makes big money to invest six figures in paid advertising, but it's important to make every dollar count.

in Taipei, Taiwan, in 2020. "In Taiwan, they didn't have COVID in 2020," he explains. Besides the brand's clothing, the first Taipei store sells black ice cream and has a vending machine selling novelty items in black, attracting guests with in-store events. Two more stores were slated to open in 2021 when we last spoke—one in Taichung, Taiwan, and the other in Miami. For the Miami store, O'hayon had partnered with Showfields, which runs the store in exchange for a fixed monthly fee. This is well worth it, from O'hayon's point of view. "We're still growing the same, but don't have the same amount of risk," he says.

With the brand more visible than ever before, Blvck Paris has also tapped another powerful marketing engine: Exclusive distributors of its products in countries such as China, Japan, Kuwait, and Taiwan that have promoted the brand to new audiences. O'hayon doesn't have to look hard to find them. Generally, the exclusive distributors are merchants who start out ordering inventory for their retail stores from a website the company has set up. Some, finding their customers love the brand, have gradually increased the size of their orders to the point it made sense for them to become the exclusive distributor for their country. "It happens naturally," says O'hayon. Several of these distributors have eventually opened their own Blvck Paris–branded e-commerce stores for their country. One advantage of working with these distributors is they know local preferences and help O'hayon customize the merchandise to the country. For instance, in Japan, Blvck Paris sells wooden chopsticks in black.

With this fast-growing marketing and distribution juggernaut in motion, Blvck Paris hit $1 million in annual revenue in 2019 and more than $4 million in 2020. And it was still attracting lots of new customers, thanks in part to the nearly one million Instagram followers on the brand's account when we last spoke. O'hayon was projecting more than $10 million in annual revenue for 2021.

Marketing a business as successfully as O'hayon has done takes creativity and ongoing commitment, particularly on a tiny business's budget. Here is a look at some additional strategies that are particularly effective for tiny businesses that want to make big money—word of mouth, content marketing, email marketing, becoming an influencer, and affiliate marketing.

GET CUSTOMERS TALKING ABOUT YOU

The simplest, most cost-effective type of marketing is word of mouth. But many entrepreneurs don't know how to get happy customers to recommend them to others. Meeting planner Alicia Schiro is a natural at it, and her relationship-driven approach offers many ideas for tiny business owners who are focused on growth.

When Schiro left her job in the startup world to launch Aced It Events, an event-planning business in New York City, in 2015, she yearned for the freedom to work on projects that were truly exciting to her. She'd been involved in booking events and had previously been an event and catering manager at an advertising agency, so meeting planning seemed like a good fit.

Schiro got off to a strong start in her business because she brought her clients from the startup she'd been working at with her to her new venture. Attracting them to her new business was simply a matter of telling them what she was doing next. She'd made a smart decision when she first accepted that job to negotiate an arrangement in which she was free to invite her clients to work with her if she left and went elsewhere. But Schiro still needed to bring on more clients. To network and socialize with other creatives, she joined SoHo House, a private club for people in creative industries. "It's important to stay informed and involved," she says.

As new business flowed in, she asked clients after each successful event for referrals to other colleagues within their companies who might need her services. In a big company, this approach was often very fruitful. Sometimes, the referrals she got from one event would lead to five new clients. To encourage referrals, Schiro offered to pay colleagues in her network who worked at event venues a 10-percent commission on any business they steered her way. "If they have a client they can't take at their venue, they will send them to me," she says.

Schiro never marketed her services aggressively to these prospects. She simply tried to get to know them as human beings and found the work flowed naturally from those relationships. She bonded with one client, for instance, over their shared hatred of hardcore intense workout classes. "We were laughing so hard!" she recalls. Her focus on building relationships

Streetfighter Strategy
TURN "LOST" CLIENTS INTO NEW BUSINESS

Because of her focus on building relationships and generating word-of-mouth recommendations, Alicia Schiro's event-planning business grows even when a client moves to another firm. "I learned very quickly this was a great thing," says Schiro. "I would ask the client to introduce me to the new person taking over their role, which they were always more than happy to do, and, in addition, I would ask to keep in touch. I would ask for their new contact information and once they got settled in their new role, I would follow up. Ninety percent of the time, they would reach out to me asking for help with an upcoming event. This has really helped grow my business."

saved her time and money on marketing. "I haven't made one cold call since I started my business," she says. "That is the long road. The short road is reaching out to people you already know and asking for introductions."

When you rely on word-of-mouth marketing, it's important to make sure you're prepared to make the most of opportunities that land in your lap. To that end, Schiro, who started out running her business as a one-woman operation, made sure she could handle bigger projects that flowed to her by staying in close touch with friends from the industry. She relied on help from a couple of contractors for work such as researching new venues. "I had to learn how to work smart," she says.

Although many meeting professionals saw their businesses devastated during the coronavirus pandemic, Schiro's grew. Early in the pandemic, she saw that clients who'd been doing live events still needed a way to meet with both their teams and clients, so she shifted her attention to online events. Planning these gatherings paid less than her usual projects, but she was glad to have an opportunity to learn how to run these events—something she'd never had time to do when she was flying all over the country for live events. "That's the key—making yourself focus on what you can do today and not

AUTOMATE YOUR WORD-OF-MOUTH MARKETING

Some entrepreneurs just can't bring themselves to "pop the question" to clients to ask them for referrals. If you've been hesitating, asking for reviews or testimonials by email or text is another great way to inspire happy customers to help spread the word about your business. One of the easiest ways to do this is to program your customer relationship management software to automatically send an email or text to those who make a purchase, asking for testimonials you can post on your website or reviews for Google, Facebook, Yelp, or TripAdvisor. It may also be worthwhile to seek a listing on a site that will verify reviewers' status as a client, such as Clutch (clutch. co) or Trustpilot (trustpilot.com). Just make sure you're confident that you'll get excellent reviews before you ask someone to vouch for you. If you're not confident, wait until you've fine-tuned your product or service to the point that you feel good about asking.

worrying how long this will go on," she told me during the early days of the pandemic.

The great part about the type of relationship-driven marketing Schiro does is that if you do have a new offering, spreading the word to existing clients is simply a matter of mentioning it during one of your normal calls. That's what Schiro did while she was working with clients to renegotiate contracts for live events that clients had to cancel. After she had held a few successful online events, she upped the ante and contacted the big companies on her client list to suggest they hire celebrities to speak at their quarterly meetings to make them more fun—an idea many took her up on. (So did A-list celebrities, who were at home sheltering in place.) Schiro soon expanded her offerings to other types of online events, such as interactive cooking classes with local chefs—helping both her clients and business owners whose restaurants were devastated by the coronavirus.

Although Schiro relies heavily on word-of-mouth marketing, she does use other methods to attract prospects outside her immediate network. When she rolled out her online events, Schiro filmed video sizzle reels with highlights of past events, as well as informational videos on how to create online events, which she shared on LinkedIn. She managed to keep up her output by hiring three traditional employees: a video editor, a content specialist, and a content creator. It paid off: Her business brought in $1.5 million in revenue in 2020—the most Aced It Events ever generated.

BUILD YOUR "PLATFORM" WITH CONTENT MARKETING

Content marketing—whether it's in writing, on video, or through live events—can also be a powerful way to market your business, and it often won't cost you anything, other than your own time. In case you're not familiar, content marketing is, essentially, sharing useful information for free, whether it's in how-to articles, op-eds, Instagram stories, videos shared on social media, or live moderated events (whether in person through a panel discussion, or on Clubhouse or LinkedIn). If your business sells information or knowledge, content marketing can be a great way to build your reputation as an expert and to attract clients who like the way you think. It is just as useful for a product-driven business. For instance, if you sell fitness gear, putting up free YouTube videos leading someone through a workout that incorporates the gear—a very subtle "call to action" to buy the gear—could be a great way to attract customers.

Denise Duffield-Thomas, an entrepreneur and author of the books *Get Rich, Lucky Bitch!* and *Chillpreneur*, is a master of content marketing. Duffield-Thomas was a life coach who had studied at Inspired Spirit Coaching Academy, run by veteran coach Sandy Forster, when she began focusing her attention on helping women build their financial know-how and entrepreneurship skills through Money Bootcamp, a course and online community she launched in 2012. Duffield-Thomas and her husband, Mark, her marketing manager, built the business to AUD $3.4 million for fiscal year 2020 (the equivalent of USD $2.6 million as of this writing), relying on the help of part-time virtual assistants and a handful of contractors, such as a bookkeeper, and funding growth out of cash flow—pulling this off while raising three children ages six and under.

A big part of her success has been content marketing. Her first foray into it was offering free workshops on goal-setting—a common challenge for people who seek life coaching. When Duffield-Thomas launched her coaching practice in 2010, she had recently moved to the Greater Newcastle area of Australia, her country of origin, from London, where she attended London Metropolitan University and worked in corporate events and new media. To get a foothold in the area and to start attracting clients to her practice, she called local gyms, health food stores, and crystal shops to see if any had a spare room where she could hold free goal-setting workshops. She put up posters around town and advertisements on Facebook and the Meetup website and, to make sure people showed up, offered attendees a free coaching session. Once they did show up, Duffield-Thomas made sure that the information she shared was truly valuable and not simply a promo for her other services. "I totally overdelivered," she recalls. That hard work paid off: Often, the attendees became paying clients.

Gradually, Duffield-Thomas built enough confidence to start charging for her workshops. She was excited to find takers for the first Saturday workshop, where she charged $97 per participant. "After that workshop, I went to the fanciest restaurant in town and bought a tall glass of champagne," she recalls. "I said, 'I can make my own money. This is amazing! And I'm helping people. That's even better!'"

Duffield-Thomas loved the flow of clients that came from her paid workshops, but she didn't enjoy the havoc the workshops were wreaking on her work/life balance. Between the prep time and follow-up, they were eating up her weekends. She began to look for another way to share her knowledge with clients that would allow her to have a life outside of work. That was when she decided to move the workshops to Facebook, which was much more convenient and a better fit. "I'm an introvert," she says. "I've always gravitated to online work."

The success of Duffield-Thomas's Facebook workshops helped her bring in coaching clients from around the world. Some signed up for one-on-one sessions; others chose group coaching. Once again, she was grateful for the work, but not happy with what it was doing to her schedule. "I was having my first coaching session at 4:30 a.m.," she recalls. "I didn't want to ask people to stay up late in the US or the UK. I was trying to do the same with my group work."

Working around the clock left her exhausted. And there was one other challenge, as her services caught on: "There were no more hours to do this," says Duffield-Thomas. She realized she needed to rethink her business model once again and to set some boundaries around her time so she could scale her message. In 2011, she wrote and self-published *Get Rich, Lucky Bitch!*, which encapsulated a lot of her teachings from the workshops and, as it quickly gained popularity, became a powerful content-marketing tool, particularly after an editor at Hay House Publishing in the UK reached out and acquired it in 2015. Unknown to her, the editor had been following her work and had joined her email list—which led to her second book, *Chillpreneur*, published in 2019. She wanted to write more and develop her group coaching program, which eventually became the foundation for her Money Bootcamp. "I needed to free up some energy," says Duffield-Thomas.

Duffield-Thomas figured out how to do that by studying the business model of an expert content marketer: entrepreneur and book author Marie Forleo, whose work she admired. She was drawn to the simplicity of Forleo's approach: running only one major educational program at a time. Duffield-Thomas decided to focus her energy on developing her course, Money Bootcamp, for which students now pay $1,997. To give that pursuit enough time and to maintain her income, she increased the price of her coaching services and then transitioned to selling six-month coaching packages, where she worked with fewer clients—just four. It was a leap of faith. "This is what I had to do to ultimately serve more people," she says.

Once Duffield-Thomas published *Get Rich, Lucky Bitch!* and started promoting it, she began getting invitations to do podcast interviews—another highly effective form of content marketing. She made herself available whenever she could be. "I did about two hundred of them in one year," she recalls. "I would get my hair done on Monday, and all day Monday and Tuesday, I would do them. It was a lot of sweat equity."

Meanwhile, Duffield-Thomas built her platform by publishing her content regularly through a blog and posting tongue-in-cheek videos on YouTube that were aimed at women entrepreneurs, like "How Women Sell in Business vs. Men."[13] "Some of the blocks we have around money—you have to laugh," she says.

Duffield-Thomas didn't expect overnight success when she started her business, though she always dreamed big: "I've always wanted to have a million-dollar business," she says. Keeping her eye on that goal gave her the patience to let her revenue grow steadily. In fiscal 2011, she brought in AUD $63,000. By 2012, she hit $146,532. That grew to $221,103 in 2013, $579,198 in 2014, $1.3 million in 2015, nearly $1.4 million by 2016, $2.6 million in 2017, then dipped to $2 million in 2018 as she adjusted her business model, and grew again to $2.8 million in 2019 and more than $3 million for 2020. Along the way, Duffield-Thomas learned an important lesson she now teaches other budding entrepreneurs: "To double, triple, or quadruple your income, you have to work less. You have to leverage the work you do." That's what content marketing allows you to do—spread your message so you can earn more money from it.

Content marketing can be a bit overwhelming to think about because there are so many ways you can go about creating it. If you're not sure where to start, check out Joe Pulizzi's book *Epic Content Marketing*, which will help you to get a better understanding and to figure out where best to direct your time and energy. Cynthia Johnson's book on personal branding, *Platform*, offers another interesting perspective taking you under the hood of a variety of online platforms so you can make the most of them to build a presence as an expert in the digital world.

---

13 "How Women Sell in Business vs. Men," Denise Duffield-Thomas, June 1, 2015, YouTube video, 9:32, https://www.youtube.com/watch?v=-oiQE7G6vNM.

BECOME AN INFLUENCER (WITHOUT POSING IN A SWIMSUIT PHOTO)

When "influencers" on Facebook, Instagram, YouTube, and other social sites first started building brands for themselves, I was a little skeptical about what their purpose was when they created a "platform," dismissing them as wannabe Kardashians. However, as I learned more, I discovered that many were building communities around sharing useful information—whether it was how to manage a chronic health condition naturally, dress stylishly at any age, stay in shape, connect with like-minded professionals, or build a thriving business in a particular field. Now it's become clear that building a "platform" on social media is a great way to meet people all over the world who have similar passions, make valuable professional connections, and bring in new business.

Jason Allan Scott, 46, a veteran events planner, is a good example of how to do this. Scott runs A Podcast Company, a London-based business where he teaches clients how to create podcasts. He also runs the *Smarter Event Planning* podcast. Beyond that, he now sells a software-as-a-service tool to help podcasters get up and running, along with a master class for aspiring hosts. He's built a strong presence as a digital influencer, as well. It's all part of living his mantra: "Never be a boss, never have a boss."

When Scott launched his podcast, he knew it would be hard to stand out if he tried to tackle a broad topic, such as business or the arts—the podcast world is too crowded—so he niched down to event planning, an area he knows well. "You have innate skills from all of the other work you've done for so long," says Scott. "Through podcasts, you can monetize that." To make sure he delivered a great experience to listeners, he invested early on in coaching by entrepreneurs and podcasters John Lee Dumas and Lewis Howes. It was from them that he learned crucial information that helped him stay motivated during the early months of establishing his podcast. "Lewis Howes said he didn't make money for his first three years in podcasting," notes Scott, "whereas John Lee Dumas told me to monetize from day one."

One critical foundation of building his podcast has been embracing the concept of "1,000 true fans," which author Kevin Kelly coined and made the subject of a book by the same name. Scott found that he could attract listeners who were not only willing to tune in, but also spread the word about his podcast by creating a two to three minute trailer that he would play before each episode—an easy way for people to sample what he was going to say without a big time commitment. As fans started following his podcast, he looked for a way to create enough valuable content for each of them to spend $1,000 with him over the year and to generate at least $100 in profit from each. "That is easier to do in some businesses than others, but it is a good creative challenge, because it is always easier and better to give your existing customers more than it is to find new fans," says Scott. For some podcasters, monetization mainly comes through selling related products and services, such as T-shirts, coaching, mentoring, or a mastermind course. For his part, Scott gradually published forty e-books in his areas of expertise, such as *The Ultimate Podcasting Guide*, on the site Bookboon; some are as short as fifteen pages long. He has also introduced a master class on the business of podcasting. "You slowly build this up over time," says Scott, who credits Ramit Sethi, author of *I Will Teach You to Be Rich*, for this insight.

Scott also enlists listeners to help attract new followers. At the end of every show, he asks listeners to take action that will help raise the visibility of the show. For instance, "If you've enjoyed me, please subscribe to the show," "Please give me a five-star review and please leave a comment," or "If you've enjoyed this, please sign up for my newsletter. I'll tell you about what I'm doing and how I can support you." The syndicates that distribute podcasts have made it difficult for people to rate podcasts, explains Scott. "If someone is willing to go from listening to the show to opening up the app, that shows to the platform you have real fans. It's not easy. It takes work."

Becoming a podcasting influencer helped Scott attract customers for other ventures. In 2015, he created his consultancy A Podcast Company in response to popular demand. As host of the *Smarter Event Planning* podcast, he kept getting inquiries from avid listeners, asking him how to create a podcast of their own for their businesses. Many were drawn by his informal style and sense of humor. "You can make it a great experience by making it a great story, where it feels like you're listening in on a conversation," he says. He focused the consultancy on teaching others how to do it themselves and to differentiate their voices by thinking about questions such as "How many people think as you do?" and "How many people ask the same questions as you do?"

Beyond these activities, Scott runs MICEOFFERS, a deals site for the meetings industry, and Lokkima, which rents cryotherapy machines to hotels and spas. He recently raised funding for Pynk, a blockchain-based investment platform. In 2020, he participated in the Y Combinator Startup School's Future Founders program. And most recently, he launched Kopus, an app that allows owners of restaurants and other public spaces to turn them into flexible spaces that can be used for work and events. Collectively, his efforts generate seven-figure revenue, he says.

It can be challenging to continue churning out content—especially if you're running other business ventures like Scott—and eventually, most influencers need help from someone else, or a team. Scott relies on assistance from seven freelancers around the world who create social media assets, produce his podcast and newsletter, handle technology work, and more. He has also taken on two "awareness ambassadors," retired professionals who work on building awareness of the business, paying them a commission for every closed sale they bring in. "I call it a smart tribe," says Scott. "We're a tribe of people working smartly, not 'hard-ly,' to get to where we want to be."

To coordinate his content team, Scott has always made his mobile phone his business hub. "My entire business is run off WhatsApp," he says. He also relies heavily on the Voice Notes app on his phone to record information on logistics, delivery, training, marketing, PR, and other tasks, and shares them with his team before directing them to a Trello board that lists projects. And he's a fan of Calendly for setting up appointments. "I try to make it as low-cost and low-tech as humanly possible," says Scott.

Streetfighter Strategy
STAY CONNECTED TO YOUR FANS

If you start a podcast, make sure to build a direct relationship with your fans—newsletters are a highly effective way to do this—and to set up a means for them to pay you directly, podcaster Jason Allan Scott suggests. Some podcasters are turning to Patreon (patreon.com) and OnlyFans (onlyfans.com), sites where fans can contribute. Podcasting makes it easy to maintain an ongoing relationship with fans because your podcast will not live on any one platform. "It's the last great medium," says Scott. "If you're on YouTube and YouTube goes down, your business is gone. With a podcast, you own your podcast. iTunes doesn't hold your podcast—they have a way of sending your podcast out."

EMBRACE EMAIL MARKETING

Many professional speakers found their businesses wilting when the COVID-19 pandemic hit. James Taylor's thrived, bringing in seven-figure revenue. Unable to log the 300,000 miles of air travel he did in 2019, he made the transition to working virtually in 2020. Throughout the pandemic, he spoke to business audiences about topics such as "SuperCreativity" and innovation from his home studio in a bucolic town near Edinburgh, Scotland, where sheep graze outside his window.

One reason Taylor did so well was a slow and steady commitment to email marketing. He has a list of 125,000 people and sends out marketing messages daily to keep business flowing. Taylor, 43, built that list gradually after starting his career as a professional keynote speaker in 2017. He'd spent his early career as a professional manager for a number of Grammy Award–winning artists after growing up in a family of musicians (his father and grandfather are jazz musicians), becoming a jazz drummer himself, and marrying an award-winning jazz singer, Alison Burns. After moving to Napa Valley, California, to work as vice president of an online music school business, Taylor began getting invitations to speak at industry conferences. He started saying yes and found he enjoyed getting up on stage. "It felt like coming home to me," he says. "Speaking isn't the same as performing but there are a lot of commonalities about connecting with the audience. There's also a love of being on the road." With a natural talent for speaking, Taylor soon found himself in high demand. "I went from being completely unknown in speaking in 2017 to doing fifty keynotes in twenty-five countries in 2019," he recalls.

By early 2020, when the coronavirus pandemic hit, Taylor generated about 70 percent of his income from in-person speeches for corporate clients. His business took off after he learned that speakers' bureaus arrange 70 percent of better-paying gigs in his field and got accepted to several. This enabled him to bring in $10,000 to $30,000 for a speech. The rest of his income came from events he organizes, such as his International Speakers Summit, a music publishing company he runs with Alison, and SpeakersU, a membership program on how to become a highly compensated global keynote that he introduced in 2018. He also hosts the *SuperCreativity* podcast, which launched in 2016.

That mix changed a bit when the COVID-19 pandemic hit. In February 2020, Taylor was in Riyadh, Saudi Arabia, after doing a talk for a soft-drink company, when the country decided to close the border. He barely made it onto the last flight out. Taylor stopped doing in-person events temporarily after that trip and transitioned to an all-virtual career almost overnight, offering his services as both a speaker and emcee. At his home in Scotland, he set up a studio, equipped with five cameras, elaborate lighting, and green screens, where he could deliver events with the highest level of polish. In some cases, he appeared at virtual events via hologram, Peter Diamandis–style, a trend he believes will be increasingly important. He also embraced technologies such as augmented reality, to add special effects that borrow from the gaming and live events worlds.

A big part of Taylor's success in building a sustainable business has been how he markets himself. Given all the time it took to prepare for his speaking work and to do it, he needed to minimize the time he spent on this to keep his business running efficiently. To that end, he thought about how to apply the 80-20 rule to marketing, asking himself, "What is the lazy way of building a speaking business?"

That question sparked an idea that still guides him. Given that his topic is creativity, he looked online for the top ten creativity speakers, did some research to find out where they were speaking, and then began an email outreach campaign to the same clients and conferences. "The smart thing is to be finding clients who have already booked speakers on exactly the same topic you speak on and who are in the same fee range or a higher fee range," he says.

Using his Ontraport, a customer relationship management software, his team began sending notes from his assistant's email address with a thirty-second promo he'd filmed, saying, "I noticed you've hired X. I'd like to introduce you to James Taylor, a top keynote speaker on creativity and innovation. Click on this video and you'll know if James is your ideal speaker." If they clicked on the video, he'd programmed Ontraport to stop sending emails and would instead send a message saying, "Let's get you time on James's calendar." Typically, about 10 percent of people respond to one of these emails marketing him as a speaker. If they don't respond, Taylor sends them another email with a link to a video. "By the fifth one, I'm talking about Scottish country dancing and its relationship to creativity!" he says. "For some people, that is the only one they respond to."

When Taylor sent his first mailing, one prospect said yes to retaining him right away. She was organizing a conference in the Middle East. She loved the title for his speech—"Creative Places." When asked if he had a video of it, he was glad she was interested but hadn't even written the speech yet. "There was no speech—there was only the title of a speech," he says. "It was a real fake-it-till-you-make-it situation."

That said, he was confident he'd be able to deliver it. "It's brand new," he responded to her. "It's very current."

"What's your fee?" she asked. Fortunately, a good friend had advised him about what to do when anyone inquired about pricing—to pick a high number and then say, "Just pay me whatever you paid last year's keynote."

"My fee is $15,000, but just pay me whatever you paid the speaker last year," he told her.

"We can't afford $15,000, but we paid last year's speaker $10,000," she told him.

To prepare for the $10,000 speaking engagement, Taylor reached out to local Rotary Clubs and asked if he could speak to them for twenty minutes on the same subject as his speech. Taylor found plenty of takers and, though he is a vegan, soon found himself on a "ham salad tour." "I would do ten in a row, sometimes two a day," he says. "I learned what worked, jokes and different things. By the end of that, I had a speech."

Taylor uses email marketing to promote his course and events, too. To engage with prospects who attend one of his free events, such as the International Authors Summit (where I first met him when I spoke there), he might first give them access to a free report, quiz, or infographic if they opt into his e-newsletter. "You might add 10,000 people to your list in the space of a month when you do those summits," he says. "Is that the perfect quality list? Sometimes not, but you know most of these people are interested in the same thing."

Once people subscribe to his e-newsletter, he offers them helpful information and tips on building their speaking career. He also mentions his paid offerings, such as membership in SpeakersU, which has a subscription model where people pay by the month or year. To keep improving his email marketing, he studies great copywriters, like David Ogilvy and Gary Halbert, and others he considers great storytellers.

That's the approach that has grown his list to 125,000 people. Taylor's team now sends out emails once a day, but not to the entire list. He has broken the list into three or four different segments by specific interests and targets them accordingly. "For our brand SpeakersU, on Tuesdays, we'll send out the new podcast episode," he says. "Then maybe two days later, we'll do another email to them about a video I've done." He uses Ontraport to make sure he's not sending emails to people who aren't opening his messages. "If we don't see much movement, we don't send them stuff anymore," he says.

Because videos are Taylor's preferred way of communicating, he develops the main messaging for his marketing communications there, then has his team turn the transcripts into blog posts, articles, and quote cards for

Instagram. His recommendation for anyone looking to market themselves is to understand which medium is most comfortable for them and to use that to build their material. Ask yourself, "Where do you instantly go to get the idea out of your head?" he asks. Once you express the idea there, you can always transform it into material for the other media, he says.

To keep all of these initiatives in motion, Taylor relies on a team of five to six freelancers. When he is getting ready for an online event, this team tackles administrative details, like setting up pre-event calls with clients and creating marketing collateral, for example, graphics and videos. He turns to a photographer in Astoria, New York—thousands of miles away—who specializes in doing virtual photoshoots that look like they were shot on location, for promotional photos. "Technology, when it's done well, should disappear," says Taylor.

Even when he factors in the cost of paying his team, speaking at online events has made his business more profitable. He found that he can do more virtual events in a week than in-person ones, which might require ten hours or more of travel to get there. "Even though, on average, the virtual keynote fee is 30 percent less, you're saving all of that time on travel and can do multiple events in a week," he notes. Although he was planning to return to in-person events when we last spoke, knowing how to build and market his online events business has given him a whole new revenue stream to help his business grow.

TAP THE POWER OF AFFILIATE MARKETING

If you subscribe to any email lists from your favorite influencers or follow them on social media sites, you've probably noticed they promote special offers for their favorite products. If you buy something by clicking on a link they provide or by using a special code, the influencer will get a commission on the sale. This is what is known as "affiliate marketing." And it can work both ways. If you've got a special offer that influencers feel good about promoting and are willing to pay them a commission to share it with their followers, affiliate marketing can be a great way to attract new, like-minded customers. If you want to learn more about affiliate marketing, the online learning site Udemy offers a variety of inexpensive courses that can help you get a taste of how it works. (Warning: This field seems to be a magnet for experts who promise "passive" income that you can make while you're sleeping. We'd all like to make money while curling up under a comforter, but realistically, there is always work involved in getting set up and maintaining the systems you put in place, even when you're doing affiliate marketing.)

Selena Soo, 39, has found that affiliate marketing has been a powerful tool for growing her business, S2 Groupe, a marketing and publicity consultancy that focuses on clients in the small-business space and has a strong representation among those involved in personal development and wellness. The three-person business brings in more than $2 million in revenue annually, through offerings such as Impacting Millions, a course on PR Soo developed, as well as her Impact Accelerator group-coaching program and PR services for select clients. Soo, who lives in Puerto Rico, relies on the help of two full-time employees and around ten contractors, depending on whether she has a big project in the works.

Soo didn't realize it at the time, but she began setting the stage for running the business as a student at Columbia University, when she created the university's first undergraduate conference on women in business. In working on that project, she found she had a knack for attracting high-profile speakers, who included Susan Lyne, chairman of Gilt Groupe; Pattie Sellers, former assistant managing editor of *Fortune* magazine; and television journalist Maria Bartiromo. Soo developed that talent further when she became a senior program manager at the Step Up Women's Network, a nonprofit organization. In that role, she organized professional mentoring events, as well as recruited junior board members who would be involved in fundraising.

Soo's knack for building relationships like these proved valuable in 2012, when she decided to launch S2 Groupe. Even though she wasn't formally trained in PR, she had a natural strength in influencing others and creating connections where both people benefited. When it was time to put up her company's website, she reached out to some of the high-profile media contacts and influencers she had gotten to know for a short, written testimonial. One came from inspirational speaker Danielle LaPorte, author of *White Hot Truth*. The other was life coach Marie Forleo, host of MarieTV. Soo found those testimonials immediately made a difference in attracting clients. "I had that instant credibility," she says.

During the early months of her business, Soo started with her first client paying her on retainer, as many PR firms do. That helped her bring in a steady income, but the relationship was stressful, and she realized it was making her miserable. Still, Soo liked publicity work and didn't want to give up on it entirely.

Fortunately, she realized that there was another way to share her expertise: teaching it. She began planning a two-day workshop in New York City around the theme "Elevate Your Brand," and promoted it on Facebook and to her email list of 150 people—which she'd built after writing a guest post for a major business publication. She charged $600 for the workshop and held it in her home. Seven people signed up for the event in the fall of 2012.

That might seem like a small number, but Soo realized something extremely important to the future growth of her business: She'd earned more in two days than she had in a month working with her retainer client—and, perhaps more important, really enjoyed the interaction with the clients in the workshop. Once she had gotten this proof of concept for her workshop idea, she repeated the event in the spring of 2013 and raised the price to $1,200—finding that demand was still high and she was still able to fill it up.

With the hope of growing her business further, Soo joined a mastermind group run by Monica Shah, a business coach who worked with business coaches, creative professionals, and entrepreneurs. Soo had noticed comments on Facebook from entrepreneurs who belonged to Shah's mastermind group, who posted about bringing in $10,000 or $20,000 a month.

Participating in the mastermind group required a substantial investment, but it helped Soo to expand her thinking about her business and inspired her to create her own six-month mastermind on PR, for which she charged $9,500. She offered one-on-one coaching, meet-the-media events, and group calls. That led to a yearlong mastermind, for which she charged $24,000.

But Soo realized not everyone could afford a high-end mastermind, so she created her first course. She was mentored by Ramit Sethi in his program called Zero to Launch. In the course, he encouraged her to do market research. "You need to validate your course idea," she says. "It's not just talking to friends who say, 'Oh, yeah—that's a good idea.'"

The real test, she learned, is if people are willing to pay for it. Sethi recommended students ask prospects if they would be willing to pay a particular price for a given course, as in "If I sold this for $297, would you be interested in purchasing this?" She paid close attention to their responses. Unless the general response was along the lines of "Please, I want to give you my money," she would not move ahead. In the course of her research, as Soo connected with more of her ideal clients, she listened carefully to what they were saying and what they needed, as Sethi recommended. She was able to develop Get Known, Get Clients, a six-month program to help students attract their ideal clients, based on what she had learned.

A business coach initially advised Soo to keep the program to three months, to set a goal of charging $1,000 for it, and to aim for signing up ten students. But Soo questioned that approach. She would need to put in three months of work ahead of time without a sufficient return on her investment—"$10,000 for six months of really hard work didn't make sense," says Soo.

She trusted her gut and opted for a six-month program, with twelve training sessions she taught live online and an additional Q&A each month. The course also came with scripts and templates to help clients with processes such as sales calls. She charged $3,000. She attracted 50 students—and made $150,000.

Once Soo knew how to create successful courses, she continued to build on her knowledge and ultimately developed her signature course, Impacting Millions, in 2016. Impacting Millions helps entrepreneurs land media coverage and become go-to experts in their industry. It includes seven video training modules, twelve months of live Q&A calls, a private Facebook community, and access to an online membership area. The yearlong course sells for $2,997.

Now that thousands of satisfied customers have taken her courses,

Soo has found that affiliate marketing is particularly helpful in spreading the word. "That's one way we keep our business lean," she says. She pays a 50-percent commission to affiliate partners who run coaching programs, courses, e-newsletters, websites, and other properties if they send her paying customers. She issues affiliate links so she can track their sales. Soo finds that graduates of her mastermind or Impacting Million courses are the ideal affiliates. Those who achieve certain sales benchmarks can win a trip to Tulum for a mastermind retreat. Not surprisingly, there are many takers. In 2021, she has more than 200 affiliates, 70 percent of whom are active promoters.

Because affiliate marketing is so dependent on the efforts of outside partners, many entrepreneurs prefer to use it in conjunction with other marketing efforts. Soo, for her part, has also gotten excellent results from appearing on podcasts, including *Entrepreneurs on Fire* and *Smart Passive Income*. She also found that guest-posting on sites like Positively Positive is extremely helpful in reaching her ideal prospects. "The people there are very into coaching," she says. "There are a lot of coaches, healers, spiritual people there. That is one of the audiences I'm looking to target." A good rule of thumb for those who want to try guest-posting, she says, is to spread the word in places your audience already hangs out. "Publicity for tech entrepreneurs is very different than for solo entrepreneurs and coaches," she says.

Soo also uses Facebook ads, but says she waited to do that until her business began bringing in revenue in the multiple six figures: "They are tricky to figure out. You can spend a lot of money and not get results if you don't know what you are doing."

Fortunately, even if you do make some mistakes, you can learn a lot from them. Ultimately, if you're open to their lessons, they can be a powerful source of the knowledge you need to ultimately build a tiny business that makes big money, as we'll explore in the final chapter.

CHAPTER 8

BECOME A LEARNING MACHINE

When Anthony Coombs founded Splendies, the underwear company you read about in Chapter 2, he knew very little about (a) selling women's lingerie or (b) the market for plus-size clothing. He was a serial entrepreneur who had run businesses in a variety of completely different industries.

But being new to the market didn't stop Coombs from building a successful business. Today, his Los Angeles–based e-commerce business brings in $13 million annually with the help of his team of contractors, and is quite profitable—and on the move. As you'll recall, Coombs was projecting $17–18 million in annual revenue for 2021 when we last spoke.

So how did Coombs go from complete newbie in his industry to the owner of a fast-growing company? Like every entrepreneur you've read about in this book, he became a learning machine, diving into experiences where he could get better and better at running and growing a business—and staying open to the many lessons available to him. He knew that working for himself meant going against the prescribed path in society. And he was willing to put in the time and effort to create a life for himself where he could not only earn a great living, but also live the way he wants. "You're in complete control," he says.

LEARN BY DIVING IN

As Coombs was quick to realize, the world of entrepreneurship rewards action over contemplation. Sometimes, you've got to simply try things and learn on the fly because there's no other way to see if they'll work. Fortunately, there is no penalty for experimenting, as long as what you're selling doesn't hurt anyone and you haven't risked more money than you can afford to lose. The more you can cultivate and hold on to that sense of experimentation as you grow your business, the more likely you are to come across knowledge that will help you achieve greater success later. Many of the entrepreneurs in this book learned how to build their tiny businesses that make big money by starting and running a series of other businesses with varying results. They understood that none of these experiences was ever wasted.

It was embracing this mindset of diving right in that ultimately led Coombs to his success in running Splendies. Coombs was a talented student who earned his BA, magna cum laude, in sociology and urban studies from the University of Pennsylvania. He interned during the summer between his sophomore and junior years for a congressman in Washington, DC, hoping to go into politics. One part of his job was stamping the congressman's signature on a postcard sent to the parents and family of military personnel being deployed overseas. Parents would sometimes write to the legislator with concerns about their children's well-being and try to meet with him in Washington. "There was no way they could ever meet their congressman," Coombs concluded. That was because the politician's schedule was full of meetings with donors. "I became extremely disillusioned with the work I was doing," he says. Coombs gave notice—"It was one of the few things I've quit," he says—and got a job waiting tables. There, he decided to put $1,000 he'd saved into starting a business.

What he learned in school, however, wasn't directly relevant. He needed to acquire a whole new set of practical knowledge, and the only way to do that was by actually trying to start a business. His first attempt was a high-end mosaic-tile import firm, which he founded in 2001 from his off-campus apartment in Philadelphia. Coombs had no special interest in mosaic tiles. He viewed the business as a classroom. "I wanted to learn and teach myself about business," he says. "I wanted to do something I had no interest in, nor any expertise in."

Initially, Coombs tried selling make-your-own-mosaic craft kits. Although he persuaded eight or nine small shops to carry them, they weren't selling rapidly, so he shifted to selling mosaic tiles to crafters on eBay. "It was highly labor-intensive to package all of it into little bags and ship them out." Coombs, then a junior in college, hired a freshman to package up the bags, but after four months, even his helper couldn't take it anymore and quit.

Then, while Coombs was away at a friend's wedding, he got an unexpected call from a woman who wanted to order tile for her pool in Arizona. Coombs had never supplied that kind of tile—or filled that size order. His average sale at the time was in the $15–20 range, and his profit on that was about $7. Coombs phoned his tile supplier in Oregon to see how they could get the tile to this new customer quickly. The postage to ship the tile to his apartment in Philadelphia would have been outrageous, but Coombs didn't want the tile to arrive in a box from another company. "No problem," the supplier told him. "We'll ship it directly." The supplier suggested a "blind" drop shipment, where the name of Coombs's company would appear on the box, an arrangement Coombs had never heard of. Even better, Coombs—who didn't have the money to pay for the tiles up front—would have thirty days to pay for the order. He'd already built a track record of paying on time after seven months of working with the supplier.

The experience brought a massive shift in Coombs's thinking. "We made $2,000 to $3,000 in profit off of two phone calls," Coombs says. He stopped shipping $15 orders and reorganized the business to focus on tiles for pools and backsplashes. Looking back, he says, "The business became very simple and way more profitable." By 2004, a construction company that had noticed the company's growing online presence came knocking, offering to buy the business. Coombs was ready to move on to his next venture and was happy to accept the offer.

That next venture was Ivy Auto Group, an online broker of used vehicles Coombs started in 2004 and ran until 2011. He got in early on the opportunity to sell cars online with that business, but encountered a problem that confounds many an innovative entrepreneur—there's a fine line between having the first-mover advantage and being a bit too early to market. "Selling used cars online was still very new," he says. "People weren't as interested at the time in going online to purchase a used vehicle." Often, Coombs worked from the early morning until the wee hours to keep the business going, and the constant toil was taking a toll on his health. At that pace, he recalls, "I was not going to make it to forty or fifty."

By chance, Coombs ran into an old friend at the airport in 2010. As they chatted about what was going on in their lives, Coombs mentioned the long hours he worked. At his friend's suggestion, Coombs read *The 4-Hour Workweek* by Tim Ferriss. He found Ferriss's ideas about working more efficiently very appealing. There was one problem: Coombs didn't think it was possible to run the online car dealership in anything like four hours a week. Some days he was working so much he was only sleeping four hours a night. "I was essentially on the golden treadmill," he says. "The business was making good money, but I was completely burned out. I felt I could make a lot more doing something else." Finally, in 2011, he called it quits. "I just ended it," he says. "It wasn't something I knew I wanted to continue. I was ready to move on."

Coombs started hunting for a new business he could build around Ferriss's philosophy. His first attempt was to build a mobile app that would allow people to find other individuals in close proximity to interact with—whether for dating, professional networking, or socializing. He launched the app, called Interact, in 2011. It failed that same year. "There were way too many options in the app, and it was way too early to market," he says. "It wasn't focused enough on one niche."

When a cousin mentioned how hard it was to find cute plus-size underwear, Coombs realized that there might be an opportunity to create an e-commerce store that targeted this gap in the marketplace. After doing some research into the industry through "a lot of Google and a lot of YouTube," Coombs came up with the idea for a subscription service where he would send customers three pairs of underwear a month: one would be a fun, limited-edition print; the others would be a sexy pair and a practical set. To build recurring revenue, he decided to sell his monthly subscriptions for an affordable $12—a price that would be accessible to women on average budgets (it's now $14.99).

At that time, women were already buying underwear online, eliminating some of the risks of being early to market. He thought there was a good chance he would be able to get shoppers to take the next step: ordering a subscription that would allow them to purchase several pairs at a time. At the time, subscription box companies were uncommon, but, he reasoned, many women would welcome the convenience of buying three pairs at a time, given that it was hard to find the items they wanted in the store. And, unlike his mobile app business, a women's plus-size underwear business would target a very narrow niche, so there was no risk of trying to become all things to all people and failing at it.

Coombs started the business in 2013, working seventy hours a week during the launch period. It was far from the four-hour workweek, but unavoidable if he wanted to launch quickly. Using $500 in startup capital, he built a simple e-commerce website on Shopify and began buying up inventory from the 99-cent bins at his local mall so he could fill the subscription boxes—a low-cost way to find out what women wanted to buy. "When I started Splendies, it was a blank canvas," he says. "We were throwing stuff on there. No one knew what was going to happen."

To promote the subscription service, Coombs taught himself to use paid Facebook advertising, learning from a $9 video tutorial course he found online. "We market it as a gift to yourself, something fun for yourself," he says. "I was surprised to learn that they can't wait to open it. It's more than just three pairs of underwear to our customers. It's something for people to look forward to, every single month."

During its first year in business, Splendies made $40 its first month—May 2013—and brought in $29,000 in annual revenue. The next year, revenue hit $275,000. "2013 was really about figuring everything out. By 2014, it was an actual business," he explains. By 2015, sales hit $474,000. They rose to nearly $1.5 million in 2016. It was in 2016 that he started online advertising. "That was a big game-changer," says Coombs.

With the average woman in the United States owning twenty-one pairs of underwear, according to one recent survey, Coombs had pulled off a big coup with his customers: selling them thirty-six pairs a year that they looked forward to receiving in the mail. But there was always a risk their dressers would get so full they would stop buying. Coombs made a continuing effort to learn all he could about his customers so he could keep inspiring them to come back. As a man more familiar with the world of boxers and tighty-whities than bikinis and G-strings, Coombs didn't have as much experience with buying women's underwear as his cousin did. So, to get ongoing feedback on what customers liked and who they were, he did surveys using SurveyMonkey, a free software tool, in 2016 and 2018. "A lot of our customers are in places brands don't think about," says Coombs. "We have a lot of people in the Midwest, a lot of people in Alaska, Hawaii, and the South. Our biggest client base is in Manhattan (Kansas!), Davenport, Iowa, and Anchorage, Alaska. Those are people who really enjoy Splendies. It may be a thirty- to-forty-minute drive to go to the store." Many have incomes below $70,000—and get ignored by lingerie brands that target the upscale market, he found.

He also paid attention to organic signs that customers loved the brand. In 2017, for instance, a group of fans started a Splendies Facebook group, without any involvement from the company. That group has grown to about 7,000 women who share what they've purchased with each other there. Another Facebook group made up of women who buy, sell, and trade unused purchases also sprung up. "Sometimes they get a pair they don't like and prefer to get something else," he says.

Over time, Coombs reduced the hours he worked to the point he could sometimes run the company in ten hours a week, automating tasks like his digital marketing. However, with the brand growing rapidly, Coombs started losing control of the schedule that he set out to create for himself and decided to make his first hire, a contractor, in 2016, to help with customer service. "My first hire was a friend of mine," he says.

Seeing how much more he could accomplish with one contractor made Coombs realize that bringing on help was the key to keeping his lifestyle going. After finding that his next hire had experience in running her own business, and that this primed her well for working in a tiny startup,

Streetfighter Strategy
EMBRACE THE GROWTH MENTALITY

As Splendies grew, founder Anthony Coombs found that he had to accept that small financial losses were part of the cost of doing business. For instance, if customers tried to make a return by calling the credit card company instead of his customer service team, he would have to respond to a chargeback from the credit card company. "One day I spent six hours fighting chargebacks," says Coombs. He may have been fighting the good fight, but when that day closed, it dawned on him that the chargebacks were worth about $100 in total—far less than his time. "That's when I realized I don't have six hours to do this," he says.

It was on that day he had an epiphany: It was time to embrace the growth mentality. "The growth mentality is saying, 'We didn't do anything wrong, we shouldn't be out this money, we shouldn't be out this time—but we have to let that go,'" he explains. "'We have to go forward. The six hours we spent fighting this would be better spent growing the business.'"

If you're tempted to prove you're right in an interaction where only a small amount of money is at stake, take a step back and think about how much time it will take, he advises. "In every single business, there comes a shift where you start to see that your time is worth more than every single penny," he says.

Coombs looked for other people who'd had similar experiences. He saw they understood the importance of addressing a complaint from a customer quickly, before the customer jumped on social media and told others not to purchase. "To someone who has run their own business, you don't have to teach that," he says. When Coombs hired team members to help with other tasks, such as social media, influencer marketing, and web development, he sought similar entrepreneurial experience. Often, he'd take stock of how they had set up their websites to get a sense of how much they understood about businesses like his own. Although Coombs communicates with them constantly on a Slack channel, he needs them to operate independently, because they are not all in the same room, and to make smart decisions that fuel the growth of the business.

By staying focused on the big picture of running his business and relying on his team to handle their specialized parts of it, Coombs has freed time and space to work on the aspects of entrepreneurship he enjoys most, like strategy. "Growing the business and seeing the numbers increase, that's fun and interesting. I can do it all day," he says. At one point, for instance, the company had outgrown its shipping partner and had a backlog of 10,000 orders. "It was going to take them at least a week to get everything fulfilled," he says. "That wasn't sufficient for me. I went and rented a storage facility. I rented a truck and some tables and chairs from a party store and found about five people off of Craigslist. I taught them how to package everything. We were able to get 10,000 orders out in two days. That's what entrepreneurship is all about."

Another time, he was at the warehouse all day working. He came back to see the company had a record day of orders and didn't have the inventory to get the orders out. "That wasn't stressful to me," he says. "That was fun. *How do we find a solution to a really cool problem?* That was when I went on a walk and came back with a solution. We would just create a waiting list. People were okay with that."

TAP THE WISDOM OF THE ENTREPRENEURIAL COMMUNITY

Coombs did a lot of his learning through experiments with running a business, but sometimes there are shortcuts to learning. One is turning to programs for entrepreneurs, both university-based and in the private sector. Many universities now offer entrepreneurship education—MBA programs and courses, executive education programs, and business incubators and accelerators—as well as events, such as business plan competitions, where you can learn a great deal about how to run a successful business and meet and learn from other entrepreneurs. Outside of college campuses, there are masterminds for entrepreneurs, online courses, and summits on topics related to entrepreneurship. Plugging in to them, in whichever form works for you, on an ongoing basis can be a great way to keep expanding your knowledge of entrepreneurs and to build a mental database of where to turn if you run into challenges in your business that you don't know how to solve.

That approach worked for Mike Brown and Jay Consalvi, graduates of the US Naval Academy in Annapolis, Maryland, who became entrepreneurs after they met while flying fighter jets for the navy on combat missions in the Persian Gulf. After leaving the military, they got into a different type of high-adrenaline pursuit: investing in oil and gas on land where it hasn't yet been discovered. At Palmares Energy, originally based in Midland, Texas, Brown and Consalvi bought mineral rights from landowners in areas where operators have secured the right to drill a well on a given property. Their goal was to amass many such properties and, ultimately, bundle them into an attractive package to sell to institutional investors. "It's a version of real estate at the end of the day," Brown says.

Investing in oil and gas isn't something you can learn by reading a textbook about it. Like many entrepreneurs who eventually start tiny businesses that make big money, Brown and Consalvi learned how to work in the energy field by doing, initially as employees of a company involved in oil and gas mineral and royalty acquisitions in Midland, Texas, where Brown is from. The president of the firm, who was to become a mentor to Brown, told him, "Right now is the best time in the history of the oil business to be in the oil business." Brown, who took his job in 2011, had soon persuaded Consalvi to join him at the firm. Working together, the two friends learned how to identify properties that were likely to be drilled in the future and to do the financial calculations involved in deal-making. "That's better than an MBA," says Brown.

When they got the itch to start their own business, their former bosses were supportive. They went into business in December 2012. "Those guys were great mentors," says Brown. "They thought the whole pie could get bigger and we could all do this."

As pilots, Brown and Consalvi knew the importance of making their fuel last, and they took that approach to their startup capital, stretching their cash to the max. As they researched and began buying property around the Permian Basin in Texas, they operated from an office in Consalvi's living room, putting up a simple website announcing to the world that they were in business.

They soon began sending direct mail to potential sellers they found in the county records. To acquire property, they would offer a lump-sum payout to a landowner in return for the royalties that would be recouped from the drilling of a successful well. They knew many landowners didn't have the financial means or risk tolerance to bet on a well—there's always a chance that it would be unproductive, known as a "dry hole"—and some would welcome the opportunity to bring on a partner to share the risk.

Brown and Consalvi thought they would be able to start turning around deals in a couple of months, but that was not as simple as they expected in a field swarming with investors. Eventually, they were able to make some smaller purchases, and when they sold them, invest the money back into the company.

Even so, it was not easy to build momentum with limited resources. Each partner had set aside about $40,000 in startup cash, but they needed most of those funds for living expenses. At one point, Brown, who has two children, got down to $2,000 in his checking account, which was scary. "It was a little different from being a twenty-two-year-old crashing on a buddy's couch," he says.

Fortunately, Palmares Energy landed a $1 million deal, bringing in some large investors at a premium so the partners could complete it. That was around Thanksgiving 2013. They sold that property a couple of years later. The company broke $1 million in annual revenue in 2013 and turned a profit. By 2015, when the profitable company had broken into eight-figure revenue, they hired an administrative assistant, and by 2016, had hit $24 million, with three employees, according to Brown. In 2017, Brown and Consalvi moved the company to Golden, Colorado, a city that offered a lifestyle they liked, but continued investing in deals in Texas, as well as Colorado and other parts of the country. After each transaction, they debriefed so that they could do even better the next time.

As it turned out, 2017 was the best year the company had. By then it had grown to five people—Brown, Consalvi, an office manager, and two contractors, with revenue "well into the eight figures," says Brown. As

Streetfighter Strategy
LEARN THROUGH CONSTANT PRACTICE

When they served in the military, Brown and Consalvi learned the importance of briefing, so they could plan for challenging scenarios, and debriefing, so they could learn from situations they navigated together.

"One thing we always did was think through the scenarios at 1G and zero miles an hour, as opposed to 500 miles per hour," Brown says. "If you think you're going to come up with this awesome plan on the flight, that's a great way to get yourself in trouble."

The partners did the same at Palmares Energy, where often five or six other companies were competing for a deal. Anytime they had a big decision ahead, they sat in their "battle chairs" in their office. They walked through every scenario that could happen to come up with a response to each one. "In the heat of battle, you don't have time to think of a response," Brown says. "You're already preprogrammed. That's the only way to stay in a fight in a jet. If A happens, you do B. If B happens, you do C."

After transactions, they debriefed. "You've got to continually try to get better," says Brown. "That's how you . . . survive. You've got to evolve."

The partners learned how important it is to prepare when a friend introduced them to a leader in the oil and gas industry to whom they hoped to market a property. Things seemed to be going well until he asked to see the deal. "He glanced it over, looked up, and said 'Okay, I'll give you X for it,'" recalls Brown. "It was a completely low-ball number. It caught me so off guard I started vomiting information to the guy—telling him what we paid and why I could never accept that."

Their would-be investor smiled and said, "Thanks, we're going to pass on this one," recalls Brown. "My partner and I were completely flabbergasted."

With 20/20 hindsight, Brown recognizes the industry titan was using a common negotiation technique on them—and now doesn't let himself get caught off guard when others use similar tactics. "After that, we practiced the art of negotiating, constantly," he says.

competition from other companies intensified, the company's revenue, which came from flipping properties and appreciation of assets in its portfolio, started declining and margins shrank. Brown and Consalvi tried concentrating on deals in the $50,000 to $5 million niche. But as larger firms ramped up their buying arms, even that space got intensely competitive. By 2019, Brown and Consalvi sold the bulk of the assets of their firm. They paused operations in March 2020 when the price of oil crashed. At that point, they had let go of the office manager and one of the contractors. "My biggest lesson was, you can't ensure growth," says Brown. "You can do things to stay ahead of the market and keep up with trends. By 2018 and 2019, we were optimized and well positioned and got squeezed by a lot of market forces out of our control. That's hard for many entrepreneurs to realize."

As they navigated this crisis and the stress it brought, Brown turned to a business coach. It helped him put what was going on in context. "People with too high an internal locus of control take what is happening to them in their business very personally," he says. "It can become a problem when you are taking full credit for all of your success and for all of your failure. It took me a lot of work with a coach to understand I can look at market forces and detach myself from them. There isn't anything we were doing wrong. It was where the market was heading."

Meanwhile, Brown began doing business coaching. As he learned this new field, he found his way to his next venture, Brute Force, a maker of fitness equipment, such as sandbags, for high-intensity workouts, run by one of his coaching clients. He became CEO in February 2021. "It was clear they needed more help," he says. He ended up buying the company in May 2021.

Brown also began immersing himself in experiences where he could learn about aspects of entrepreneurship that were new to him. One of his best decisions was joining the Baby Bathwater Institute, a private membership group for entrepreneurs that offers events and a mastermind. Many are involved in e-commerce, an area that interested Brown. "I've been learning by osmosis by being around people in this space," he says. "We've started sharing knowledge. We eventually start doing business together. It's inevitable. When you make great friends that are really smart, you start seeing opportunities."

Brown also became a partner and investor in a digital marketing agency. Besides being fun, it came with a side benefit: "I get to learn how to leverage online advertising for e-commerce," he says. That's a great skill to have in his new venture. And fortunately, if he needs more help, he'll know where to turn.

TURN YOUR CUSTOMERS INTO A BRAIN TRUST

When Kish Vasnani, now 36, got fired from his sales job selling software in August 2016, he didn't want to get out of bed. It was the second time he'd lost a sales position under similar circumstances. "I was working for a venture-backed software company," he says. "If you didn't hit your quota or it was a bad month, they fired you. Those types of organizations tend to be very short-sighted."

Rather than jump back into a similar pressure cooker, he decided to go into business with his wife, Vanessa Jeswani, now 34. She'd already ditched her corporate marketing career to run an e-commerce business on Etsy from their tiny New York City apartment, doing digital marketing consulting on the side to help pay her bills. Vasnani quickly arranged to do part-time sales consulting in exchange for health insurance at a friend's marketing agency while they built the company. "I didn't want to have a boss again," Vasnani says. But they had some trepidation. "Definitely, in the beginning, we were very, very scared," says Vasnani. "We didn't know if and when we would be able to support ourselves again fully."

Their e-commerce business morphed into Nomad Lane, a brand that sells travel bags online. In 2020, it generated just under $1 million in annual revenue (earned almost entirely in the first three months of the year, before COVID-19 all but shut down travel), after hitting $3 million in 2019—but was on its way back to growing when we spoke. Embracing their love of travel, Vasnani and Jeswani were living in Miami, Florida, at the time we spoke, after an extended stay in Bali, and had a new baby in May 2021.

The couple managed to build their business to the point it could survive COVID-19 by letting their customers educate them every step of the way. Initially, when Jeswani started the business, she sold a variety of accessories. However, it quickly became clear that her travel-related products—such as pillowcases with travel photos on them, passport holders, and travel pouches—tended to sell best. Once Vasnani joined her in the business, they decided to focus on travel products and to eliminate the rest. From their constant study of entrepreneurship, says Jeswani, "We had learned there were riches in niches." Nomad Lane's growing revenue told them they were on the right track. They brought in about $23,000 in sales in 2016, their first year working together. By year two, they hit about $40,000 in revenue by paring down their merchandise to travel items, like travel socks.

As they gathered confidence that focusing on travel products was the way to go, the couple liquidated Vasnani's 401(k)—which they estimated would cover twelve to fifteen months of frugal living—and began developing a new product, the Bento Bag. It is a unisex travel tote designed to help frequent fliers pack in an organized way and to make the most of the space under an airplane seat.

Both knew the world of frequent travel firsthand. They had met at a Cinco de Mayo party in New York in 2012, just before Vasnani, then a traveling salesman, had to move to Mumbai to fulfill a contract to work there until 2013. Once he relocated, they met each other in both India and the United States, and many destinations in between, until they could reunite in New York.

They also shared some knowledge of the garment industry, picked up through osmosis while growing up. Vasnani's father ran his own men's clothing stores in Atlanta, where the family moved from India when Vasnani was a small boy. "I understood how to sell to people, how to budget, how to forecast," Vasnani says. Jeswani's parents did garment manufacturing in the Philippines, supplying big-box retailers in the United States with children's clothing. "I saw the other side of the business—manufacturing and production," she says.

Nomad Lane's founders extended their $10,000 in initial startup cash

Streetfighter Strategy
SPEED THE LEARNING CURVE BY READING (AND LISTENING!)

To grow their business as quickly as possible, Nomad Lane's founders read approximately fifty books on entrepreneurship to learn how other entrepreneurs built their brands. Among their favorites:

Shoe Dog by Phil Knight

Never Split the Difference by Chris Voss

From Zero to One by Peter Thiel

Principles by Ray Dalio

They also subscribe to newsletters. Two of their favorites:

Lean Luxe (leanluxe.com)—A source of luxury business intelligence.

The Hustle (thehustle.co)—A dispatch on business and tech news.

They're also fans of podcasts on entrepreneurship and industry trends. Their favorites:

How I Built This—Host Guy Raz delves in to the stories behind some of the world's most famous companies.

Glossy—The latest on fashion, luxury, and tech.

Loose Threads—Conversations with the leaders defining the consumer economy.

My First Million—A mashup on the latest business ideas, with a smattering of celebrity guests.

Planet Money—NPR's take on cash, capitalism, and consumerism.

Well Made by Lumi—A look at the people and ideas influencing our consumption patterns.

The James Altucher Show—Altucher, an investor known for his sense of humor, speaks with business luminaries like Ray Dalio, Mark Cuban, and Arianna Huffington.

The Tim Ferriss Show—This one probably needs no explanation, but in case it's new to you, it deconstructs the habits of world-class performers in all areas of their life, so you can borrow from them.

by putting as many charges as they could on credit cards, but paying the bills in full each month. This has allowed them to accumulate millions of credit card rewards points they use to fund purchases, such as flights to their factory and even their date nights. With about twenty credit cards between them, they keep their credit utilization down to 1 to 2 percent, which protects their credit rating, and avoid overspending. "We carefully watch all of our costs, all of our expenses, all of our overhead," says Vasnani. "We've been focused on sustainable profit growth since day one."

With the help of a designer they hired for $400 on the freelance platform Upwork, the couple created a blueprint known as a tech pack for the Bento Bag. They designed it from water-resistant, premium nylon to allow enough room for a fifteen-inch laptop. It also has a built-in phone charger. "We wanted to design something functional but aesthetically pleasing," says Vasnani. "I sit in a lot of business meetings and often when someone walks in with a backpack, they look like they'll be going to the top of the Himalayas after the meeting."

Investing about $3,200 of their savings, the couple found a manufacturer in Asia at a trade show and hired that factory to create a sample. To fund their company's growth, Nomad Lane's founders planned a campaign on the crowdfunding site Indiegogo, intending to raise $15,000. Many entrepreneurs who sell products allow supporters to place preorders for their products, essentially obtaining customer financing for the manufacture.

Three months before they launched the campaign, they started building an email list. They did this by running Facebook ads that targeted people interested in travel bags and keeping in touch by sending them design previews as their idea evolved. Jeswani had experience running Facebook campaigns from her previous corporate marketing job and knew how to manage spending on the platform carefully.

After investing about $1,000 in the ads, they had built a list of about 5,000 people. When they got ready to start their campaign, they sent out a calendar invite for the day of the launch, to remind their contacts of the campaign. Their jaws dropped when, within the first hour, Nomad Lane achieved $20,000 in sales. "The rest was a blur," recalls Vasnani.

Noticing the momentum, Indiegogo's internal team helped the cou-

Streetfighter Strategy
STAY MOTIVATED

One of the most important keys to success in a tiny business is showing up—but staying inspired to do that is hard sometimes. To renew their commitment every day, Nomad Lane's founders took a moment to think about the day's goals and to pump themselves up every morning as they were starting the business. "Our main goal was really to go to bed every night feeling we had accomplished something—a happy customer, a new sale, an Instagram influencer mention," says Vasnani. "Every little victory or accomplishment we had, we celebrated in a big way."

When the entrepreneurs both lived in New York City, they also attended as many entrepreneurial events as possible. One favorite was Founders Friday NYC, where they met many like-minded entrepreneurs. Surrounding themselves with entrepreneurial thinkers reminded them they were not alone when they hit inevitable setbacks, such as manufacturing errors—a problem many direct-to-consumer brands have faced. "We watched and saw how they communicated and how they fixed the problem, so we can learn from them," says Jeswani. There was another benefit, adds Vasnani: "We saw there were other people who had gone through worse. They were able to recover." Once in Florida, they had to improvise when it came to meeting entrepreneurs. Vasnani reached out to fellow members of Entrepreneurs' Organization and joined a cycling group made up of e-commerce business owners. He stays in on Friday nights to get up in time for the rides: 5:00 a.m. on Saturdays.

ple market the campaign and to extend it from June 2018 to March 2019. Expecting to raise $15,000, the duo came away with $2.1 million. With that money included, their revenue hit about $1 million in 2018, they say.

Initially, Nomad Lane's founders priced the Bento Bag at about half of its current $198 price. However, when customers gave them feedback that they were underpricing it, they listened, realizing the business would be more sustainable if they raised it to a price customers suggested it was worth.

With the company growing quickly, Nomad Lane built a team of ten regular contractors and vendors: their designer, their quality control/factory agent, a social media manager, a paid-ad manager, an email-marketing manager, a customer service person, a bookkeeper, an accountant, a web developer, and an outsourced warehouse and shipping partner. They communicate with this team about deliverables using Airtable, a project management tool. They automated several apps connected to Shopify, their e-commerce platform, for tasks such as soliciting customer reviews and feedback. They also automated emails, such as the thank-you emails they send, using their CRM, Klaviyo. To keep track of customer data, they use an e-commerce help-desk software called Gorgias. "If a customer messages us, we can see the whole history of that customer—what they bought, how much they bought, where they live, how they found us," says Vasnani.

By fine-tuning their pricing, Nomad Lane's founders put their revenue on an upward trajectory. The company had grown rapidly during the first three months of 2020, just before COVID-19 hit, with world-travelers snapping up their bags as quickly as they could make them. Then the pandemic hit, and sales fell off a cliff. They hunkered down. Fortunately, notes Vasnani, "We make money faster than we spend it."

During the slow months that followed, they devoted themselves to market research. They started a Zoom call that fans of their bags could subscribe to. About thirty to forty people signed up. "They were business travelers, used to being on a train all the time," says Vasnani. "Now they are all of a sudden sitting at home."

They chatted with the subscribers, mostly women, about travel and their latest business ideas. On those calls, some of the women mentioned they needed a basic black tote bag where things wouldn't disappear into the "black hole." Those conversations led to their latest product, a new Nomad Lane Origami Tote Pack, complete with their signature pockets inside. They launched the bag on Indiegogo in early June 2021, eager to diversify outside of the travel sector, finding it was simpler than they thought to find a way forward. "We just started listening to our customers," says Vasnani.

They had raised $231,534 at the time I finished writing this book, fully funding their campaign.

In the end, no matter what tiny business you run, that's what it's all about— the people you serve. If you are passionate about making their lives better with your product or service and about building a sustainable business that allows you to deliver it to them, you'll be surprised at how the ideas, strategies, resources, and help you need will materialize. There's a magic to running a tiny business that makes big money—and all you need to do to tap in to it is keep showing up, pay attention to what it's teaching you, and keep applying what you're learning. You may not get to your planned destination in the exact time frame you expect, but if you're open to the journey, you'll be surprised at how many gifts it brings you. I'll be rooting for you.

TINY BUSINESSES THAT MAKE BIG MONEY

As you know if you've read my earlier work, I love data. In case you like to geek out on it, too, here is our analysis showing which microbusinesses with up to twenty employees had the most money left over after making payroll. Bear in mind that many of them have substantial overhead.

There is one main chart for all the businesses up to twenty employees, as well as one for businesses with fewer than five employees, five to nine employees, and ten to nineteen employees. How big a team is needed is relevant if you have limited startup funds. Payroll is the biggest cost in many businesses, so if your budget is limited, the list of businesses with fewer than five employees will be most helpful to you, unless you can secure outside financing.

BUSINESS WITH FEWER THAN FIVE EMPLOYEES

Rank	NAICS Code	NAICS Description	Average Receipts Per Firm	Average Payroll Per Firm	Receipts Minus Payroll
1	73210	Casinos (except Casino Hotels)	28,101,667	316,458	27,785,208
2	311512	Creamery Butter Manufacturing	26,257,923	849,538	25,408,385
3	325193	Ethyl Alcohol Manufacturing	10,400,000	172,917	10,227,083
4	622110	General Medical and Surgical Hospitals	12,580,855	3,203,255	9,377,600
5	221112	Fossil Fuel Electric Power Generation	9,431,962	202,346	9,229,615
6	311930	Flavoring Syrup and Concentrate Manufacturing	7,031,860	84,442	6,947,419
7	622	Hospitals	8,934,831	2,267,94	6,666,892
8	311221	Wet Corn Milling	6,486,182	80,545	6,405,636
9	423520	Coal and Other Mineral and Ore Merchant Wholesalers	6,500,569	145,342	6,355,228
10	721120	Casino Hotels	7,054,455	1,230,818	5,823,636
11	551111	Offices of Bank Holding Companies	5,503,940	226,731	5,277,209
12	322130	Paperboard Mills	5,734,500	1,015,833	4,718,667
13	311230	Breakfast Cereal Manufacturing	4,853,368	227,105	4,626,263
14	424720	Petroleum and Petroleum Products Merchant Wholesalers (except Bulk Stations and Terminals)	4,714,142	122,628	4,591,514
15	4247	Petroleum and Petroleum Products Merchant Wholesalers	4,683,795	118,515	4,565,280
16	424710	Petroleum Bulk Stations and Terminals	4,625,051	111,569	4,513,482
17	221122	Electric Power Distribution	4,442,113	131,352	4,310,761
18	22112	Electric Power Transmission, Control, and Distribution	4,258,635	132,152	4,126,483
19	424110	Printing and Writing Paper Merchant Wholesalers	4,150,209	100,620	4,049,589
20	424440	Poultry and Poultry Products Merchant Wholesalers	3,879,931	131,017	3,748,914
21	336992	Military Armored Vehicle, Tank, and Tank Component Manufacturing	4,068,167	575,833	3,492,333

22	424510	Grain and Field Bean Merchant Wholesalers	3,441,178	97,984	3,343,193
23	333618	Other Engine Equipment Manufacturing	3,895,926	573,146	3,322,780
24	211130	Natural Gas Extraction	3,359,975	167,457	3,192,517
25	325110	Petrochemical Manufacturing	3,189,667	180,333	3,009,333
26	424420	Packaged Frozen Food Merchant Wholesalers	3,093,281	107,371	2,985,910
27	441110	New Car Dealers	3,131,379	187,037	2,944,342
28	32519	Other Basic Organic Chemical Manufacturing	3,089,912	184,372	2,905,540
29	31122	Starch and Vegetable Fats and Oils Manufacturing	2,966,400	71,909	2,894,491
30	486990	All Other Pipeline Transportation	2,974,333	99,000	2,875,333
31	4245	Farm Products Raw Material Merchant Wholesalers	2,950,069	92,727	2,857,343
32	311422	Specialty Canning	3,144,270	455,162	2,689,108
33	2211	Electric Power Generation, Transmission, and Distribution	2,832,981	144,230	2,688,750
34	325180	Other Basic Inorganic Chemical Manufacturing	2,899,918	213,820	2,686,098
35	333921	Elevator and Moving Stairway Manufacturing	3,241,733	616,556	2,625,178
36	31151	Dairy Products (except Frozen) Manufacturing	2,694,119	131,069	2,563,049
37	332431	Metal Can Manufacturing	2,635,950	92,900	2,543,050
38	425120	Wholesale Trade Agents and Brokers	2,630,076	97,319	2,532,757
39	4251	Wholesale Electronic Markets and Agents and Brokers	2,601,100	96,999	2,504,100
40	212111	Bituminous Coal and Lignite Surface Mining	2,641,929	158,821	2,483,107
41	3251	Basic Chemical Manufacturing	2,626,645	173,394	2,453,251
42	424520	Livestock Merchant Wholesalers	2,519,146	69,979	2,449,167
43	423110	Automobile and Other Motor Vehicle Merchant Wholesalers	2,420,364	77,668	2,342,695
44	221210	Natural Gas Distribution	2,457,358	134,784	2,322,574
45	424480	Fresh Fruit and Vegetable Merchant Wholesalers	2,381,292	103,882	2,277,410

BUSINESS WITH FEWER THAN FIVE EMPLOYEES continued

Rank	NAICS Code	NAICS Description	Average Receipts Per Firm	Average Payroll Per Firm	Receipts Minus Payroll
46	424590	Other Farm Products Raw Material Merchant Wholesalers	2,377,290	100,832	2,276,458
47	3112	Grain and Oilseed Milling	2,363,607	91,693	2,271,913
48	336120	Heavy-Duty Truck Manufacturing	2,416,000	171,714	2,244,286
49	325199	All Other Basic Organic Chemical Manufacturing	2,414,391	182,191	2,232,200
50	324121	Asphalt Paving Mixture and Block Manufacturing	2,414,598	190,383	2,224,214
51	622210	Psychiatric and Substance Abuse Hospitals	2,641,000	450,363	2,190,636
52	424610	Plastics Materials and Basic Forms and Shapes Merchant Wholesalers	2,291,497	121,925	2,169,573
53	31131	Sugar Manufacturing	2,285,100	197,900	2,087,200
54	424940	Tobacco and Tobacco Products Merchant Wholesalers	2,164,934	79,171	2,085,764
55	311224	Soybean and Other Oilseed Processing	2,149,304	64,696	2,084,609
56	524130	Reinsurance Carriers	2,163,731	149,404	2,014,327
57	424470	Meat and Meat Products Merchant Wholesalers	2,063,064	89,377	1,973,687
58	322291	Sanitary Paper Products Manufacturing	2,079,267	121,533	1,957,733
59	32412	Asphalt Paving, Roofing, and Saturated Materials Manufacturing	2,125,459	168,678	1,956,781
60	311314	Cane Sugar Manufacturing	2,108,000	164,444	1,943,556
61	311225	Fats and Oils Refining and Blending	2,017,619	75,286	1,942,333
62	4235	Metal and Mineral (except Petroleum) Merchant Wholesalers	2,056,309	121,800	1,934,509
63	33361	Engine, Turbine, and Power Transmission Equipment Manufacturing	2,289,188	355,756	1,933,431
64	424910	Farm Supplies Merchant Wholesalers	2,020,322	93,289	1,927,033

65	424460	Fish and Seafood Merchant Wholesalers	1,992,079	83,541	1,908,538
66	522294	Secondary Market Financing	2,014,293	112,561	1,901,732
67	21211	Coal Mining	2,043,581	165,044	1,878,537
68	325194	Cyclic Crude, Intermediate, and Gum and Wood Chemical Manufacturing	2,086,300	223,200	1,863,100
69	221121	Electric Bulk Power Transmission and Control	1,959,765	142,176	1,817,588
70	481211	Nonscheduled Chartered Passenger Air Transportation	1,930,390	134,811	1,795,579
71	332117	Powder Metallurgy Part Manufacturing	2,129,800	344,200	1,785,600
72	4246	Chemical and Allied Products Merchant Wholesalers	1,871,127	118,866	1,752,261
73	3221	Pulp, Paper, and Paperboard Mills	2,078,536	355,143	1,723,393
74	423510	Metal Service Centers and Other Metal Merchant Wholesalers	1,829,061	120,596	1,708,466
75	336510	Railroad Rolling Stock Manufacturing	1,960,667	274,095	1,686,571
76	3241	Petroleum and Coal Products Manufacturing	1,832,017	152,276	1,679,741
77	325520	Adhesive Manufacturing	1,822,856	148,990	1,673,866
78	3115	Dairy Products Manufacturing	1,750,997	95,908	1,655,089
79	311514	Dry, Condensed, and Evaporated Dairy Products Manufacturing	1,765,462	115,115	1,650,346
80	486210	Pipeline Transportation of Natural Gas	1,781,692	151,205	1,630,487
81	423310	Lumber, Plywood, Millwork, and Wood Panel Merchant Wholesalers	1,714,181	97,573	1,616,608
82	311119	Other Animal Food Manufacturing	1,706,913	94,083	1,612,830
83	424690	Other Chemical and Allied Products Merchant Wholesalers	1,726,217	117,811	1,608,405
84	4244	Grocery and Related Products Merchant Wholesalers	1,685,873	82,465	1,603,409
85	311615	Poultry Processing	1,709,852	120,407	1,589,444
86	326140	Polystyrene Foam Products Manufacturing	1,897,304	316,058	1,581,246
87	221115	Wind Electric Power Generation	1,765,979	187,311	1,578,667

BUSINESS WITH FEWER THAN FIVE EMPLOYEES continued

Rank	NAICS Code	NAICS Description	Average Receipts Per Firm	Average Payroll Per Firm	Receipts Minus Payroll
88	22111	Electric Power Generation	1,715,639	153,128	1,562,510
89	711211	Sports Teams and Clubs	1,829,188	274,671	1,554,517
90	212230	Copper, Nickel, Lead, and Zinc Mining	1,689,727	162,818	1,526,909
91	424430	Dairy Products (except Dried or Canned) Merchant Wholesalers	1,606,896	89,857	1,517,038
92	481111	Scheduled Passenger Air Transportation	1,577,504	99,421	1,478,083
93	31111	Animal Food Manufacturing	1,556,884	83,491	1,473,393
94	311211	Flour Milling	1,535,577	78,942	1,456,635
95	325991	Custom Compounding of Purchased Resins	1,590,671	152,89	1,437,776
96	423940	Jewelry, Watch, Precious Stone, and Precious Metal Merchant Wholesalers	1,506,999	80,349	1,426,650
97	7132	Gambling Industries	1,497,590	73,440	1,424,150
98	331492	Secondary Smelting, Refining, and Alloying of Nonferrous Metal (except Copper and Aluminum)	1,538,774	116,000	1,422,774
99	424	Merchant Wholesalers, Nondurable Goods	1,504,314	87,745	1,416,569
100	42	Wholesale Trade	1,502,378	93,196	1,409,181
101	4411	Automobile Dealers	1,486,419	77,516	1,408,903
102	447190	Other Gasoline Stations	1,455,251	55,172	1,400,079
103	424210	Drugs and Druggists' Sundries Merchant Wholesalers	1,493,139	103,772	1,389,367
104	325311	Nitrogenous Fertilizer Manufacturing	1,534,819	150,907	1,383,907
105	4471	Gasoline Stations	1,428,389	48,189	1,380,200
106	4231	Motor Vehicle and Motor Vehicle Parts and Supplies Merchant Wholesalers	1,455,769	77,806	1,377,963
107	447110	Gasoline Stations with Convenience Stores	1,423,202	46,926	1,376,276
108	3361	Motor Vehicle Manufacturing	1,514,752	145,853	1,368,899

109	115111	Cotton Ginning	1,565,957	202,304	1,363,652
110	48121	Nonscheduled Air Transportation	1,482,907	120,254	1,362,653
111	423860	Transportation Equipment and Supplies (except Motor Vehicle) Merchant Wholesalers	1,483,441	124,588	1,358,853
112	561599	All Other Travel Arrangement and Reservation Services	1,457,952	105,600	1,352,352
113	533110	Lessors of Nonfinancial Intangible Assets (except Copyrighted Works)	1,455,001	108,552	1,346,448
114	326160	Plastics Bottle Manufacturing	1,529,091	185,515	1,343,576
115	481	Air Transportation	1,456,102	116,715	1,339,387
116	336112	Light Truck and Utility Vehicle Manufacturing	1,407,417	74,167	1,333,250
117	322211	Corrugated and Solid Fiber Box Manufacturing	1,812,271	480,500	1,331,771
118	322212	Folding Paperboard Box Manufacturing	1,534,500	210,147	1,324,353
119	115115	Farm Labor Contractors and Crew Leaders	1,529,552	206,037	1,323,515
120	324199	All Other Petroleum and Coal Products Manufacturing	1,388,565	73,565	1,315,000
121	312230	Tobacco Manufacturing	1,367,000	58,978	1,308,022
122	423130	Tire and Tube Merchant Wholesalers	1,381,487	76,987	1,304,500
123	327992	Ground or Treated Mineral and Earth Manufacturing	1,555,658	260,579	1,295,079
124	335912	Primary Battery Manufacturing	1,571,476	297,143	1,274,333
125	221116	Geothermal Electric Power Generation	1,610,500	338,500	1,272,000
126	32419	Other Petroleum and Coal Products Manufacturing	1,396,654	129,716	1,266,938
127	325414	Biological Products (except Diagnostic) Manufacturing	1,412,639	159,778	1,252,861
128	813211	Grantmaking Foundations	1,355,159	104,209	1,250,950
129	324191	Petroleum Lubricating Oil and Grease Manufacturing	1,399,862	151,983	1,247,879
130	336360	Motor Vehicle Seating and Interior Trim Manufacturing	1,484,932	239,831	1,245,102
131	483111	Deep Sea Freight Transportation	1,372,362	134,790	1,237,571

BUSINESS WITH FEWER THAN FIVE EMPLOYEES *continued*

Rank	NAICS Code	NAICS Description	Average Receipts Per Firm	Average Payroll Per Firm	Receipts Minus Payroll
132	311111	Dog and Cat Food Manufacturing	1,301,367	65,453	1,235,914
133	423810	Construction and Mining (except Oil Well) Machinery and Equipment Merchant Wholesalers	1,340,800	106,255	1,234,545
134	31121	Flour Milling and Malt Manufacturing	1,304,934	72,158	1,232,776
135	221330	Steam and Air-Conditioning Supply	1,511,400	280,900	1,230,500
136	333120	Construction Machinery Manufacturing	1,393,153	165,973	1,227,180
137	48111	Scheduled Air Transportation	1,324,966	99,401	1,225,565
138	424410	General Line Grocery Merchant Wholesalers	1,294,372	69,282	1,225,091
139	4233	Lumber and Other Construction Materials Merchant Wholesalers	1,318,555	96,745	1,221,809
140	32221	Paperboard Container Manufacturing	1,572,795	353,081	1,219,714
141	33591	Battery Manufacturing	1,470,481	251,574	1,218,907
142	441210	Recreational Vehicle Dealers	1,281,706	78,465	1,203,242
143	311613	Rendering and Meat Byproduct Processing	1,293,733	92,067	1,201,667
144	446110	Pharmacies and Drugstores	1,303,836	115,493	1,188,343
145	335911	Storage Battery Manufacturing	1,406,212	222,576	1,183,636
146	423330	Roofing, Siding, and Insulation Materials Merchant Wholesalers	1,282,730	102,111	1,180,618
147	424130	Industrial and Personal Service Paper Merchant Wholesalers	1,275,586	103,840	1,171,746
148	486	Pipeline Transportation	1,295,978	132,099	1,163,879
149	424450	Confectionery Merchant Wholesalers	1,218,571	58,003	1,160,569
150	33611	Automobile and Light-Duty Motor Vehicle Manufacturing	1,299,682	139,682	1,160,000
151	331315	Aluminum Sheet, Plate, and Foil Manufacturing	1,310,385	152,308	1,158,077

152	532411	Commercial Air, Rail, and Water Transportation Equipment Rental and Leasing	1,270,003	120,945	1,149,058
153	441120	Used Car Dealers	1,201,100	58,520	1,142,580
154	336111	Automobile Manufacturing	1,282,671	150,026	1,132,645
155	424320	Men's and Boys' Clothing and Furnishings Merchant Wholesalers	1,223,088	91,546	1,131,542
156	55111	Management of Companies and Enterprises	1,321,329	189,966	1,131,364
157	424810	Beer and Ale Merchant Wholesalers	1,219,635	93,833	1,125,803
158	335932	Noncurrent-Carrying Wiring Device Manufacturing	1,223,067	106,633	1,116,433
159	313320	Fabric Coating Mills	1,401,075	285,325	1,115,750
160	423620	Household Appliances, Electric Housewares, and Consumer Electronics Merchant Wholesalers	1,202,013	86,886	1,115,127
161	424490	Other Grocery and Related Products Merchant Wholesalers	1,178,858	74,037	1,104,822
162	325212	Synthetic Rubber Manufacturing	1,255,250	151,925	1,103,325
163	4241	Paper and Paper Products Merchant Wholesalers	1,192,859	91,260	1,101,599
164	424330	Women's, Children's, and Infants' Clothing and Accessories Merchant Wholesalers	1,169,038	78,602	1,090,436
165	324122	Asphalt Shingle and Coating Materials Manufacturing	1,173,000	97,176	1,075,824
166	423920	Toy and Hobby Goods and Supplies Merchant Wholesalers	1,161,252	86,462	1,074,790
167	551112	Offices of Other Holding Companies	1,261,007	188,166	1,072,841
168	325120	Industrial Gas Manufacturing	1,192,050	121,100	1,070,950
169	311411	Frozen Fruit, Juice, and Vegetable Manufacturing	1,219,303	149,091	1,070,212
170	4243	Apparel, Piece Goods, and Notions Merchant Wholesalers	1,137,099	82,0312	1,055,067
171	4248	Beer, Wine, and Distilled Alcoholic Beverages Merchant Wholesalers	1,146,738	94,518	1,052,220
172	423730	Warm Air Heating and Air-Conditioning Equipment and Supplies Merchant Wholesalers	1,174,299	126,883	1,047,415

BUSINESS WITH FEWER THAN FIVE EMPLOYEES *continued*

Rank	NAICS Code	NAICS Description	Average Receipts Per Firm	Average Payroll Per Firm	Receipts Minus Payroll
173	221117	Biomass Electric Power Generation	1,243,739	197,957	1,045,783
174	423690	Other Electronic Parts and Equipment Merchant Wholesalers	1,151,041	105,601	1,045,440
175	325613	Surface Active Agent Manufacturing	1,142,065	101,968	1,040,097
176	212112	Bituminous Coal Underground Mining	1,249,111	209,556	1,039,556
177	423930	Recyclable Materials Merchant Wholesalers	1,117,649	80,190	1,037,459
178	424820	Wine and Distilled Alcoholic Beverages Merchant Wholesalers	1,122,253	94,747	1,027,505
179	423	Merchant Wholesalers, Durable Goods	1,120,965	95,170	1,025,795
180	4239	Miscellaneous Durable Goods Merchant Wholesalers	1,102,368	78,95	1,023,412
181	333991	Power-Driven Handtool Manufacturing	1,165,000	143,028	1,021,972
182	325412	Pharmaceutical Preparation Manufacturing	1,183,985	165,677	1,018,308
183	4236	Household Appliances and Electrical and Electronic Goods Merchant Wholesalers	1,121,113	103,958	1,017,155
184	311212	Rice Milling	1,113,000	101,000	1,012,000
185	326220	Rubber and Plastics Hoses and Belting Manufacturing	1,219,702	207,860	1,011,842
186	326150	Urethane and Other Foam Products (except Polystyrene) Manufacturing	1,176,287	164,809	1,011,479
187	325910	Printing Ink Manufacturing	1,200,549	190,608	1,009,941
188	325320	Pesticide and Other Agricultural Chemical Manufacturing	1,113,667	104,293	1,009,373
189	56159	Other Travel Arrangement and Reservation Services	1,100,619	99,131	1,001,488
190	423220	Home Furnishing Merchant Wholesalers	1,091,345	95,731	995,614
191	331110	Iron and Steel Mills and Ferroalloy Manufacturing	1,104,972	109,710	995,262

192	81321	Grantmaking and Giving Services	1,090,100	96,990	993,109
193	423840	Industrial Supplies Merchant Wholesalers	1,101,460	108,718	992,742
194	311511	Fluid Milk Manufacturing	1,096,492	108,770	987,721
195	4249	Miscellaneous Nondurable Goods Merchant Wholesalers	1,062,586	77,077	985,509
196	32521	Resin and Synthetic Rubber Manufacturing	1,114,665	133,568	981,097
197	335220	Major Household Appliance Manufacturing	1,173,571	198,107	975,464
198	483211	Inland Water Freight Transportation	1,141,313	168,190	973,124
199	331314	Secondary Smelting and Alloying of Aluminum	1,109,308	138,615	970,692
200	325620	Toilet Preparation Manufacturing	1,071,984	107,668	964,316

BUSINESS WITH FIVE TO NINE EMPLOYEES

Rank	NAICS Code	NAICS Description	Average Receipts Per Firm	Average Payroll Per Firm	Receipts Minus Payroll
1	424720	Petroleum and Petroleum Products Merchant Wholesalers (except Bulk Stations and Terminals)	29,700,982	447,787	29,253,1945
2	4247	Petroleum and Petroleum Products Merchant Wholesalers	23,072,444	370,256	22,702,189
3	551111	Offices of Bank Holding Companies	21,298,333	569,000	20,729,333
4	424710	Petroleum Bulk Stations and Terminals	18,561,169	316,764	18,244,405
5	423520	Coal and Other Mineral and Ore Merchant Wholesalers	18,678,878	434,796	18,244,082
6	424440	Poultry and Poultry Products Merchant Wholesalers	17,347,574	394,902	16,952,672
7	425110	Business-to-Business Electronic Markets	16,561,083	331,000	16,230,083
8	483111	Deep Sea Freight Transportation	14,499,682	580,409	13,919,273
9	4251	Wholesale Electronic Markets and Agents and Brokers	13,988,690	494,414	13,494,276
10	425120	Wholesale Trade Agents and Brokers	13,944,853	496,839	13,448,015
11	424520	Livestock Merchant Wholesalers	13,710,574	328,138	13,382,436
12	311224	Soybean and Other Oilseed Processing	10,760,000	237,895	10,522,105
13	4245	Farm Products Raw Material Merchant Wholesalers	10,506,762	315,806	10,190,955
14	424510	Grain and Field Bean Merchant Wholesalers	10,360,859	308,259	10,052,600
15	424420	Packaged Frozen Food Merchant Wholesalers	10,368,231	363,138	10,005,092
16	424940	Tobacco and Tobacco Products Merchant Wholesalers	10,231,386	231,350	10,000,036
17	524130	Reinsurance Carriers	9,289,333	859,467	8,429,867
18	424590	Other Farm Products Raw Material Merchant Wholesalers	8,323,481	336,380	7,987,102
19	31122	Starch and Vegetable Fats and Oils Manufacturing	8,185,917	225,083	7,960,833

20	486110	Pipeline Transportation of Crude Oil	8,117,500	643,250	7,474,250
21	311225	Fats and Oils Refining and Blending	7,501,125	244,750	7,256,375
22	424480	Fresh Fruit and Vegetable Merchant Wholesalers	7,527,884	335,206	7,192,678
23	325312	Phosphatic Fertilizer Manufacturing	7,756,000	710,400	7,045,600
24	424110	Printing and Writing Paper Merchant Wholesalers	7,343,260	319,208	7,024,052
25	424460	Fish and Seafood Merchant Wholesalers	6,897,366	283,480	6,613,886
26	423110	Automobile and Other Motor Vehicle Merchant Wholesalers	6,946,447	342,838	6,603,608
27	325194	Cyclic Crude, Intermediate, and Gum and Wood Chemical Manufacturing	6,953,400	351,400	6,602,000
28	331315	Aluminum Sheet, Plate, and Foil Manufacturing	7,481,222	951,111	6,530,111
29	336112	Light Truck and Utility Vehicle Manufacturing	6,736,857	329,571	6,407,286
30	424470	Meat and Meat Products Merchant Wholesalers	6,407,718	310,359	6,097,359
31	4235	Metal and Mineral (except Petroleum) Merchant Wholesalers	6,414,094	416,108	5,997,986
32	424430	Dairy Products (except Dried or Canned) Merchant Wholesalers	6,320,428	330,428	5,990,000
33	4244	Grocery and Related Products Merchant Wholesalers	6,177,072	311,979	5,865,093
34	423940	Jewelry, Watch, Precious Stone, and Precious Metal Merchant Wholesalers	6,182,691	334,494	5,848,197
35	331492	Secondary Smelting, Refining, and Alloying of Nonferrous Metal (except Copper and Aluminum)	6,141,955	346,182	5,795,773
36	212112	Bituminous Coal Underground Mining	6,885,100	1,206,300	5,678,800
37	424610	Plastics Materials and Basic Forms and Shapes Merchant Wholesalers	6,069,408	421,863	5,647,544
38	311512	Creamery Butter Manufacturing	5,904,600	272,400	5,632,200
39	324121	Asphalt Paving Mixture and Block Manufacturing	6,139,986	574,214	5,565,771

BUSINESS WITH FIVE TO NINE EMPLOYEES *continued*

Rank	NAICS Code	NAICS Description	Average Receipts Per Firm	Average Payroll Per Firm	Receipts Minus Payroll
40	423510	Metal Service Centers and Other Metal Merchant Wholesalers	5,939,391	415,385	5,524,006
41	212230	Copper, Nickel, Lead, and Zinc Mining	6,618,667	1,163,833	5,454,833
42	424	Merchant Wholesalers, Nondurable Goods	5,742,251	332,299	5,409,953
43	32412	Asphalt Paving, Roofing, and Saturated Materials Manufacturing	5,920,488	537,884	5,382,605
44	3112	Grain and Oilseed Milling	5,329,107	208,907	5,120,200
45	813211	Grantmaking Foundations	5,450,658	418,833	5,031,825
46	4246	Chemical and Allied Products Merchant Wholesalers	5,347,452	443,472	4,903,980
47	561599	All Other Travel Arrangement and Reservation Services	5,277,548	431,204	4,846,344
48	3241	Petroleum and Coal Products Manufacturing	5,335,561	499,167	4,836,394
49	524114	Direct Health and Medical Insurance Carriers	5,286,660	503,358	4,783,301
50	424210	Drugs and Druggists' Sundries Merchant Wholesalers	5,144,257	396,088	4,748,169
51	325414	Biological Products (except Diagnostic) Manufacturing	5,273,081	562,676	4,710,405
52	42	Wholesale Trade	5,023,488	364,003	4,659,485
53	221210	Natural Gas Distribution	5,124,119	466,186	4,657,932
54	311111	Dog and Cat Food Manufacturing	4,914,615	272,154	4,642,462
55	424910	Farm Supplies Merchant Wholesalers	4,981,614	339,994	4,641,620
56	424690	Other Chemical and Allied Products Merchant Wholesalers	5,076,890	451,570	4,625,320
57	324122	Asphalt Shingle and Coating Materials Manufacturing	4,960,188	378,938	4,581,250
58	486	Pipeline Transportation	5,067,857	545,357	4,522,500
59	423130	Tire and Tube Merchant Wholesalers	4,763,696	281,608	4,482,088

60	423310	Lumber, Plywood, Millwork, and Wood Panel Merchant Wholesalers	4,840,051	366,365	4,473,686
61	311514	Dry, Condensed, and Evaporated Dairy Products Manufacturing	4,765,000	319,583	4,445,417
62	236117	New Housing For-Sale Builders	4,753,527	338,063	4,415,465
63	325311	Nitrogenous Fertilizer Manufacturing	4,851,896	442,517	4,409,379
64	32519	Other Basic Organic Chemical Manufacturing	4,834,667	438,600	4,396,067
65	52411	Direct Life, Health, and Medical Insurance Carriers	4,786,200	410,610	4,375,590
66	551112	Offices of Other Holding Companies	5,253,518	888,069	4,365,449
67	48311	Deep Sea, Coastal, and Great Lakes Water Transportation	4,769,180	436,348	4,332,831
68	236116	New Multifamily Housing Construction (except For-Sale Builders)	4,715,081	382,756	4,332,326
69	486210	Pipeline Transportation of Natural Gas	4,812,462	483,308	4,329,154
70	324199	All Other Petroleum and Coal Products Manufacturing	4,628,778	308,444	4,320,333
71	325320	Pesticide and Other Agricultural Chemical Manufacturing	4,718,696	431,217	4,287,478
72	31111	Animal Food Manufacturing	4,444,274	244,310	4,199,964
73	424820	Wine and Distilled Alcoholic Beverages Merchant Wholesalers	4,536,465	383,380	4,153,085
74	311119	Other Animal Food Manufacturing	4,328,177	237,437	4,090,741
75	441110	New Car Dealers	4,383,077	295,087	4,087,990
76	424490	Other Grocery and Related Products Merchant Wholesalers	4,353,815	302,395	4,051,420
77	334517	Irradiation Apparatus Manufacturing	4,439,8512	406,889	4,032,963
78	327211	Flat Glass Manufacturing	4,495,333	515,333	3,980,000
79	524113	Direct Life Insurance Carriers	4,221,851	306,021	3,915,830
80	424340	Footwear Merchant Wholesalers	4,244,954	332,621	3,912,333
81	423860	Transportation Equipment and Supplies (except Motor Vehicle) Merchant Wholesalers	4,351,526	458,760	3,892,766

BUSINESS WITH FIVE TO NINE EMPLOYEES continued

Rank	NAICS Code	NAICS Description	Average Receipts Per Firm	Average Payroll Per Firm	Receipts Minus Payroll
82	4248	Beer, Wine, and Distilled Alcoholic Beverages Merchant Wholesalers	4,241,002	359,264	3,881,738
83	311911	Roasted Nuts and Peanut Butter Manufacturing	4,058,143	221,821	3,836,321
84	423620	Household Appliances, Electric Housewares, and Consumer Electronics Merchant Wholesalers	4,188,772	363,891	3,824,881
85	524126	Direct Property and Casualty Insurance Carriers	4,072,446	296,079	3,776,367
86	221112	Fossil Fuel Electric Power Generation	4,311,941	601,530	3,710,411
87	424450	Confectionery Merchant Wholesalers	3,997,407	290,032	3,707,375
88	33611	Automobile and Light-Duty Motor Vehicle Manufacturing	3,982,514	305,514	3,677,000
89	32419	Other Petroleum and Coal Products Manufacturing	4,091,267	416,911	3,674,356
90	81321	Grantmaking and Giving Services	4,038,634	380,671	3,657,963
91	211130	Natural Gas Extraction	4,050,632	431,868	3,618,763
92	3251	Basic Chemical Manufacturing	4,053,808	442,308	3,611,500
93	424130	Industrial and Personal Service Paper Merchant Wholesalers	3,937,272	361,088	3,576,185
94	325199	All Other Basic Organic Chemical Manufacturing	3,968,412	442,750	3,525,662
95	331110	Iron and Steel Mills and Ferroalloy Manufacturing	3,857,980	336,294	3,521,686
96	522293	International Trade Financing	3,789,579	273,895	3,515,684
97	324191	Petroleum Lubricating Oil and Grease Manufacturing	3,956,889	444,028	3,512,861
98	4411	Automobile Dealers	3,754,128	247,852	3,506,275
99	424410	General Line Grocery Merchant Wholesalers	3,678,000	221,185	3,456,815
100	33149	Nonferrous Metal (except Copper and Aluminum) Rolling, Drawing, Extruding, and Alloying	3,800,036	360,691	3,439,345
101	312230	Tobacco Manufacturing	3,723,609	287,260	3,436,348

102	4249	Miscellaneous Nondurable Goods Merchant Wholesalers	3,719,861	292,832	3,427,028
103	4233	Lumber and Other Construction Materials Merchant Wholesalers	3,769,746	365,535	3,404,211
104	423330	Roofing, Siding, and Insulation Materials Merchant Wholesalers	3,803,403	414,201	3,389,201
105	4239	Miscellaneous Durable Goods Merchant Wholesalers	3,675,90	303,680	3,372,220
106	3361	Motor Vehicle Manufacturing	3,654,933	293,778	3,361,156
107	4231	Motor Vehicle and Motor Vehicle Parts and Supplies Merchant Wholesalers	3,641,506	290,593	3,350,912
108	424320	Men's and Boys' Clothing and Furnishings Merchant Wholesalers	3,661,259	313,193	3,348,066
109	441120	Used Car Dealers	3,574,234	234,342	3,339,892
110	481211	Nonscheduled Chartered Passenger Air Transportation	3,865,283	550,934	3,314,349
111	424330	Women's, Children's, and Infants' Clothing and Accessories Merchant Wholesalers	3,625,528	311,387	3,314,141
112	4243	Apparel, Piece Goods, and Notions Merchant Wholesalers	3,629,757	317,822	3,311,935
113	423690	Other Electronic Parts and Equipment Merchant Wholesalers	3,661,131	395,3411	3,265,790
114	483	Water Transportation	3,679,595	418,7189	3,260,876
115	55111	Management of Companies and Enterprises	3,896,960	639,070	3,257,890
116	423920	Toy and Hobby Goods and Supplies Merchant Wholesalers	3,574,450	338,156	3,236,294
117	311211	Flour Milling	3,443,391	215,304	3,228,087
118	5241	Insurance Carriers	3,554,660	329,793	3,224,868
119	423810	Construction and Mining (except Oil Well) Machinery and Equipment Merchant Wholesalers	3,608,400	393,984	3,214,416
120	322219	Other Paperboard Container Manufacturing	3,667,889	458,500	3,209,389
121	311613	Rendering and Meat Byproduct Processing	3,563,444	357,556	3,205,889
122	311221	Wet Corn Milling	3,360,444	180,556	3,179,889
123	522110	Commercial Banking	3,720,376	542,408	3,177,967

BUSINESS WITH FIVE TO NINE EMPLOYEES *continued*

Rank	NAICS Code	NAICS Description	Average Receipts Per Firm	Average Payroll Per Firm	Receipts Minus Payroll
124	4241	Paper and Paper Products Merchant Wholesalers	3,502,236	331,633	3,170,602
125	22112	Electric Power Transmission, Control, and Distribution	3,574,098	413,262	3,160,836
126	311930	Flavoring Syrup and Concentrate Manufacturing	3,502,875	345,250	3,157,625
127	3253	Pesticide, Fertilizer, and Other Agricultural Chemical Manufacturing	3,518,956	371,380	3,147,575
128	4236	Household Appliances and Electrical and Electronic Goods Merchant Wholesalers	3,534,548	399,154	3,135,393
129	221122	Electric Power Distribution	3,540,717	407,867	3,132,850
130	447190	Other Gasoline Stations	3,287,898	168,406	3,119,491
131	2111	Oil and Gas Extraction	3,568,393	449,858	3,118,535
132	3314	Nonferrous Metal (except Aluminum) Production and Processing	3,446,369	354,762	3,091,607
133	481111	Scheduled Passenger Air Transportation	3,591,107	503,929	3,087,179
134	424810	Beer and Ale Merchant Wholesalers	3,371,850	288,325	3,083,525
135	31121	Flour Milling and Malt Manufacturing	3,295,222	216,963	3,078,259
136	336340	Motor Vehicle Brake System Manufacturing	3,330,700	268,600	3,062,100
137	423	Merchant Wholesalers, Durable Goods	3,412,492	362,792	3,049,699
138	115111	Cotton Ginning	3,507,581	458,871	3,048,710
139	336111	Automobile Manufacturing	3,339,833	299,900	3,039,933
140	532411	Commercial Air, Rail, and Water Transportation Equipment Rental and Leasing	3,440,076	409,621	3,030,455
141	325130	Synthetic Dye and Pigment Manufacturing	3,439,250	420,900	3,018,350
142	211120	Crude Petroleum Extraction	3,466,737	451,741	3,014,995

143	325211	Plastics Materials and Resin Manufacturing	3,484,478	479,196	3,005,283
144	483211	Inland Water Freight Transportation	3,461,938	463,250	2,998,688
145	48121	Nonscheduled Air Transportation	3,505,186	510,732	2,994,455
146	423220	Home Furnishing Merchant Wholesalers	3,327,815	347,038	2,980,777
147	423430	Computer and Computer Peripheral Equipment and Software Merchant Wholesalers	3,406,071	427,682	2,978,390
148	56159	Other Travel Arrangement and Reservation Services	3,342,117	365,138	2,976,978
149	32521	Resin and Synthetic Rubber Manufacturing	3,433,417	466,000	2,967,417
150	42431	Piece Goods, Notions, and Other Dry Goods Merchant Wholesalers	3,285,085	333,439	2,951,646
151	424310	Piece Goods, Notions, and Other Dry Goods Merchant Wholesalers	3,285,085	333,439	2,951,646
152	481	Air Transportation	3,443,954	494,920	2,949,034
153	523130	Commodity Contracts Dealing	3,649,900	711,471	2,938,429
154	423910	Sporting and Recreational Goods and Supplies Merchant Wholesalers	3,228,113	326,394	2,901,719
155	423410	Photographic Equipment and Supplies Merchant Wholesalers	3,302,880	405,370	2,897,509
156	52412	Direct Insurance (except Life, Health, and Medical) Carriers	3,198,317	302,490	2,895,826
157	3252	Resin, Synthetic Rubber, and Artificial and Synthetic Fibers and Filaments Manufacturing	3,330,246	447,992	2,882,254
158	423840	Industrial Supplies Merchant Wholesalers	3,278,000	399,138	2,878,862
159	4232	Furniture and Home Furnishing Merchant Wholesalers	3,205,740	348,342	2,857,398
160	32531	Fertilizer Manufacturing	3,212,355	356,089	2,856,267
161	325180	Other Basic Inorganic Chemical Manufacturing	3,300,940	453,900	2,847,040
162	423610	Electrical Apparatus and Equipment, Wiring Supplies, and Related Equipment Merchant Wholesalers	3,249,341	409,449	2,839,892
163	2122	Metal Ore Mining	3,613,649	779,243	2,834,405

BUSINESS WITH FIVE TO NINE EMPLOYEES continued

Rank	NAICS Code	NAICS Description	Average Receipts Per Firm	Average Payroll Per Firm	Receipts Minus Payroll
164	325120	Industrial Gas Manufacturing	3,269,273	453,818	2,815,455
165	331420	Copper Rolling, Drawing, Extruding, and Alloying	3,154,818	347,455	2,807,363
166	4471	Gasoline Stations	2,934,037	127,883	2,806,154
167	424990	Other Miscellaneous Nondurable Goods Merchant Wholesalers	3,070,217	283,640	2,786,578
168	332993	Ammunition (except Small Arms) Manufacturing	3,268,000	494,333	2,773,667
169	447110	Gasoline Stations with Convenience Stores	2,878,896	121,847	2,757,049
170	423930	Recyclable Material Merchant Wholesalers	3,020,915	265,619	2,755,296
171	311213	Malt Manufacturing	2,954,333	220,000	2,734,333
172	48111	Scheduled Air Transportation	3,144,600	417,622	2,726,978
173	423730	Warm Air Heating and Air-Conditioning Equipment and Supplies Merchant Wholesalers	3,156,244	433,218	2,723,025
174	325613	Surface Active Agent Manufacturing	3,140,333	437,778	2,702,556
175	423720	Plumbing and Heating Equipment and Supplies (Hydronics) Merchant Wholesalers	3,102,053	399,932	2,702,122
176	423210	Furniture Merchant Wholesalers	3,038,619	349,645	2,688,973
177	453930	Manufactured (Mobile) Home Dealers	2,930,168	262,287	2,667,881
178	325212	Synthetic Rubber Manufacturing	3,006,363	355,636	2,650,727
179	423450	Medical, Dental, and Hospital Equipment and Supplies Merchant Wholesalers	3,065,787	417,828	2,647,959
180	4238	Machinery, Equipment, and Supplies Merchant Wholesalers	3,012,372	380,616	2,631,756
181	441210	Recreational Vehicle Dealers	2,899,547	269,537	2,630,010
182	423390	Other Construction Materials Merchant Wholesalers	2,993,293	377,453	2,615,841
183	236220	Commercial and Institutional Building Construction	2,981,453	371,514	2,609,939

184	321219	Reconstituted Wood Products Manufacturing	2,886,353	282,235	2,604,118
185	446110	Pharmacies and Drugstores	2,882,771	285,297	2,597,475
186	326122	Plastics Pipe and Pipe Fitting Manufacturing	2,893,761	305,405	2,588,357
187	2211	Electric Power Generation, Transmission, and Distribution	3,060,459	472,459	2,588,000
188	335929	Other Communication and Energy Wire Manufacturing	2,920,800	337,680	2,583,120
189	2362	Nonresidential Building Construction	2,943,019	371,493	2,571,526
190	423820	Farm and Garden Machinery and Equipment Merchant Wholesalers	2,849,187	288,348	2,560,839
191	312111	Soft Drink Manufacturing	2,818,850	268,000	2,550,850
192	441222	Boat Dealers	2,824,705	278,466	2,546,239
193	532112	Passenger Car Leasing	2,875,485	330,636	2,544,848
194	423830	Industrial Machinery and Equipment Merchant Wholesalers	2,930,737	399,979	2,530,758
195	335220	Major Household Appliance Manufacturing	2,975,286	452,429	2,522,857
196	325520	Adhesive Manufacturing	2,927,639	412,098	2,515,541
197	33131	Alumina and Aluminum Production and Processing	2,915,111	433,400	2,481,711
198	336360	Motor Vehicle Seating and Interior Trim Manufacturing	2,716,457	261,886	2,454,571
199	32541	Pharmaceutical and Medicine Manufacturing	2,917,479	463,858	2,453,621
200	21211	Coal Mining	2,912,053	475,035	2,437,018

BUSINESS WITH TEN TO NINETEEN EMPLOYEES

Rank	NAICS Code	NAICS Description	Average Receipts Per Firm	Average Payroll Per Firm	Receipts Minus Payroll
1	524130	Reinsurance Carriers	192,077,875	1,266,875	190,811,000
2	423520	Coal and Other Mineral and Ore Merchant Wholesalers	57,511,810	1,035,571	56,476,238
3	336111	Automobile Manufacturing	44,935,529	932,882	44,002,647
4	424720	Petroleum and Petroleum Products Merchant Wholesalers (except Bulk Stations and Terminals)	41,326,515	841,185	40,485,330
5	425110	Business-to-Business Electronic Markets	38,400,900	1,111,775	37,289,125
6	424590	Other Farm Products Raw Material Merchant Wholesalers	38,093,721	890,574	37,203,148
7	33611	Automobile and Light-Duty Motor Vehicle Manufacturing	34,812,167	807,917	34,004,250
8	4251	Wholesale Electronic Markets and Agents and Brokers	31,023,112	1,031,637	29,991,474
9	425120	Wholesale Trade Agents and Brokers	30,851,190	1,029,404	29,821,787
10	4247	Petroleum and Petroleum Products Merchant Wholesalers	28,602,383	751,428	27,850,955
11	221210	Natural Gas Distribution	29,063,241	1,348,517	27,714,724
12	3361	Motor Vehicle Manufacturing	28,439,031	822,813	27,616,219
13	4245	Farm Products Raw Material Merchant Wholesalers	23,373,288	667,218	22,706,069
14	424520	Livestock Merchant Wholesalers	22,284,885	356,197	21,928,689
15	424710	Petroleum Bulk Stations and Terminals	21,714,669	689,467	21,025,202
16	424510	Grain and Field Bean Merchant Wholesalers	21,196,445	681,217	20,515,228
17	324110	Petroleum Refineries	21,389,500	1,486,500	19,903,000
18	522293	International Trade Financing	20,382,600	1,461,400	18,921,200
19	424940	Tobacco and Tobacco Products Merchant Wholesalers	19,144,468	559,942	18,584,526
20	424420	Packaged Frozen Food Merchant Wholesalers	18,510,237	779,363	17,730,874

21	311224	Soybean and Other Oilseed Processing	16,094,091	528,818	15,565,273
22	31122	Starch and Vegetable Fats and Oils Manufacturing	15,894,792	655,042	15,239,750
23	424440	Poultry and Poultry Products Merchant Wholesalers	15,937,980	702,706	15,235,275
24	424480	Fresh Fruit and Vegetable Merchant Wholesalers	14,594,283	754,457	13,839,826
25	331410	Nonferrous Metal (except Aluminum) Smelting and Refining	14,217,412	806,706	13,410,706
26	336992	Military Armored Vehicle, Tank, and Tank Component Manufacturing	14,458,667	1,180,333	13,278,333
27	311512	Creamery Butter Manufacturing	13,542,000	484,750	13,057,250
28	236116	New Multifamily Housing Construction (except For-Sale Builders)	13,869,082	963,066	12,906,016
29	212230	Copper, Nickel, Lead, and Zinc Mining	14,445,833	1,561,000	12,884,833
30	481111	Scheduled Passenger Air Transportation	13,370,407	800,037	12,570,370
31	221122	Electric Power Distribution	13,654,760	1,119,798	12,534,962
32	813211	Grantmaking Foundations	13,353,396	851,216	12,502,180
33	486	Pipeline Transportation	13,989,250	1,679,833	12,309,417
34	424470	Meat and Meat Products Merchant Wholesalers	12,935,789	642,276	12,293,513
35	486210	Pipeline Transportation of Natural Gas	13,833,700	1,794,900	12,038,800
36	311225	Fats and Oils Refining and Blending	12,698,273	732,091	11,966,182
37	423940	Jewelry, Watch, Precious Stone, and Precious Metal Merchant Wholesalers	12,549,539	725,529	11,824,011
38	424690	Other Chemical and Allied Products Merchant Wholesalers	12,624,881	898,676	11,726,205
39	4246	Chemical and Allied Products Merchant Wholesalers	12,433,560	898,218	11,535,341
40	424610	Plastics Materials and Basic Forms and Shapes Merchant Wholesalers	11,908,934	893,937	11,014,997
41	515210	Cable and Other Subscription Programming	11,552,071	704,405	10,847,667

BUSINESS WITH TEN TO NINETEEN EMPLOYEES *continued*

Rank	NAICS Code	NAICS Description	Average Receipts Per Firm	Average Payroll Per Firm	Receipts Minus Payroll
42	48111	Scheduled Air Transportation	11,607,216	782,351	10,824,865
43	4244	Grocery and Related Products Merchant Wholesalers	11,437,215	651,508	10,785,706
44	325193	Ethyl Alcohol Manufacturing	11,317,000	643,000	10,674,000
45	4235	Metal and Mineral (except Petroleum) Merchant Wholesalers	11,519,356	860,647	10,658,708
46	311422	Specialty Canning	10,921,067	399,467	10,521,600
47	5241	Insurance Carriers	11,366,982	873,504	10,493,478
48	424460	Fish and Seafood Merchant Wholesalers	10,836,369	579,594	10,256,774
49	423110	Automobile and Other Motor Vehicle Merchant Wholesalers	10,889,590	658,655	10,230,935
50	424	Merchant Wholesalers, Nondurable Goods	10,799,565	701,639	10,097,926
51	236117	New Housing For-Sale Builders	10,794,915	796,982	9,997,934
52	424430	Dairy Products (except Dried or Canned) Merchant Wholesalers	10,604,036	653,442	9,950,594
53	2211	Electric Power Generation, Transmission, and Distribution	11,017,726	1,163,369	9,854,357
54	3112	Grain and Oilseed Milling	10,471,792	660,688	9,811,104
55	336112	Light Truck and Utility Vehicle Manufacturing	10,226,857	504,429	9,722,429
56	423510	Metal Service Centers and Other Metal Merchant Wholesalers	10,561,180	857,003	9,704,177
57	532411	Commercial Air, Rail, and Water Transportation Equipment Rental and Leasing	10,716,606	1,283,455	9,433,152
58	324122	Asphalt Shingle and Coating Materials Manufacturing	10,150,412	832,059	9,318,353
59	81321	Grantmaking and Giving Services	10,040,463	805,301	9,235,162
60	424410	General Line Grocery Merchant Wholesalers	9,640,440	493,500	9,146,940
61	211130	Natural Gas Extraction	10,106,910	997,761	9,109,149
62	423620	Household Appliances, Electric Housewares, and Consumer Electronics Merchant Wholesalers	9,829,020	844,170	8,984,850

63	2111	Oil and Gas Extraction	10,187,659	1,231,504	8,956,154
64	42	Wholesale Trade	9,634,355	775,070	8,859,285
65	311119	Other Animal Food Manufacturing	9,475,018	643,000	8,832,018
66	211120	Crude Petroleum Extraction	10,072,167	1,266,585	8,805,582
67	524114	Direct Health and Medical Insurance Carriers	9,699,023	911,682	8,787,341
68	483111	Deep Sea Freight Transportation	9,473,813	795,500	8,678,313
69	441110	New Car Dealers	9,229,814	601,759	8,628,055
70	52411	Direct Life, Health, and Medical Insurance Carriers	9,460,969	848,469	8,612,500
71	423690	Other Electronic Parts and Equipment Merchant Wholesalers	9,498,856	898,704	8,600,152
72	424910	Farm Supplies Merchant Wholesalers	9,273,399	702,519	8,570,880
73	32412	Asphalt Paving, Roofing, and Saturated Materials Manufacturing	9,515,618	960,294	8,555,324
74	424210	Drugs and Druggists' Sundries Merchant Wholesalers	9,331,456	858,475	8,472,981
75	331420	Copper Rolling, Drawing, Extruding, and Alloying	9,170,727	713,364	8,457,364
76	336120	Heavy-Duty Truck Manufacturing	9,319,625	867,500	8,452,125
77	325110	Petrochemical Manufacturing	10,596,500	2,215,250	8,381,250
78	325320	Pesticide and Other Agricultural Chemical Manufacturing	9,323,722	942,889	8,380,833
79	31111	Animal Food Manufacturing	8,977,428	617,096	8,360,332
80	324121	Asphalt Paving Mixture and Block Manufacturing	9,304,020	1,003,039	8,300,980
81	524113	Direct Life Insurance Carriers	8,937,250	709,400	8,227,850
82	311211	Flour Milling	8,783,844	625,125	8,158,719
83	115111	Cotton Ginning	8,927,135	774,514	8,152,622
84	533110	Lessors of Nonfinancial Intangible Assets (except Copyrighted Works)	9,040,895	941,025	8,099,869
85	423920	Toy and Hobby Goods and Supplies Merchant Wholesalers	8,775,308	714,210	8,061,098
86	311212	Rice Milling	8,900,846	914,846	7,986,000

BUSINESS WITH TEN TO NINETEEN EMPLOYEES *continued*

Rank	NAICS Code	NAICS Description	Average Receipts Per Firm	Average Payroll Per Firm	Receipts Minus Payroll
87	31121	Flour Milling and Malt Manufacturing	8,636,543	700,435	7,936,109
88	3241	Petroleum and Coal Products Manufacturing	8,914,547	1,012,496	7,902,051
89	524126	Direct Property and Casualty Insurance Carriers	8,780,506	957,047	7,823,459
90	523110	Investment Banking and Securities Dealing	10,383,085	2,590,644	7,792,441
91	325412	Pharmaceutical Preparation Manufacturing	9,072,607	1,350,321	7,722,286
92	424110	Printing and Writing Paper Merchant Wholesalers	8,511,159	796,174	7,714,986
93	312111	Soft Drink Manufacturing	8,314,118	621,735	7,692,382
94	423330	Roofing, Siding, and Insulation Materials Merchant Wholesalers	8,530,566	857,762	7,672,803
95	532112	Passenger Car Leasing	8,455,030	844,333	7,610,697
96	4411	Automobile Dealers	8,079,196	560,231	7,518,965
97	483114	Coastal and Great Lakes Passenger Transportation	8,588,714	1,103,786	7,484,929
98	424490	Other Grocery and Related Products Merchant Wholesalers	8,109,913	625,050	7,484,863
99	4236	Household Appliances and Electrical and Electronic Goods Merchant Wholesalers	8,345,746	888,985	7,456,761
100	423310	Lumber, Plywood, Millwork, and Wood Panel Merchant Wholesalers	8,190,486	749,713	7,440,773
101	221	Utilities	8,288,282	877,908	7,410,374
102	424340	Footwear Merchant Wholesalers	8,072,284	663,664	7,408,619
103	3314	Nonferrous Metal (except Aluminum) Production and Processing	8,141,691	741,064	7,400,628
104	331492	Secondary Smelting, Refining, and Alloying of Nonferrous Metal (except Copper and Aluminum)	8,192,609	898,609	7,294,000
105	561599	All Other Travel Arrangement and Reservation Services	7,967,612	736,713	7,230,899

106	424130	Industrial and Personal Service Paper Merchant Wholesalers	8,056,856	829,906	7,226,950
107	423430	Computer and Computer Peripheral Equipment and Software Merchant Wholesalers	8,156,726	1,008,353	7,148,372
108	311514	Dry, Condensed, and Evaporated Dairy Products Manufacturing	7,703,100	608,900	7,094,200
109	423130	Tire and Tube Merchant Wholesalers	7,709,864	652,891	7,056,973
110	324199	All Other Petroleum and Coal Products Manufacturing	7,797,200	896,000	6,901,200
111	325414	Biological Products (except Diagnostic) Manufacturing	7,927,296	1,084,630	6,842,667
112	312230	Tobacco Manufacturing	7,290,846	462,000	6,828,846
113	423860	Transportation Equipment and Supplies (except Motor Vehicle) Merchant Wholesalers	7,761,764	941,692	6,820,072
114	4239	Miscellaneous Durable Goods Merchant Wholesalers	7,413,312	661,794	6,751,518
115	424450	Confectionery Merchant Wholesalers	7,066,304	509,619	6,556,686
116	562213	Solid Waste Combustors and Incinerators	7,409,250	857,000	6,552,250
117	424310	Piece Goods, Notions, and Other Dry Goods Merchant Wholesalers	7,220,942	678,354	6,542,588
118	311911	Roasted Nuts and Peanut Butter Manufacturing	6,940,133	410,833	6,529,300
119	441120	Used Car Dealers	7,051,145	522,083	6,529,062
120	423930	Recyclable Material Merchant Wholesalers	7,097,608	611,581	6,486,027
121	525990	Other Financial Vehicles	9,147,957	2,681,261	6,466,696
122	325212	Synthetic Rubber Manufacturing	7,273,846	838,308	6,435,538
123	4243	Apparel, Piece Goods, and Notions Merchant Wholesalers	6,983,461	663,051	6,320,410
124	311111	Dog and Cat Food Manufacturing	6,821,205	504,846	6,316,359
125	424820	Wine and Distilled Alcoholic Beverages Merchant Wholesalers	7,107,813	796,034	6,311,779
126	4249	Miscellaneous Nondurable Goods Merchant Wholesalers	6,927,998	624,476	6,303,522

BUSINESS WITH TEN TO NINETEEN EMPLOYEES *continued*

Rank	NAICS Code	NAICS Description	Average Receipts Per Firm	Average Payroll Per Firm	Receipts Minus Payroll
127	423730	Warm Air Heating and Air-Conditioning Equipment and Supplies Merchant Wholesalers	7,223,564	959,108	6,264,456
128	236220	Commercial and Institutional Building Construction	7,091,836	847,768	6,244,068
129	523130	Commodity Contracts Dealing	7,380,692	1,139,769	6,240,923
130	423	Merchant Wholesalers, Durable Goods	6,989,665	785,990	6,203,675
131	212393	Other Chemical and Fertilizer Mineral Mining	7,459,200	1,260,400	6,198,800
132	424320	Men's and Boys' Clothing and Furnishings Merchant Wholesalers	6,841,104	649,093	6,192,011
133	311411	Frozen Fruit, Juice, and Vegetable Manufacturing	6,954,941	800,882	6,154,059
134	221112	Fossil Fuel Electric Power Generation	7,061,526	932,789	6,128,737
135	4231	Motor Vehicle and Motor Vehicle Parts and Supplies Merchant Wholesalers	6,731,706	611,698	6,120,008
136	2362	Nonresidential Building Construction	6,959,793	845,455	6,114,338
137	481112	Scheduled Freight Air Transportation	6,846,600	734,600	6,112,000
138	423810	Construction and Mining (except Oil Well) Machinery and Equipment Merchant Wholesalers	6,905,599	808,430	6,097,169
139	4248	Beer, Wine, and Distilled Alcoholic Beverages Merchant Wholesalers	6,816,757	723,781	6,092,976
140	423210	Furniture Merchant Wholesalers	6,840,139	750,647	6,089,492
141	32519	Other Basic Organic Chemical Manufacturing	6,893,779	821,116	6,072,663
142	3253	Pesticide, Fertilizer, and Other Agricultural Chemical Manufacturing	6,856,745	785,266	6,071,479
143	424330	Women's, Children's, and Infants' Clothing and Accessories Merchant Wholesalers	6,731,297	660,709	6,070,588

144	4233	Lumber and Other Construction Materials Merchant Wholesalers	6,794,762	743,333	6,051,429
145	4232	Furniture and Home Furnishing Merchant Wholesalers	6,747,641	738,697	6,008,944
146	332913	Plumbing Fixture Fitting and Trim Manufacturing	6,733,000	724,800	6,008,200
147	325199	All Other Basic Organic Chemical Manufacturing	6,824,909	858,156	5,966,754
148	423720	Plumbing and Heating Equipment and Supplies (Hydronics) Merchant Wholesalers	6,836,773	883,775	5,952,997
149	331221	Rolled Steel Shape Manufacturing	6,649,591	704,182	5,945,409
150	423220	Home Furnishing Merchant Wholesalers	6,667,320	728,487	5,938,832
151	423610	Electrical Apparatus and Equipment, Wiring Supplies, and Related Equipment Merchant Wholesalers	6,766,659	881,981	5,884,679
152	221330	Steam and Air-Conditioning Supply	7,021,000	1,136,500	5,884,500
153	423840	Industrial Supplies Merchant Wholesalers	6,729,115	853,747	5,875,368
154	3251	Basic Chemical Manufacturing	6,744,213	894,426	5,849,787
155	32419	Other Petroleum and Coal Products Manufacturing	6,897,378	1,049,244	5,848,133
156	114111	Finfish Fishing	6,780,727	1,006,455	5,774,273
157	4241	Paper and Paper Products Merchant Wholesalers	6,498,302	742,765	5,755,536
158	333912	Air and Gas Compressor Manufacturing	6,489,947	737,263	5,752,684
159	424810	Beer and Ale Merchant Wholesalers	6,341,771	605,868	5,735,903
160	324191	Petroleum Lubricating Oil and Grease Manufacturing	6,784,900	1,068,400	5,716,500
161	335991	Carbon and Graphite Products Manufacturing	6,442,250	774,500	5,667,750
162	32541	Pharmaceutical and Medicine Manufacturing	6,740,000	1,076,633	5,663,367
163	441210	Recreational Vehicle Dealers	6,257,582	601,819	5,655,764
164	325314	Fertilizer (Mixing Only) Manufacturing	6,417,018	765,429	5,651,589

BUSINESS WITH TEN TO NINETEEN EMPLOYEES *continued*

Rank	NAICS Code	NAICS Description	Average Receipts Per Firm	Average Payroll Per Firm	Receipts Minus Payroll
165	325130	Synthetic Dye and Pigment Manufacturing	6,579,625	978,125	5,601,500
166	423820	Farm and Garden Machinery and Equipment Merchant Wholesalers	6,224,006	641,193	5,582,812
167	523910	Miscellaneous Intermediation	8,040,614	2,477,801	5,562,812
168	52412	Direct Insurance (except Life, Health, and Medical) Carriers	6,422,281	864,548	5,557,733
169	221115	Wind Electric Power Generation	6,950,231	1,397,385	5,552,846
170	31151	Dairy Products (except Frozen) Manufacturing	6,045,300	499,600	5,545,700
171	3221	Pulp, Paper, and Paperboard Mills	6,306,333	764,778	5,541,556
172	32531	Fertilizer Manufacturing	6,272,460	747,934	5,524,526
173	33131	Alumina and Aluminum Production and Processing	6,097,097	591,677	5,505,419
174	447190	Other Gasoline Stations	5,844,043	346,368	5,497,674
175	813219	Other Grantmaking and Giving Services	6,129,963	668,814	5,461,149
176	311930	Flavoring Syrup and Concentrate Manufacturing	6,153,696	715,173	5,438,521
177	525	Funds, Trusts, and Other Financial Vehicles	7,877,167	2,441,800	5,435,367
178	5259	Other Investment Pools and Funds	7,877,167	2,441,800	5,435,366
179	48311	Deep Sea, Coastal, and Great Lakes Water Transportation	6,462,560	1,028,849	5,433,712
180	11411	Fishing	6,375,935	973,871	5,402,064
181	423450	Medical, Dental, and Hospital Equipment and Supplies Merchant Wholesalers	6,283,095	889,485	5,393,609
182	325620	Toilet Preparation Manufacturing	6,043,148	676,528	5,366,620
183	4238	Machinery, Equipment, and Supplies Merchant Wholesalers	6,170,443	813,297	5,357,145
184	212111	Bituminous Coal and Lignite Surface Mining	6,053,229	742,114	5,311,114
185	4237	Hardware, and Plumbing and Heating Equipment and Supplies Merchant Wholesalers	6,156,677	856,318	5,300,359

186	423410	Photographic Equipment and Supplies Merchant Wholesalers	6,038,038	763,582	5,274,456
187	423910	Sporting and Recreational Goods and Supplies Merchant Wholesalers	5,929,992	680,745	5,249,247
188	5231	Securities and Commodity Contracts Intermediation and Brokerage	7,129,955	1,885,875	5,244,080
189	441222	Boat Dealers	5,844,150	603,970	5,240,179
190	336360	Motor Vehicle Seating and Interior Trim Manufacturing	5,799,725	568,850	5,230,875
191	332431	Metal Can Manufacturing	5,838,600	610,800	5,227,800
192	325180	Other Basic Inorganic Chemical Manufacturing	6,106,200	884,686	5,221,514
193	481212	Nonscheduled Chartered Freight Air Transportation	5,934,333	736,333	5,198,000
194	325120	Industrial Gas Manufacturing	6,166,125	981,000	5,185,125
195	22111	Electric Power Generation	6,366,984	1,201,905	5,165,079
196	423830	Industrial Machinery and Equipment Merchant Wholesalers	6,001,958	861,467	5,140,491
197	325991	Custom Compounding of Purchased Resins	5,759,929	626,321	5,133,607
198	33149	Nonferrous Metal (except Copper and Aluminum) Rolling, Drawing, Extruding, and Alloying	5,852,127	731,855	5,120,273
199	311513	Cheese Manufacturing	5,575,221	462,014	5,113,206
200	4234	Professional and Commercial Equipment and Supplies Merchant Wholesalers	5,935,594	852,718	5,082,876

BUSINESS WITH FEWER THAN TWENTY EMPLOYEES

Rank	NAICS Code	NAICS Description	Average Receipts Per Firm	Average Payroll Per Firm	Receipts Minus Payroll
1	524130	Reinsurance Carriers	23,846,360	410,613	23,435,747
2	311512	Creamery Butter Manufacturing	19,320,182	652,045	18,668,136
3	713210	Casinos (except Casino Hotels)	18,026,500	274,737	17,751,763
4	424720	Petroleum and Petroleum Products Merchant Wholesalers (except Bulk Stations and Terminals)	15,566,483	301,071	15,265,411
5	4247	Petroleum and Petroleum Products Merchant Wholesalers	14,967,239	329,340	14,637,900
6	424710	Petroleum Bulk Stations and Terminals	14,225,742	353,452	13,872,290
7	423520	Coal and Other Mineral and Ore Merchant Wholesalers	13,816,241	289,544	13,526,697
8	325193	Ethyl Alcohol Manufacturing	12,669,389	315,444	12,353,944
9	424510	Grain and Field Bean Merchant Wholesalers	9,526,479	293,180	9,233,299
10	424440	Poultry and Poultry Products Merchant Wholesalers	8,902,612	289,245	8,613,367
11	221210	Natural Gas Distribution	8,874,264	474,215	8,400,049
12	4245	Farm Products Raw Material Merchant Wholesalers	8,556,689	252,957	8,303,732
13	324110	Petroleum Refineries	8,924,091	637,364	8,286,727
14	311224	Soybean and Other Oilseed Processing	8,130,358	223,113	7,907,245
15	336111	Automobile Manufacturing	7,817,740	294,780	7,522,959
16	311221	Wet Corn Milling	7,561,409	198,273	7,363,136
17	622110	General Medical and Surgical Hospitals	9,653,273	2,404,597	7,248,675
18	33611	Automobile and Light-Duty Motor Vehicle Manufacturing	7,363,872	288,497	7,075,376
19	31122	Starch and Vegetable Fats and Oils Manufacturing	7,298,435	241,557	7,056,878
20	424520	Livestock Merchant Wholesalers	7,117,322	154,961	6,962,360
21	424590	Other Farm Products Raw Material Merchant Wholesalers	7,102,400	224,137	6,878,263

22	424420	Packaged Frozen Food Merchant Wholesalers	7,113,282	269,523	6,843,758
23	221112	Fossil Fuel Electric Power Generation	7,301,661	535,645	6,766,016
24	424940	Tobacco and Tobacco Products Merchant Wholesalers	6,717,034	191,608	6,525,426
25	221122	Electric Power Distribution	6,840,074	448,034	6,392,040
26	3361	Motor Vehicle Manufacturing	6,664,672	298,108	6,366,565
27	22112	Electric Power Transmission, Control, and Distribution	6,668,423	441,637	6,226,786
28	336992	Military Armored Vehicle, Tank, and Tank Component Manufacturing	6,919,000	710,900	6,208,100
29	325110	Petrochemical Manufacturing	7,422,143	1,343,143	6,079,000
30	551111	Offices of Bank Holding Companies	6,276,908	279,655	5,997,252
31	311930	Flavoring Syrup and Concentrate Manufacturing	6,096,963	312,244	5,784,720
32	311225	Fats and Oils Refining and Blending	6,051,500	289,800	5,761,700
33	212230	Copper, Nickel, Lead, and Zinc Mining	6,303,217	788,696	5,514,522
34	424480	Fresh Fruit and Vegetable Merchant Wholesalers	5,734,506	272,737	5,461,769
35	322130	Paperboard Mills	6,336,429	958,000	5,378,429
36	311212	Rice Milling	5,924,381	611,714	5,312,667
37	622	Hospitals	7,108,850	1,812,973	5,295,876
38	424470	Meat and Meat Products Merchant Wholesalers	5,477,243	263,006	5,214,238
39	425120	Wholesale Trade Agents and Brokers	5,368,505	190,563	5,177,942
40	4251	Wholesale Electronic Markets and Agents and Brokers	5,359,770	190,198	5,169,572
41	424110	Printing and Writing Paper Merchant Wholesalers	5,400,082	242,549	5,157,533
42	523210	Securities and Commodity Exchanges	5,907,200	892,600	5,014,600
43	336112	Light Truck and Utility Vehicle Manufacturing	5,216,731	258,769	4,957,962
44	325312	Phosphatic Fertilizer Manufacturing	5,441,909	536,182	4,905,727

BUSINESS WITH FEWER THAN TWENTY EMPLOYEES *continued*

Rank	NAICS Code	NAICS Description	Average Receipts Per Firm	Average Payroll Per Firm	Receipts Minus Payroll
45	3112	Grain and Oilseed Milling	5,167,391	265,877	4,901,513
46	441110	New Car Dealers	5,087,967	324,496	4,763,471
47	425110	Business-to-Business Electronic Markets	4,833,863	168,452	4,665,412
48	311119	Other Animal Food Manufacturing	4,875,664	305,857	4,569,807
49	324121	Asphalt Paving Mixture and Block Manufacturing	5,041,798	483,575	4,558,223
50	4235	Metal and Mineral (except Petroleum) Merchant Wholesalers	4,822,396	326,966	4,495,431
51	32412	Asphalt Paving, Roofing, and Saturated Materials Manufacturing	4,888,470	453,950	4,434,520
52	424610	Plastics Materials and Basic Forms and Shapes Merchant Wholesalers	4,677,849	312,746	4,365,103
53	32519	Other Basic Organic Chemical Manufacturing	4,626,789	432,114	4,194,675
54	211130	Natural Gas Extraction	4,511,341	353,516	4,157,824
55	2211	Electric Power Generation, Transmission, and Distribution	4,554,195	403,444	4,150,751
56	721120	Casino Hotels	4,981,889	869,611	4,112,278
57	423510	Metal Service Centers and Other Metal Merchant Wholesalers	4,440,108	328,556	4,111,551
58	31111	Animal Food Manufacturing	4,369,519	273,466	4,096,053
59	331314	Secondary Smelting and Alloying of Aluminum	4,297,000	233,474	4,063,526
60	3241	Petroleum and Coal Products Manufacturing	4,516,266	456,715	4,059,551
61	311422	Specialty Canning	4,462,551	404,913	4,057,638
62	483111	Deep Sea Freight Transportation	4,298,406	277,273	4,021,133
63	324122	Asphalt Shingle and Coating Materials Manufacturing	4,355,254	350,925	4,004,328
64	423110	Automobile and Other Motor Vehicle Merchant Wholesalers	4,191,950	191,951	3,999,999
65	331410	Nonferrous Metal (except Aluminum) Smelting and Refining	4,223,474	306,921	3,916,553

66	424460	Fish and Seafood Merchant Wholesalers	4,090,767	187,343	3,903,424
67	4246	Chemical and Allied Products Merchant Wholesalers	4,195,390	304,986	3,890,403
68	486210	Pipeline Transportation of Natural Gas	4,361,048	485,952	3,875,097
69	311211	Flour Milling	4,113,374	271,598	3,841,776
70	331420	Copper Rolling, Drawing, Extruding, and Alloying	4,158,603	346,968	3,811,635
71	331315	Aluminum Sheet, Plate, and Foil Manufacturing	4,300,935	496,903	3,804,032
72	331492	Secondary Smelting, Refining, and Alloying of Nonferrous Metal (except Copper and Aluminum)	4,133,755	351,347	3,782,408
73	424430	Dairy Products (except Dried or Canned) Merchant Wholesalers	3,965,496	225,123	3,740,373
74	4244	Grocery and Related Products Merchant Wholesalers	3,948,143	208,311	3,739,831
75	424690	Other Chemical and Allied Products Merchant Wholesalers	4,021,454	302,141	3,719,313
76	325199	All Other Basic Organic Chemical Manufacturing	4,127,019	450,527	3,676,492
77	3251	Basic Chemical Manufacturing	4,092,365	435,467	3,656,898
78	31121	Flour Milling and Malt Manufacturing	3,929,040	292,362	3,636,678
79	325194	Cyclic Crude, Intermediate, and Gum and Wood Chemical Manufacturing	3,885,450	297,750	3,587,700
80	424910	Farm Supplies Merchant Wholesalers	3,807,585	242,959	3,564,626
81	336120	Heavy-Duty Truck Manufacturing	3,848,973	336,811	3,512,162
82	311514	Dry, Condensed, and Evaporated Dairy Products Manufacturing	3,752,354	269,104	3,483,250
83	115111	Cotton Ginning	3,903,720	423,012	3,480,708
84	424	Merchant Wholesalers, Nondurable Goods	3,632,229	221,3356	3,410,899
85	325180	Other Basic Inorganic Chemical Manufacturing	3,805,884	456,863	3,349,021
86	311230	Breakfast Cereal Manufacturing	3,573,816	235,632	3,338,184
87	423310	Lumber, Plywood, Millwork, and Wood Panel Merchant Wholesalers	3,601,126	277,527	3,323,598

BUSINESS WITH FEWER THAN TWENTY EMPLOYEES continued

Rank	NAICS Code	NAICS Description	Average Receipts Per Firm	Average Payroll Per Firm	Receipts Minus Payroll
88	481111	Scheduled Passenger Air Transportation	3,571,064	260,287	3,310,777
89	325414	Biological Products (except Diagnostic) Manufacturing	3,756,257	453,000	3,303,257
90	31151	Dairy Products (except Frozen) Manufacturing	3,502,295	243,211	3,259,084
91	324191	Petroleum Lubricating Oil and Grease Manufacturing	3,694,299	504,000	3,190,299
92	311911	Roasted Nuts and Peanut Butter Manufacturing	3,383,148	208,102	3,175,046
93	221121	Electric Bulk Power Transmission and Control	3,432,800	321,050	3,111,750
94	32419	Other Petroleum and Coal Products Manufacturing	3,553,322	447,275	3,106,047
95	486110	Pipeline Transportation of Crude Oil	3,333,171	292,200	3,040,971
96	212393	Other Chemical and Fertilizer Mineral Mining	3,664,538	630,538	3,034,000
97	42	Wholesale Trade	3,268,475	236,602	3,031,872
98	423130	Tire and Tube Merchant Wholesalers	3,219,749	221,082	2,998,666
99	424210	Drugs and Druggists' Sundries Merchant Wholesalers	3,259,495	262,125	2,997,370
100	3314	Nonferrous Metal (except Aluminum) Production and Processing	3,305,778	315,519	2,990,259
101	423330	Roofing, Siding, and Insulation Materials Merchant Wholesalers	3,269,732	320,013	2,949,719
102	212111	Bituminous Coal and Lignite Surface Mining	3,274,777	328,166	2,946,611
103	333618	Other Engine Equipment Manufacturing	3,460,975	520,093	2,940,883
104	236116	New Multifamily Housing Construction (except For-Sale Builders)	3,184,408	253,375	2,931,033
105	486	Pipeline Transportation	3,264,924	362,206	2,902,718

106	325311	Nitrogenous Fertilizer Manufacturing	3,229,158	331,317	2,897,842
107	332431	Metal Can Manufacturing	3,110,394	213,636	2,896,758
108	423620	Household Appliances, Electric Housewares, and Consumer Electronics Merchant Wholesalers	3,122,750	258,498	2,864,252
109	424410	General Line Grocery Merchant Wholesalers	3,013,969	161,873	2,852,096
110	311111	Dog and Cat Food Manufacturing	3,030,447	187,772	2,842,675
111	212210	Iron Ore Mining	3,443,500	632,500	2,811,000
112	423940	Jewelry, Watch, Precious Stone, and Precious Metal Merchant Wholesalers	2,972,061	163,104	2,808,957
113	325320	Pesticide and Other Agricultural Chemical Manufacturing	3,102,431	299,241	2,803,190
114	324199	All Other Petroleum and Coal Products Manufacturing	3,042,757	241,838	2,800,919
115	312230	Tobacco Manufacturing	2,967,146	186,902	2,780,244
116	325211	Plastics Materials and Resin Manufacturing	3,190,507	432,974	2,757,533
117	336360	Motor Vehicle Seating and Interior Trim Manufacturing	3,094,597	343,806	2,750,791
118	212112	Bituminous Coal Underground Mining	3,342,738	606,400	2,736,338
119	441210	Recreational Vehicle Dealers	2,995,604	264,832	2,730,772
120	424130	Industrial and Personal Service Paper Merchant Wholesalers	2,997,447	282,335	2,715,112
121	32521	Resin and Synthetic Rubber Manufacturing	3,126,700	416,453	2,710,247
122	311411	Frozen Fruit, Juice, and Vegetable Manufacturing	3,045,828	345,641	2,700,188
123	221330	Steam and Air-Conditioning Supply	3,232,333	538,476	2,693,857
124	21211	Coal Mining	3,069,968	389,313	2,680,655
125	3252	Resin, Synthetic Rubber, and Artificial and Synthetic Fibers and Filaments Manufacturing	3,082,422	406,278	2,676,143
126	423860	Transportation Equipment and Supplies (except Motor Vehicle) Merchant Wholesalers	2,987,840	312,148	2,675,692

BUSINESS WITH FEWER THAN TWENTY EMPLOYEES *continued*

Rank	NAICS Code	NAICS Description	Average Receipts Per Firm	Average Payroll Per Firm	Receipts Minus Payroll
127	325991	Custom Compounding of Purchased Resins	2,993,615	331,760	2,661,855
128	423730	Warm Air Heating and Air-Conditioning Equipment and Supplies Merchant Wholesalers	3,045,491	393,371	2,652,120
129	325412	Pharmaceutical Preparation Manufacturing	3,090,604	461,055	2,629,549
130	336414	Guided Missile and Space Vehicle Manufacturing	3,271,500	656,000	2,615,500
131	423690	Other Electronic Parts and Equipment Merchant Wholesalers	2,897,618	282,386	2,615,232
132	4233	Lumber and Other Construction Materials Merchant Wholesalers	2,892,920	277,924	2,614,996
133	313230	Nonwoven Fabric Mills	2,969,000	374,356	2,594,644
134	48111	Scheduled Air Transportation	2,797,344	225,481	2,571,863
135	3221	Pulp, Paper, and Paperboard Mills	2,988,718	438,256	2,550,462
136	813211	Grantmaking Foundations	2,746,208	198,907	2,547,302
137	322211	Corrugated and Solid Fiber Box Manufacturing	3,027,432	496,618	2,530,815
138	423810	Construction and Mining (except Oil Well) Machinery and Equipment Merchant Wholesalers	2,821,443	293,424	2,528,019
139	3253	Pesticide, Fertilizer, and Other Agricultural Chemical Manufacturing	2,823,870	312,499	2,511,371
140	334517	Irradiation Apparatus Manufacturing	2,842,671	335,658	2,507,013
141	4231	Motor Vehicle and Motor Vehicle Parts and Supplies Merchant Wholesalers	2,706,747	202,670	2,504,077
142	4411	Automobile Dealers	2,668,406	164,797	2,503,609
143	212391	Potash, Soda, and Borate Mineral Mining	2,883,167	384,333	2,498,833
144	325520	Adhesive Manufacturing	2,927,509	432,771	2,494,738
145	424810	Beer and Ale Merchant Wholesalers	2,730,794	241,135	2,489,659

146	33149	Nonferrous Metal (except Copper and Aluminum) Rolling, Drawing, Extruding, and Alloying	2,789,155	309,962	2,479,192
147	423820	Farm and Garden Machinery and Equipment Merchant Wholesalers	2,741,051	271,926	2,469,125
148	312111	Soft Drink Manufacturing	2,691,005	224,473	2,466,533
149	4236	Household Appliances and Electrical and Electronic Goods Merchant Wholesalers	2,745,550	287,625	2,457,925
150	325212	Synthetic Rubber Manufacturing	2,778,750	326,359	2,452,391
151	446110	Pharmacies and Drugstores	2,720,302	273,076	2,447,226
152	561599	All Other Travel Arrangement and Reservation Services	2,646,291	213,837	2,432,454
153	331110	Iron and Steel Mills and Ferroalloy Manufacturing	2,708,076	285,853	2,422,223
154	32531	Fertilizer Manufacturing	2,730,749	316,931	2,413,818
155	333921	Elevator and Moving Stairway Manufacturing	3,021,178	607,792	2,413,386
156	423930	Recyclable Materials Merchant Wholesalers	2,630,029	218,323	2,411,706
157	221115	Wind Electric Power Generation	2,879,688	469,063	2,410,625
158	325120	Industrial Gas Manufacturing	2,798,256	391,333	2,406,923
159	333912	Air and Gas Compressor Manufacturing	2,741,055	335,027	2,406,027
160	311513	Cheese Manufacturing	2,604,251	210,845	2,393,406
161	4248	Beer, Wine, and Distilled Alcoholic Beverages Merchant Wholesalers	2,637,668	244,627	2,393,041
162	311615	Poultry Processing	2,593,979	210,350	2,383,629
163	423920	Toy and Hobby Goods and Supplies Merchant Wholesalers	2,583,032	214,229	2,368,803
164	336510	Railroad Rolling Stock Manufacturing	2,831,250	469,467	2,361,783
165	424490	Other Grocery and Related Products Merchant Wholesalers	2,535,099	177,826	2,357,273
166	424820	Wine and Distilled Alcoholic Beverages Merchant Wholesalers	2,602,878	245,932	2,356,946
167	326122	Plastics Pipe and Pipe Fitting Manufacturing	2,664,896	314,374	2,350,522
168	32221	Paperboard Container Manufacturing	2,805,481	456,582	2,348,900

BUSINESS WITH FEWER THAN TWENTY EMPLOYEES *continued*

Rank	NAICS Code	NAICS Description	Average Receipts Per Firm	Average Payroll Per Firm	Receipts Minus Payroll
169	447190	Other Gasoline Stations	2,455,395	119,441	2,335,954
170	335929	Other Communication and Energy Wire Manufacturing	2,750,013	414,267	2,335,747
171	325220	Artificial and Synthetic Fibers and Filaments Manufacturing	2,625,250	301,225	2,324,025
172	423720	Plumbing and Heating Equipment and Supplies (Hydronics) Merchant Wholesalers	2,644,029	330,549	2,313,481
173	3115	Dairy Products Manufacturing	2,517,132	204,729	2,312,403
174	424340	Footwear Merchant Wholesalers	2,486,308	197,787	2,288,520
175	423840	Industrial Supplies Merchant Wholesalers	2,595,333	307,009	2,288,324
176	32541	Pharmaceutical and Medicine Manufacturing	2,681,727	422,171	2,259,556
177	322212	Folding Paperboard Box Manufacturing	2,709,490	451,582	2,257,908
178	481211	Nonscheduled Chartered Passenger Air Transportation	2,558,196	302,880	2,255,316
179	423	Merchant Wholesalers, Durable Goods	2,502,073	257,297	2,244,776
180	533110	Lessors of Nonfinancial Intangible Assets (except Copyrighted Works)	2,489,763	258,449	2,231,314
181	321114	Wood Preservation	2,487,990	259,555	2,228,435
182	423220	Home Furnishing Merchant Wholesalers	2,476,110	252,339	2,223,771
183	423430	Computer and Computer Peripheral Equipment and Software Merchant Wholesalers	2,522,956	300,110	2,222,846
184	325130	Synthetic Dye and Pigment Manufacturing	2,535,983	318,966	2,217,017
185	331221	Rolled Steel Shape Manufacturing	2,508,459	297,941	2,210,518
186	4241	Paper and Paper Products Merchant Wholesalers	2,444,644	236,385	2,208,259
187	424450	Confectionery Merchant Wholesalers	2,354,236	148,433	2,205,803

188	335991	Carbon and Graphite Products Manufacturing	2,587,262	384,662	2,202,600
189	4471	Gasoline Stations	2,297,743	99,236	2,198,506
190	236220	Commercial and Institutional Building Construction	2,487,359	299,407	2,187,952
191	33131	Alumina and Aluminum Production and Processing	2,475,425	293,875	2,181,550
192	423610	Electrical Apparatus and Equipment, Wiring Supplies, and Related Equipment Merchant Wholesalers	2,478,208	299,942	2,178,266
193	424320	Men's and Boys' Clothing and Furnishings Merchant Wholesalers	2,379,003	202,526	2,176,477
194	326111	Plastics Bag and Pouch Manufacturing	2,480,366	307,696	2,172,670
195	447110	Gasoline Stations with Convenience Stores	2,267,367	95,744	2,171,623
196	22111	Electric Power Generation	2,534,060	365,421	2,168,638
197	325613	Surface Active Agent Manufacturing	2,489,881	332,000	2,157,881
198	2362	Nonresidential Building Construction	2,439,159	297,940	2,141,220
199	522110	Commercial Banking	2,711,467	573,991	2,137,476
200	31191	Snack Food Manufacturing	2,359,099	226,631	2,132,468

WHAT TINY BUSINESSES THAT MAKE BIG MONEY HAVE IN COMMON

As part of the research for this book, I surveyed many of the entrepreneurs who shared their stories to find out what common threads exist in their experiences, habits, and best practices. Forty-nine entrepreneurs completed the survey.

Here are some of the most interesting findings:

- It took the businesses an average of almost four years to get to $1 million in annual revenue.
- They spent an average of four years as nonemployer businesses (meaning those with no payroll); 18 percent of them never hired traditional, W-2 employees.
- All of them use contractors in their businesses.
- 90% use automation in their business.
- 88% exercise in some way. Their most popular workouts: yoga (22%), gym workouts (18%), strength training (14%), and walking (14%).
- Many (64%) have a mind/body/spiritual or religious practice (such as meditation or prayer).

- 34% meditate.
- 37% have a business coach.
- 45% belong to an entrepreneurship group.

You can find the specific responses of the forty-nine entrepreneurs who participated at tinybusinessbigmoney.com.

ACKNOWLEDGMENTS

Like many a tiny business, this book never would have come to fruition without the support and contributions of many people.

An immense thank you to all the entrepreneurs who shared your inspiring stories and to the experts who helped me make sense of the trends and data in this book.

Thank you also to the team at W. W. Norton: Michael Tizzano, who believed in the book enough to fight for it during the auction process; to Ann Treistman, Editorial Director of The Countryman Press; and Isabel McCarthy, Assistant Editor, who brought it over the finish line; and to Allison Chi, Devon Zahn, and Ken Hansen.

Thank you also to my husband, Robert Sicoli, and my children, Anna, Emily, Sarah, and Robert, for all you did to help me finish writing this book. Anna and Emily, thank you for programming the spreadsheets in the Appendices and for your research assistance with the survey. Sarah, thank you for your research assistance and for helping me keep my business going when I was writing nonstop. Robert, thank you for brainstorming ideas for how to express the streetfighting concept. Thank you to my parents, Francine and Walter, for always encouraging me in my writing endeavors, and to my brother, Michael (an entrepreneur himself), for your ideas and feedback.

This book never would have been published without the support of Leila Campoli, my tireless literary agent at Stonesong. Thank you, Leila, for the many phone calls where we sharpened the idea for the book and for helping me to find the ideal publisher. You are truly an inspiration.

Thank you also to retired police officers Jim Whitaker and Patrick O'Connor and martial artist/entrepreneur Dan Faggella for your insights into streetfighting, which informed the streetfighting tips throughout the book.

Thank you also to all the other supportive friends and advisors who supported me throughout: my mentor, Verne Harnish; Elizabeth MacBride, my business partner and coauthor of *The New Builders*; and Doug Wick, my business coach at Positioning Systems. Thank you to my friends, June Avignone and Gregory Van Maanen, and fellow writers, Anne Field, Lori Ioannou, and Eilene Zimmerman, for your creative inspiration and support.

Thank you to the folks who helped me recharge my batteries and keep myself in one piece during the writing process: the team at Hot Yoga Revolution; Andrew Amigo, CEO and founder of The Accomplished Brain; my Taekwondo Master Jim Cahill; Advanced Rolfer Chuck Carpenter; chiropractor Mike Teytelbaum, acupuncturist An Ying, and the wonderful team at the Therapeutic Massage & Training Center; among many others.

Thank you to pod teacher, Matt Meyer, and fellow pod parents, Shannon and Wilson Caldwell, Marian and Alan Sepinwall, and Natalie and George Theocharopoulou, for coming together to create a great experience for our sons, so I had the peace of mind to work on the book while we all juggled online school and pandemic life.

And, ultimately, I'd like to thank you, the reader, for becoming part of the entrepreneurial community around this book. A book can be a powerful catalyst for bringing people together, and I hope I'll hear from you about your experiences in starting your own tiny business—one that allows you to go after your dreams and to achieve your full potential.

INDEX